Strategic Chess

MASTERING THE
CLOSED GAME

Strategic Chess

MASTERING THE CLOSED GAME

Grandmaster
Edmar Mednis

SUMMIT PUBLISHING
Los Angeles

First Summit Publishing Edition

ISBN: 0-945806-11-6

Cover design by Heidi Frieder

Printed and bound in the United States of America

SUMMIT PUBLISHING

To Milton and Marilyn Finkelstein

Contents

Preface

To the question "Who wins more tournament games?" the correct answer is: "The player who knows what is going on." This means that if you know the strategic theme of your opening well, understand how to apply it in middlegame play, and if necessary can also make use of your knowledge in the thematic endgame to follow, then you will be a very successful tournament player.

Players bent on improving their practical results have told me numerous times that their greatest need is a book that can take them through their opening variation into and through the middlegame and if needed, also the endgame that follows. Otherwise, once they are out of their "book," i.e. the opponent varies in the opening from the main line or the line simply ends, they start to flounder. This book is aimed to fill their need. The mechanism is complete games of strong players. First I describe, as clearly as I know how, the important strategic theme(s) of the opening and then demonstrate how the theme(s) should be carried through all the applicable phases of that game.

This is not a book of perfect games. Though perfect games do exist, they form a minute part of games played and therefore do not reflect the real life. In real life errors are made and it is important to learn how to minimize the frequency of them and how to take advantage of errors by the opponent. The emphasis on strategic themes is the major tool for furthering both of these goals.

The criteria for selecting the individual games have been as follows:

(1) The game should be instructive in terms of both good and bad decisions made.

(2) I should have done a large amount of work on the game already so that I can give a deeper and more accurate reflection of what actually happened. Of necessity, this means that my own games and games previously analyzed by me have been preferred. Every time I go over a game I learn more about it. In some cases this leads to the overturning of a previous conclusion—this being the inevitable result of the search for truth in the science of chess.

(3) Because in real life some games effectively end already in the opening, while in others the decisive element comes in the middlegame or endgame, this kind of mix also appears here.

A much more difficult decision has been: which openings and variations thereof to include? The closed games universe is wide, deep and varied. My decision has been based on the amount of valuable help that I felt I could give to the reader. The guiding principle has been: select unbalanced, yet strategically clear openings. Therefore I have avoided openings such as the main line of the Botvinnik Variation of the Queen's Gambit Declined (1 d4 d5 2 c4 e6 3 Nc3 Nf6 4 Nf3 c6 5 Bg5 dxc4 6 e4 b5 7 e5 h6 8 Bh4 g5 9 Nxg5) because it is "too specifically tactical" and minimized coverage of e.g. the Orthodox Defense to the QGD ("too simple"), Benko Gambit and Benoni Defense ("too deeply sophisticated") etc.

This same principle has been applied to the specific variations chosen. Thus, in the King's Indian Defense, the Classical Variation is featured and Game 14 demonstrates the strategically important dxe5 exchange by White, while Game 15 shows the ins and outs of the strategically equally important d5 advance. The variations selected are important, purely strategic ones. Perhaps I should clarify what I mean by the term "strategic." It refers to the structural elements of a position rather than the specific tactical possibilities.

There is one particular element in the book that may strike some readers as surprising: a large number of games will travel early on quite an "unconventional" road before a well known opening position is reached. This is because the science of move orders has become a very important part of the professional chess scene. The professional player uses this science to try to ensure that he reaches the opening variation that he is striving for, while preventing his opponent from achieving his aim. Because nowadays in tournament play move orders are so important, I devote a considerable amount of attention to them. What good will it do you to learn a variation perfectly, if your opponents, by using a perceptive move order, prevent you from reaching your variation?

There are two more specific items I should mention regarding use of this book:

 (1) The opening references consulted were current through the end of 1991.

 (2) The rather detailed table of contents lists openings alphabetically.

Please note that under Queen's Gambit Declined appear a total of six openings.

Some of the material in this book has been published before, but in every case has been enlarged and adapted to fit the book's theme: playing unbalanced, strategically clear openings more successfully.

In general the following standard sources have been utilized in the preparation of this book: personal knowledge, personal contacts, leading chess periodicals and chess books. When appropriate, direct credit is given in the text.

To ensure that the reader and the author are on the same wavelength regarding the meaning of the question and exclamation marks as they are used in the characterization of moves, these are the presently accepted meanings:

!	=	a strong move
!!	=	a very strong move; a fantastic move
?	=	a bad move; a weak move
??	=	a horrible move; a blunder
!?	=	an enterprising move; a move worthy of consideration
?!	=	a dubious move, for theoretical or practical reasons

In an undertaking of such scope, some errors are almost inevitable. The author accepts responsibility for all of these. Your assistance in bringing them to my attention will be appreciated.

As always, my deepest gratitude goes to my wonderful blonde wife, Baiba, not only for typing the entire manuscript but also for never-ending physical and moral support.

This is my second book for Summit Publishing. I am very happy to be associated with this fine publishing firm and its president, Dodd M. Darin.

Edmar Mednis
New York, 1992

Benko Gambit
Game 1

White: Maxim Dlugy
Black: Lev Alburt
Played at U.S 1990 Closed (Match) Championship, Jacksonville, Florida,
Match Game 3

1	d4	Nf6
2	c4	c5
3	d5	b5

It it this move that turns the Benoni Defense into the Benko Gambit.
It is a relatively new opening, which I date from 1967, when GM Pal
Benko—the true pathfinder—started playing it with great success. The
immediate point of the move is obvious: Black wants to undermine the
support of the d-pawn even at the cost of a pawn.

4	cxb5	a6

This is the normal starting point of the Benko Gambit. We can already
express the over-all objectives of each side as follows:

BLACK will use the open a- and b- files to put White's Queenside
under pressure. Of necessity, this is a relatively long term strategic plan.

WHITE will work to consolidate his one pawn advantage.

A thematic example of the play after 5 bxa6 g6 is: 6 Nc3 Bxa6
7 Nf3 Bg7 8 g3 d6 9 Bg2 Nbd7 10 0-0 0-0 11 Bf4 Qb6 12 Rb1 Qb7 13
Re1 Rfb8 when Black has good compensation for the pawn (GM Wilder).

5	f3!?

[diag. 1]

A relatively new idea with a very clear strategic plan:
WHITE will play e2-e4, safeguarding d5 and establishing a powerful
center.

White's spatial advantage derives from having his d-pawn in Black's part of the board. With 3...b5, Black has undermined the support from c4 - therefore White rushes to provide new support from e4. Moreover, the e-pawn, being a primary central pawn, further enhances White's central superiority. White's plan is direct—it can even be called "naively simple"—yet based on well known strategic principles. With Black being simple and direct on the Queenside, it is in general sound strategy to respond in a direct way in the center.

5   ...   g6

Aiming for a traditional type of Benko Gambit. The two significant alternatives are:

(1) 5...axb5?!: Black wins back the pawn all right, but loses valuable time and in general just forgets what the Benko is about. Punishment was swift in M. Gurvich - A. Miles, Manila Interzonal 1990: 6 e4 Qa5+ 7 Bd2 b4 8 Na3! Ba6?! (Black cannot afford this additional loss of time. In order is 8...d6.) 9 Nc4 Qc7 10 Nh3 d6 11 a3! Bxc4 12 Bxc4 bxa3 13 Rxa3 Rxa3 14 bxa3 g6 15 Qa4+ Nbd7 16 Qa8+ Qb8 17 Qxb8+ Nxb8 18 Ke2 Bg7 19 Rb1. White dominates the Queenside and the a-pawn is a terror. Black resigned after 19 ...0-0 20 Rb7 Rc8 21 a4 Ne8 22 Rxe7 Nc7 23 Ba5 Nba6 24 Rd7.

(2) 5...e6: Black again strikes at White's center, without paying attention to completing his own development. I would expect that White can retain an opening advantage after 6 e4 exd5 7 e5 Qe7 8 Qe2 Ng8 9 Nc3 Bb7 10 Nh3, e.g. 10...c4 11 Be3! axb5 12 0-0-0! Qxe5 13 f4! Qe7 14 Rxd5!, Dlugy - Alburt, U.S. Championship 1991.

6   e4   Bg7

Black rushes his Kingside development without taking time out for 6...d6. Then White safeguards his Queenside and completes his development with 7 Na3! Bg7 8 Ne2 Nbd7 9 Nc3! 0-0 10 Be2 Ne8 11 0-0, keeping a normal opening advantage.

7   Na3!

Being ready to recapture on b5 while keeping c3 free for the smooth development of the KN.

7   ...   0-0

There is no reason why Black should be successful with the premature 7...e6?!, as in Dlugy - Alburt, New York Open 1990. In the game White self-blocked with 8 d6? and went on to lose. Subsequently, GM Dlugy recommended 8 dxe6 fxe6 9 Be3! d6 when Black is full of weaknesses while being a pawn down.

Of course, the normal 7...d6 transposes back into the note given after Black's 6th.

8	Ne2!	Ne8
9	Nc3	Nd6?

Again, the normal 9...d6 transposes into the position given earlier. The text has scant chances for success, because White has the superior center, harmonious Knight placements and no weaknesses. Black's error is that instead of playing in the well tested sound long term strategic way, he is looking for a short term successful tactical trick.

10 Be3!

Simple, logical and strong: White develops the QB to its primary central square while attacking the c-pawn. Because 10...Nb7 is just silly and 10...Qb6 11 Na4 Qa5+ 12 Bd2 Qc7 13 b6 is downright bad, Black might as well continue with his idea.

10	...	axb5
11	Bxc5	Nb7
12	Bd4	

White controls the center, has superior piece development (three active vs. two less active), plus a pawn advantage. Under such conditions he can feel confident that Black will not have any unpleasant surprises. For instance, 12...b4? is refuted by 13 Bxg7 Kxg7 14 Qd4+ followed by 15 Qxb4.

12	...	e5
13	dxe6	Bxd4
14	Qxd4	Nc6

[diag. 2]

Black hopes to win a piece with 15...b4 after White moves his Queen. Yet note the key features of the position: White has more space, more center, active development, two extra pawns, whereas Black's Kingside lacks dark square protection as does the center and Queenside, the QB is undeveloped and the Nb7 underdeveloped. Under such conditions, it is hardly surprising that White has a devastating tactical shot.

15	e7!	Qxe7
16	Qd2	b4
17	Nd5	Qc5
18	Rc1!	

Because of the Black deficiencies enumerated above, White correctly goes for the kill.

18	...	Qa7
19	Nb5	Qxa2
20	Bc4!	

White's material advantage has been exchanged for a mammoth edge in development. If now 20...b3, White takes advantage of Black's dark square weaknesses everywhere with 21 Nbc7 Ra7 22 Nf6+ Kg7 23 Nce8+ Kh8 24 Qh6.

20	...	Qa5
21	Nbc7	Kg7

After 21...Ra7 White mates with 22 Qh6 followed by 23 Nf6.

22	Nxa8	Qxa8
23	Nxb4	Qa7
24	Nd5	f5
25	Qc3+	Kh6
26	Qe3+!	

Up the Exchange and pawn, White simplifies into a securely won endgame. This is always the safest way of winning a won game. In the following endgame White perfectly executes the dual goals of preventing counterplay while simplifying by exchanging pieces.

26	...	Qxe3+
27	Nxe3	fxe4
28	fxe4	Nd6
29	Bd5	Ne5
30	Rf1!	Re8
31	Kd2	Ba6
32	Rf6!	Re6
33	Rxe6	dxe6

34	Ba8	Kg5
35	Rc5	Kf6
36	b3	Bb5
37	Kc3	Nd7
38	Ng4+	Ke7
39	Rc7	Be2
40	Bc6	Nb5+
41	Bxb5	Bxb5
42	Ne5	Kd6
43	Rxd7+	Bxd7
44	Nxd7	Black resigns

The K & P endgame after 44...Kxd7 45 Kd4 is elementary.

Benoni Defense

Game 2

White: Lev Alburt
Black: Dmitry Gurevich
Played at U.S. 1989 Closed Championship, Long Beach, California

1	d4	Nf6
2	c4	e6

At present a large majority of Benoni experts avoid the pure Benoni move order 2...c5 3 d5 e6 because they dislike playing against the sharp variation: 4 Nc3 exd5 5 cxd5 d6 6 e4 g6 7 f4 Bg7 8 Bb5+. Therefore, they start off with 2...e6 and only follow up with 3...c5 after 3 g3 or 3 Nf3. If White plays 3 Nc3, then Black switches into the Nimzo-Indian with 3...Bb4.

3	g3	c5
4	d5	

Bringing about the characteristic Benoni pawn formation. White can, of course, avoid this by 4 Nf3, leading most likely into the English Opening.

4	...	exd5
5	cxd5	d6

Already here the strategic features of the Benoni have been set. Black has brought about an unbalanced central pawn formation by, in effect, exchanging his e-pawn for White's c-pawn. Therefore Black's primary central influence has decreased. The resulting double-edged situation features these over-all strategic themes:

WHITE'S PRIMARY goal is to mobilize his e-pawn—the extra central pawn—for a properly timed e4 and e5 advance.

White's SECONDARY goal is to apply pressure against Black's d-pawn.

BLACK must create counterplay on the Queenside because this is where his pawn majority is. Moreover, he must also prevent White from effectively carrying out the central pawn thrust. It is exceedingly difficult to properly carry out both of these requirements.

6	Nc3	g6
7	Nf3	Bg7
8	Bg2	0-0
9	0-0	

[diag. 3]

There are two major themes for White behind the KB fianchetto variation:

(1) White's KB is pointing in the direction of the centrally important e4 and d5 squares. Therefore an e2-e4 advance can be more readily supported, while also preventing Black from controlling the e4 square. Moreover, once White has gotten in e4, a further advance to e5 is easier to achieve since the KB will be protecting the d5 pawn.

(2) If White executes the e4, f4, e5 pawn advance, White's King position could be weakened. The presence of the KB on g2 helps protect the King.

9   ...   Na6

One of Black's main line variations. The Knight will either retreat to c7 to assist the ...b5 advance or head to c5 after a later ...c4. Moreover, from any of these locations (a6, c7, c5) the Knight does not interfere with the development of the QB. The other main line alternatives are:

a) 9...Nbd7. From here the Knight controls the important e5 square but blocks development of the QB. This means that the Knight will have to move again, to either b6 or e5 - depending on the variation.

b) 9...a6 prepares 10...b5. Of course, White prevents that with 10 a4. Then Black's only way of developing the QN is to d7.

c) 9...Re8. Black's attempt to control e4 is easily repulsed by 10 Nd2. Nevertheless, Black's KR is well placed on e8 to impede White's central pawn advances.

After the text, White's most frequent line continues with 10 Nd2. From here the Knight heads to c4, applying pressure to d6 and being in position to assist in a later e5 advance.

10 h3!?

This modest looking move actually has a sophisticated strategic point. In the Benoni, g4 is an important square for Black because, depending on the situation, it could be advantageous either for Black's QB or KN to occupy it. This would be particularly so if White aims for an early e4, since Black's ...Bg4 would be an effective pin.

10 ...   Bd7?!

At the time of this game, the text was the move recommended by theory. Yet, if Black would pay attention to the strategic themes of the Benoni he would hardly choose it. On d7 the QB is both modestly and awkwardly placed, e.g. the d-pawn is now unprotected. Instead 10...Nc7 would remove the Knight from the edge while preparing Queenside play via ...b5; 10...Re8 would hinder White's e-pawn advance.

11 e4!   Qc8?!

Again, blindly following "theory." Also 11...c4 does not work well because 12 Bf4 occurs with gain of time. The best move is 11...Re8, paying the necessary attention to the center.

The problems with the text are threefold: 1) The Queen is awkwardly placed here, 2) Black's vulnerable point—the d6 pawn—is left even more vulnerable, and 3) Black uses up a valuable tempo to basically achieve nothing.

12 Bf4!!

The strategic refutation of Black's play. Instead, the earlier game had gone 12 Kh2 Re8 13 Re1 c4 with good counterplay for Black after 14 e5?! dxe5 15 Nxe5 Bf5 16 Bg5 Nb4, Marovic - Planinc, Amsterdam 1973 or after 14 Bf4 Nc5 (analysis).

In strategic positions demanding maximum speed and energy, one tempo can make the whole difference between achieving one's strategic goal or getting nothing. By not wasting a tempo with 12 Kh2, White achieves his goal of powerful central initiative.

12 ...   Bxh3?!

To me this move looks like psychological resignation. Black realizes that his previous play has been refuted and now decides that he should try for "complications". Nevertheless, necessary was to protect the d-pawn by 12...Ne8. It is true that after 13 Kh2 Black's minor pieces stand both passively and awkwardly, yet he has not been blown away in the center.

Black's position after the text will soon be shown to be hopeless. GM Gurevich is among the country's leading experts on the Benoni, but in this game he seems to be playing some other opening. I have not been appending? marks to Black's moves because of themselves they are not so bad. Yet in all of his decisions Black is not paying attention to the strategic themes of the Benoni and thus the decisions turn out to be wrong. The Benoni demands perfection from Black to be playable—otherwise, as here, Black's situation very quickly becomes hopeless.

13	Bxd6	Bxg2
14	Kxg2	Re8
15	Re1	

[diag. 4]

White's unopposed d- and e- pawns give him a huge central superiority which is ready to suffocate Black. White's only weakness is the missing h-pawn, but Black is in no position to try to do anything about it because he has no way of getting at White's King.

15	...	Qd7?!

Black cannot hope to withstand White's onslaught without the help of the QN. He had to try 15...c4, hoping to continue with 16...Nc5.

16	e5!	Ng4
17	Ne4	Rad8

Obviously 17...Nxe5? 18 Nxe5 Bxe5? 19 Bxe5 Rxe5 fails to 20 Nf6+.

18	Rc1	b6
19	e6!	

In strategically overwhelming positions there often is a special tactical crushing sequence. White's position is overwhelming because of his domineering center and completely developed, actively placed forces. The advance of the e-pawn wins by force. If Black avoids capturing the pawn by 19...Qb7, White wins as follows: 20 exf7+ Qxf7 21 Nfg5 Qf5 22 f3 Ne5 23 Ne6 Rc8 24 g4 Qf7 25 N4g5.

19	...	fxe6
20	dxe6	Rxe6

The win is straightforward after 20...Qxe6 21 Nfg5 Qf5 22 Qb3+ Kh8 23 Nf7+. Throughout the game Black is handicapped by, in effect, playing without his QN.

21	Nfg5!	Nxf2

Obviously 21...R6e8 is refuted by 22 Qb3+. With the text Black hopes for some chances after 22 Kxf2?! Bd4+ followed by 23...Rxd6.

22 Qb3!!

As I already mentioned a bit earlier, in vastly superior positions there often is a devastating tactical shot. The text is exactly that.

22	...	Nxe4
23	Rxe4	Qxd6
24	Rd1!	Bd4

24...Qxd1 allows smothered mate after 25 Qxe6+ Kh8 26 Nf7+ Kg8 27 Nh6+ Kh8 28 Qg8+ Rxg8 29 Nf7.

25	Nxe6	Black resigns

After 25...Kh8 26 Nxd8 Qxd8 27 Qf7 Qa8 28 Kh2! there is no reasonable defense to 29 Re8+.

Bogo - Indian Defense
Game 3

White: Lev Polugaevsky
Black: Viktor Korchnoi
Played at 1977 Semi-Final Candidates Match, Evian, France, Game 12.

1 d4   e6
2 c4   Bb4+

This check on the second move is played by uncompromising strategists on a some-time basis. If Black follows up with a ...Nf6, then by transposition of moves the game will lead to the Nimzo-Indian or Bogo-Indian Defenses; if he follows up with an early ...f5, then we get less explored irregular waters. Yet the choice is always Black's. What is certain about the text is that Black is ready—in fact he must be ready—to exchange off his KB. Whether it is for White's QB or QN is White's choice.

3 Bd2

This and 3 Nd2 usually lead to the Bogo-Indian; 3 Nc3 Nf6 leads to the Nimzo-Indian. Of course, after both 3 Nc3 and 3 Nd2 Black can enter a quasi-Dutch Defense with 3 ...f5.

3 ...   Qe7
4 g3   Nc6
5 Nf3   Nf6

Via transposition of moves a well known variation of the Bogo-Indian Defense has arisen. (The normal move order is 1 d4 Nf6 2 c4 e6 3 Nf3 Bb4+ 4 Bd2 Qe7 5 g3 Nc6.) The Bogo-Indian is named after the Russian-German grandmaster Efim Bogoljubov who introduced it into international play in the 1920s. It can be considered a sister opening to the Nimzo-Indian: Black develops his KB to b4 and is ready to complete his Kingside development by castling. However, the Bogo-Indian is inherently "less threatening" to White since there is no risk of winding up with doubled c-pawns.

In general, the Bogo-Indian is an equalizing opening for Black. He exchanges off a minor piece, completes Kingside development by early castling, does not create any weaknesses and satisfies himself with a solid, slightly inferior center, with the characteristic central pawn formation being d6 and e5.

White's objective is to use his moderate central superiority as a basis for activity on the left side of the board, i.e. a- through d- files.

At this point White can choose whether to exchange off his QB or QN for Black's KB. Historically, White's most common plan has been to allow his QB to be exchanged. The main line then goes: 6 Bg2 Bxd2+! (Black must rush this exchange since after 6...0-0?! 7 0-0 Bxd2 White can play 8 Qxd2 followed by the active development of the QN to c3.) 7 Nbxd2 (Forced because after 7 Qxd2? Ne4 8 Qc2 Qb4+ White either loses a pawn or must play 9 Kf1.) 7 ...d6 8 0-0 0-0 9 e4 e5 10 d5 Nb8. By virtue of having his d-pawn on d5 White already has more space on the Queens' side of center and will aim to gain additional space there with 11 b4. White is, however, handicapped by a poorly placed QN. Black's position is inherently solid and he has the "correct" Bishop for his central pawn formation, because the QB is not boxed in by the pawns. Note that, unlike the King's Indian Defense, Black is not left with a passive KB. This factor shows up much of the strategic thinking behind the Bogo-Indian. The over-all conclusion is that the position after 10...Nb8 offers Black, in due course, excellent chances for equalization, without undue risk of being blown away.

6   Nc3

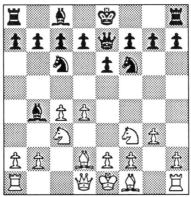

[diag. 5]

The text has recently become increasingly popular. The strategic ideas behind it are the following:

    (1) The QN assumes an active location, establishing control of e4. Therefore Black will have no choice but soon to play ...Bxc3.

    (2) With White's QB then actively placed on c3, Black will not be able to execute the thematic ...d6 and ...e5 central advance, as this will simply increase the scope of the QB.

    (3) Therefore, Black will have to rush to exchange off White's QB with ...Ne4. The net result will be that even though two sets of minor pieces will have been exchanged off, White's

two remaining minor pieces will be well placed.

(4) White's slight central superiority and well placed pieces will give a modest yet pleasant initiative on the left side of the board, while carrying little risk of a loss.

6 ... Bxc3

In conjunction with the next move Black's most thematic plan. Black can, however, completely change the character of the position by playing 6...d5, bringing about positions more characteristic of the Ragozin variation of the Queens Gambit Declined (1 d4 d5 2 c4 e6 3 Nc3 Nf6 4 Nf3 Bb4). White's best then is 7 cxd5 exd5 8 Bg2, with the normal opening plus. In this position Black's QN on c6 is not well placed since the smooth protection of the d-pawn is hindered.

7 Bxc3 Ne4
8 Rc1 d6

About equivalent is the immediate 8 ... 0-0, to be followed a bit later by ...d6 and ...Nxc3. However, recent attempts at complications with 8...Nb4?! have not been successful, e.g. 9 Qa4 a5 10 Bg2 0-0 11 Nd2! Nxc3 12 bxc3! Nc6 13 c5! d5 14 cxd6 cxd6 15 Rb1, Tukmakov - Belyavsky, USSR Championship 1987. White has strong pressure against Black's weakened Queenside and an enhanced central presence himself and therefore a clear advantage. Because 8...Nb4?! disregards the strategic ideas behind the Bogo-Indian, it is hardly surprising that it is unsatisfactory.

9 d5 Nxc3
10 Rxc3 Nd8?!

Of course, inferior is 10...exd5? 11 cxd5 with White getting very strong pressure along the half-open c-file. However, the text has the disadvantage of deadening the Knight since it has little future both on and from d8. The passage of time has taught that correct is 10...Nb8, with the likely continuation 11 Bg2 e5 12 0-0 0-0 13 Nd2 Nd7 14 b4 f5, Vyzmanavin - A. Petrosian, Moscow 1989. White's space advantage on the Queenside gives him a slight edge after 15 c5! (15...bxc5?! 16 Qb3! Kh8 17 bxc5 Nxc5 18 Qa3 b6 19 Nb3 leads to a large advantage for White), yet with 15...e4 Black gains sufficient chances in the center to keep his disadvantage at a minimum. The above sequence shows off both sides' potential very well: White expands on the Queenside where he has more space while Black makes use of having more influence on the e-file.

11 Bg2 0-0
12 dxe6?!

White unnecessarily allows Black's Knight to return to the fray.

Thematic is 12 0-0 and after 12...e5, 13 b4!. Because of the clumsy location of his Knight, Black then has a harder time ahead than in the above variation.

12   ...   Nxe6!

Korchnoi only needed two draws to clinch the match and thus is quite happy to choose the weakness-free text. Under "must win" conditions, 12...fxe6 also would be satisfactory,. By voluntarily exchanging his center pawn on the fifth rank for a center pawn on the third rank, White has forfeited the bulk of his opening advantage.

13   0-0   Bd7

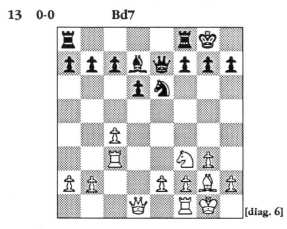

[diag. 6]

The nature of the position now is quite different from those considered earlier where White's d-pawn is on Black's side of the board. Black has completed his minor piece development and has no structural weaknesses. White still has a tiny edge because the c-pawn gives him control of the important d5 square. GM Keene now suggests 14 Nd4 as the best way of retaining this edge.

14   Nh4   Bc6
15   Nf5   Qf6
16   Ne3   Bxg2
17   Kxg2

This early middlegame position shows Black well ahead in time (he has used 40 minutes, whereas White has already taken 72 minutes - with the time limit being 40 moves in 2½ hours) and White with the slight positional superiority referred to earlier. In addition to his c-pawn on the 4th rank controlling more central space than Black's d-pawn on the 3rd rank, White's QR is more active than Black's and White's Knight can establish itself at least temporarily on d5. Nevertheless, Black's position is comfortable and remains free of weaknesses and there is no chess reason why he should not obtain the desired draw.

17	...	Rfe8
18	Nd5	Qg6
19	Qb1	

The prospects of winning such an endgame are slight. If White is playing to win, in order is 19 Re3.

19	...	c6
20	Qxg6	hxg6
21	Ne3	

On move 19 Black made the following decisions: (1) He did not mind the resulting doubled g-pawns as that helps to keep White's Knight out of f5, and (2) He decided to play ...c6 because the Knight's position on d5 was too cramping for Black to tolerate.

This endgame can be judged to be theoretically slightly in White's favor, because Black's d-pawn now is "weak." Yet White cannot attack it that easily, whereas Black can defend it well enough. Therefore, in a practical sense White's winning prospects are minute.

21	...	Nc5!
22	Rd1	a5

Ensuring the Knight's active location for some time to come. Obviously 23 Rxd6?? is refuted by 23...Ne4.

23	Ra3	Red8
24	Nc2	Kf8
25	h4	Ra6
26	Ne1	Re8!
27	Kf3	Ke7!
28	Re3+	Ne6
29	b3	Raa8

With perceptive maneuvering Black has safeguarded the d-pawn while not allowing White to progress anywhere else either. Not a trace of White's advantage has remained. Korchnoi now offered a draw—in every way a logical step. Yet Polugaevsky, needing a win, after a brief moment of thought turned it down. This soon has a dramatic effect on the course of the game.

30	Nd3	Rad8
31	Nb2	Kd7
32	Na4	Kc7
33	Nc3	

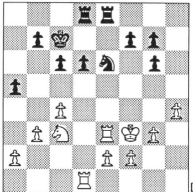

[diag. 7]

Up to here Black has defended carefully and well; after the simple 33...Nc5 White wouldn't have a prayer of achieving anything. However, Korchnoi's ego must have been insulted by the draw refusal. Being well ahead on time—30 minutes left to White's 10—he decides to punish Polugaevsky for his insolence by lashing out with ...

33 ...   g5?

This pseudo-activity has the immediate effect of giving White a cramp on Black's Kingside and Black a permanently vulnerable g5 pawn. It is always most dangerous to allow one's emotions to take over from the head in making chess decisions.

34	h5	f5
35	g4!	f4
36	Red3	Nc5
37	Rd4	Nd7
38	Ne4!	Ne5+
39	Kg2	Nf7

An ignominious conclusion to Black's "activity." Instead 39...Nxg4? makes matters worse after 40 Nxd6 since 40...Rxe2? loses outright to 41 Kf3.

40	f3	Re5
41	Kf2	b5

The results of 33...g5? are apparent to a naked eye: not only is g5 a permanent weakness, but, moreover, White's Knight has been allowed a fantastic unassailable location on e4. The text, played just before the end of the playing session, is a risky attempt at some activity on the Queenside. After 10 minutes' thought White sealed ...

42   Rc1?!

Inexact. The correct Rook redeployment is 42 R4d2 followed by Rc2 as this keeps the e-pawn protected. Even stronger is 42 a3! as given by GM Keene. White prevents the blocking of the Queenside via ...b4 and gets ready to double Rooks on the c-file. Black cannot afford 42...bxc4?! 43 bxc4 as this will allow White to decisively double Rooks on the b-file.

42   ...   b4!
43   a4?

An incomprehensible move after adjournment analysis. By voluntarily closing the Queenside, White denies himself chances there. Black can just hold the center and Kingside.

GM Keene, Korchnoi's second at the match, correctly points out that after 43 Rd2, followed by a3 White still keeps the advantage.

43   ...   Rde8!

Of course, Black is not about to help White by opening the Queenside with 43...bxa3?. By doubling on the e-file Black gets counterplay against White's backward e-pawn.

44   Rcd1   R8e6
45   R1d2   Re7!

White's position looks nice, but Black can protect the vulnerable d6 and g5 pawns comfortably enough. After 21 minutes' thought White saw no way to progress and acquiesced to a drawn K & P endgame.

46   Nxd6   Nxd6
47   Rxd6   Rxe2+
48   Rxe2   Rxe2+
49   Kxe2   Kxd6
50   Kd2   c5   Draw

Catalan Opening

Game 4

White: Ulf Andersson
Black: Gilles Miralles
Played at Cannes (France) International Tournament 1989

1	c4	Nf6
2	Nf3	e6
3	g3	d5
4	Bg2	Be7
5	0-0	0-0
6	d4	

By means of a frequently used transposition of moves, the current main line position in the Catalan Opening has arisen. (The usual move order is 1 d4 Nf6 2 c4 e6 3 g3 d5 4 Bg2 Be7 5 Nf3 0-0 6 0-0.) Many grandmasters, including me, prefer to use the move order of this game because we feel that it is easier for Black to equalize by playing 4...dxc4 if White's d-pawn has already been advanced (i.e. 1 d4 Nf6 2 c4 e6 3 g3 d5 4 Bg2 dxc4) than if it has not (i.e. 1 c4 Nf6 2 Nf3 e6 3 g3 d5 4 Bg2). See Game 7 for an illustration of the latter case.

The Catalan Opening has White using a completely different approach than in the typical Queen's Gambit Declined variations. There White first mobilizes his Queenside pieces so as to put immediate pressure on d5, as well as on Black's Queenside. In the Catalan White first completes the relatively modest development of his Kingside forces. The key minor piece is White's KB. From its fianchettoed location it bears down on the important e4 - b7 squares. Depending on the variation that Black chooses, the KB will support the e4 advance, pressure d5 or aim at Black's Queenside. Often two of these features come into play.

Because the Catalan is inherently less aggressive at the start than are the lines in the Queen's Gambit Declined, from a purely theoretical view it should be easier for Black to equalize against the Catalan than in the QGD. Yet in real life this is not so. The Catalan is a thematically logical, sophisticated and sound opening and unless Black fully understands the positions that result, he will quickly find himself in a most uncomfortable situation.

If White does not play an early d4, then the resulting variations are considered to be part of the Reti Opening. For instance, a build-up with 6 b3, 7 Bb2 8 e3, 9 Qe2, 10 d3 etc. is a Reti.

6	...	dxc4

This delayed capture was for a long time thought to be unpleasantly passive, but was returned to respectability by World Champion Anatoly Karpov in the 1970s. He showed that Black's smooth active development of the Queenside pieces puts him very close to comfortable equality. Black reasons that the time White will use to recover the pawn will allow Black to do "his thing."

The alternative, which is currently less popular, is to hold the center with 6...Nbd7 and 7...c6, followed by developing the QB after 8...b6 and 9...Bb7/Ba6. This theoretically important approach will be covered in Game 6.

7   Qc2

White will recover the pawn in the strategically most straight-forward way. More ambitious alternatives are: (1) 7 Na3, after which Black should play 7...Bxa3 8 bxa3 Bd7! with the idea 9 Ne5 Bc6!, and (2) 7 Ne5 when 7...Nc6! is correct. In both cases Black will have equal chances in rather unbalanced positions. The steady text is White's most frequent and best move.

7   ...   a6
8   Qxc4

White can prevent Black's ....b5 by 8 a4, but over the past ten years this has pretty much disappeared from GM play. There are two reasons for this:

    (1) The permanent weakening of the important b4 square, and
    (2) It has become recognized that ...b5 can lead to a slight, yet permanent weakening of Black's Queenside.

8   ...   b5
9   Qc2   Bb7

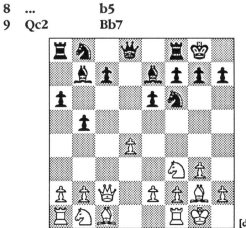

[diag. 8]

This is the starting point of the current main line. The strategic themes are very clear:

Black must try to free his Queenside by getting in ...c5. If he can achieve that without cost, he is assured full equality. Otherwise, White's central superiority will leave Black cramped for the rest of the game. White's over-all objective is to prevent Black's freeing ...c5. Since often it cannot be prevented, White wants to ensure that he has other tools in his tool box. In aiming to retain an opening advantage, White will try for the following goals:

- Take advantage of the hole on c5 by placing his QN there.
- Build a substantial central superiority by getting in e4.
- Take advantage of the Queenside weakening ...b5 advance by a properly timed a4.
- Go for pressure against c7 by having a Q + R battery on the c-file.
- Weaken Black's Queenside by an exchange of light square Bishops. Then very often the key square becomes c6. White wants to dominate it by having a Knight or major piece there.

Of course, White is not going to get anywhere without developing his Queenside forces. Therefore, his first order of business is to develop his QB. The choices are:

(1) 10 Bf4. White develops with gain of time by hitting the c-pawn. Rather than the obvious 10...Nd5 or 10...Bd6, Black's highest rated response is 10...Nc6 11 Rd1 Rc8.

(2) 10 Bd2. A sophisticated idea, introduced by Dutch GM Sosonko. White plans to immobilize the c-pawn by the pin after a Ba5. Black's most reliable response is 10...Be4 and then after 11 Qc1, either the the retreat 11...Bb7 or the developmental 11...Nbd7.

(3) 10 Bg5. See the game.

10   Bg5

Because White's QB is his least useful minor piece (for instance, it does not directly help with any of the goals enumerated above), White is happy to exchange it off. This will help in the fight for both the e4 and c5 squares.

10   ...   Nbd7

Unlike the variation after 10 Bd2, here 10...Be4?! works out badly: 11 Qc1 Qc8 12 Nbd2 Bb7 13 e4! h6 14 Bxf6 Bxf6 15 Qc2, Mednis - K. Burger, Brighton 1983. White has achieved mastery of both e4 and c5 and has a substantial advantage.

11   Bxf6

This immediate capture makes it more difficult for Black to get in ...c5, since both 11...Bxf6?! and 11...gxf6 are met by 12 Ng5!, followed by 13 Bxb7 and 14 Bc6, blocking the c-pawn. On the other hand, the developmental 11 Nbd2 can be met by 11...c5!? and it is not all clear whether White can achieve an advantage after 12 Bxf6 gxf6 or even 12...Bxf6 13 dxc5 Rc8.

11	...	Nxf6
12	Nbd2	Rc8
13	Nb3	

The fight is continuing over the crucial c5 square. Black can try to break loose with 13...c5!?, with the possible continuation being 14 dxc5 a5 15 a4 Be4 16 Qc3 b4 17 Qe3 Bd5, Andersson - Petursson, Reggio Emilia 1989/90. White should be slightly better after the continuing game course 18 Rfd1 Qc7 19 Nfd4 Bxg2 20 Kxg2 Bxc5 21 Rac1 because his pieces are more active and Black's a-pawn is vulnerable.

Instead, Black selects a less committing course and bides his time before breaking with ...c5.

13	...	Be4
14	Qc3	Nd5
15	Qd2	Nb4

The immediate 15...c5 16 Nxc5 Bxc5 17 dxc5 Rxc5 leads to an endgame advantage for White after 18 Rac1 Rxc1 19 Rxc1 Nf6 20 Qxd8 Rxd8 21 Ne5! Bxg2 22 Kxg2, Larsen - Tal, Naestved 1985. White's three remaining pieces are better placed than Black's and, moreover, Black's Queenside pawns are more vulnerable than White's.

However, I believe that Black can improve on the above line by first playing 15...Bb4! and only after 16 Qd1, 16...c5, as in Dlugy - de Firmian, New York Open 1985. Because White's Rooks are connected no more, Black has excellent prospects for full equality.

16	Rfc1	Bd5
17	Qd1	a5?

An instructive strategic error: Black weakens some more his already tender Queenside and this is enough to cause irreparable damage. Black must keep remembering that his objective is to free his game with ...c5. Therefore mandatory is 17...Bxb3! 18 Qxb3 c5! (GM Kouatly) because after 19 dxc5 Black has 19...Rxc5 (20 Qxb4?? Rxc1+), when White's advantage is minute.

18	a3	a4
19	Nc5	Nc6
20	Nb7!!	

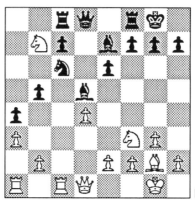

[diag. 9]

After the game GM Andersson told me that he liked this move very much and that it turned out to be even stronger than he had originally thought. The idea is to paralyze Black's Queenside while keeping complete control over c5. White has totally accomplished his strategic objective; Black has been a failure in achieving his goal. Still, of course, White must transform his success into something tangible, i.e. material advantage. As is generally true in the Catalan, so here too White's prospects do not lie against Black's King but on the Queenside.

20	...	Qd7
21	e3	Rb8
22	Nc5	Qc8
23	Nd2!	

Black's QB is the glue that holds the light squares in the center and on the Queenside together. Therefore it is thematic for White to exchange off his less active KB for Black's QB.

| 23 | ... | Rd8 |
| 24 | b4! | |

Continuing the strategically masterful play. If Black avoids exchanging, then White's pressure along the c-file will be unbearable; if Black exchanges, then White's pieces will gain infiltaration squares for entering Black's weakened Queenside. Black selects the second evil.

24	...	axb3
25	Ndxb3	Rb6
26	Bxd5	Rxd5
27	a4!	

Consistently continuing the plan initiated on move 24. White is satisfied to exchange his scraggly a-pawn for Black's b-pawn as that will allow him to train all his effort on Black's c-pawn. Note how crystal clear White's plan has been: by preventing ...c5, he has turned Black's c-pawn into a backward pawn. By opening the Queenside he is increasing the c-pawn's vulnerability. White's minimum goal is to capture that pawn for nothing.

27	...	bxa4
28	Nxa4	Ra6
29	Qc2	

The Q + R battery on the c-file is now in place. The opening of the Queenside has given White key squares there and extremely strong pressure against the c-pawn. The odds are at least 99% that White will capture it. Therefore, Black should aim to lose it in a "favorable" manner. According to Andersson, Black's only hope is to allow the capture of the c-pawn in such a way as to bring about an endgame. Then Black's drawing chances would be based on the fact that all the remaining pawns are on the same side. Even so, that pawn configuration is the for White very favorable 5P vs 4P one. These endgames almost invariably go lost in real life, even if at the start they may not be 100% theoretically lost. The defensive job is so onerous and the need for perfection so absolute that, assuming good play by the stronger side, the defender can't be up to it and loses.

29	...	Bd6?!

Hereafter the KR will not be able to participate in the defense of the Queenside. Therefore, in order is 29...Rd8.

30	Nc3!	Nb4
31	Qe2	Rg5
32	Rxa6!	

A well known strategy: by exchanging off the Queenside defending Rook, White's remaining Rook will have a much more decisive effect on the Queenside. For instance, Black cannot respond with 32...Qxa6? because White wins immediately after 33 Qxa6 Nxa6 34 Ra1, e.g. 34...Nb8 35 Ra8 c6 36 Nc5 or 34...Nb4 35 Ne4 followed by 36 Nxd6 and 37 Ra8+. Note how already in these variations Black's Queenside misses its wayward Rook.

32	...	Nxa6
33	Ne4	Rd5
34	Ra1	Nb8

After 34...Nb4, decisive is 35 Qc4.

35	Nc3	Rg5

36	Ne4	Rd5
37	Nc3	Rg5
38	Qc4!	

[diag. 10]

White's current objective is to establish overwhelming supremacy on the Queenside. He now has all four of his pieces actively placed there, whereas Black is, in effect, playing without his Rook. White need not rush to concentrate on the c-pawn - that will drop in due course in any event. White's immediate threat is 39 Ra7.

38	...	Qb7
39	Rb1!	

The threat now is 40 Nc5 Qc8 41 N5e4 followed by 42 Nxd6. Black's scattered forces are no match for White's concentrated small army.

39	...	Qc6
40	Nc5	Nd7

The end is equally near after 40...Qe8, e.g. 41 Qa4! Nc6 42 N5e4 Ra5 43 Nxd6 cxd6 44 Qxc6! etc.

41	Nxd7!	Qxd7
42	Ne4	Black resigns

The killer after a Rook move is 43 Nxd6.

Game 5

White: Viktor Korchnoi
Black: Tigran Petrosian
Played at 1977 Quarter-Final Candidates Match, Il Ciocco, Italy, Game 3

1	c4	e6
2	g3	d5
3	Bg2	Nf6
4	Nf3	Be7
5	d4	

The game is about to reach—after transposition of moves—the main line position. (The "pure" Catalan move order would have been 1 d4 Nf6 2 c4 e6 3 g3 d5 4 Bg2 Be7 5 Nf3.) After the normal 5...0-0 6 0-0 the main line is reached—see the previous game. Instead ...

5 ...   dxc4?!

Played infrequently and for good reason. If Black wants to choose one of the open defenses (i.e. involving ...dxc4) to the Catalan, then he should capture either on the 4th move or on the 6th (as in Game 4). By capturing on move 4 (i.e. after 1 d4 Nf6 2 c4 e6 3 g3 d5 4 Bg2) Black aims for quick development of the Queenside, e.g. 5 Qa4+ Nbd7 6 Qxc4 a6, planning an early ...b5 and possibly ...c5. The capture on move 6 means that White also has castled and thus has not started mobilizing his Queenside forces. For Black to capture on move 5 mixes up the two systems. Compared to the variation given after Black's 4th move, the development of Black's KB to e7 has done nothing to further Queenside play and thus Black is a tempo behind. Moreover after the text White can improve on the non-committal castling (6 0-0) by starting Queenside and central play a move earlier.

6 Nc3!

6 Qa4+ is also good, but the developmental text is stronger because White can recover the c-pawn under more favorable conditions. For instance, 6...Nc6 7 Qa4 or 6...Nbd7 7 Nd2! Nb6 8 Nxc4 Nxc4 9 Qa4+ - in each case White's superior central influence and powerful KB give him a clear advantage.

6 ...   0-0
7 Ne5!

By recovering the c-pawn with the KN, White opens the diagonal of his KB.

7 ...   c5

Black tries to exploit White's lack of castling with this central challenge. In general, such an approach is thematic, but here the results are disappointing. Therefore, worth exploring is 7...Nc6!?, an idea analogous to that in the main line (5...0-0 6 0-0 dxc4 7 Ne5 Nc6!).

8 dxc5!   Qxd1+

Leads to an unpleasant endgame, as does 8...Bxc5 9 Qxd8 Rxd8 10 Nxc4 Nc6 11 0-0, transposing into Filip-Unzicker, Nice Olympiad 1974. Yet the middlegame after 8...Qc7 9 Nxc4 is equally unpleasant:
1) 9...Qxc5 10 b3!, or
2) 9...Bxc5 10 0-0! when 10...Bxf2+? 11 Rxf2 Qxc4 is refuted by 12 Rxf6!! gxf6 13 Bh6 Nc6 14 e3! Rd8 15 Qh5 e5 16 Ne4 Qe6 17 Qh4 Black resigns, Ivkov - Robatsch, Vinkovci 1968. In each of these variations White —thanks to his fantastic KB— has extremely strong pressure against Black's Queenside.

9 Nxd1

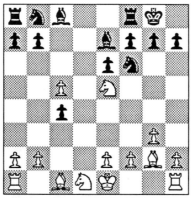

[diag. 11]

This is a position very easy to misjudge by those not steeped in the potential of the Catalan. Because White is not yet castled and his QN is "underdeveloped" Black appears to be well off as far as development is concerned. Moreover, the pawn formation is essentially symmetrical. Yet any apparent equality is very misleading. What matters is that White's KB is raking Black's Queenside, in particular b7, making it very difficult for Black to complete his development there. Therefore, White has a clear advantage and the best that Black can hope for is laborious equality far down the line.

The strategic themes are:

WHITE will attempt to put Black's Queenside under siege. White's immediate weapon is the KB, which will be joined early by both Knights and later by the QB and Rooks.

BLACK must work to get his Queenside developed. At least some of the power of White's KB must be neutralized to achieve this.

9 ... Nbd7?!

This cannot be right since White's KB is allowed to remain lord of his diagonal. To mitigate that power, Black's QN will have to be developed to c6. In order is 9...Bxc5, whereupon White has two ways of retaining his pleasant advantage:

(1) 10 0-0 Nc6 11 Nxc4 Bd7 12 Be3 Be7 (12...Nd4 is met by 13 Nc3) 13 Nc3 Rac8 (Slightly better is 13...Rfd8 14 Rac1 with a continuing edge for White.) 14 Rad1 Rfd8 15 Bf4 Be8 16 Nd6 Bxd6 17 Bxd6, Shcherbakov - Gavrilyuk, USSR 1988. The active Bishops in an open position give White a very strong initiative.

(2) 10 Nxc4 Nc6 11 0-0 Bd7 12 Nc3 (12 Be3 transposes into the above game.) 12...Rad8 13 Bf4 b6 14 Rfd1, F. Olafsson - Donner, Amsterdam 1976. White's piece activity is much superior to Black's, leading to a clear advantage.

10 Nxc4 Nxc5
11 Nc3!

With the simplest of moves White has made Black's position close to critical. Because White's KB controls the key e4, d5 and b7 squares, Black's difficulties in completing his development are manifest. His only chance is 11...Rd8, to be able to follow up with 12...Nd5.

11 ... Bd7?!

After the routine text Black's position becomes critical. The 28 minutes Petrosian spent on it signifies his unhappiness with what he himself had sowed. If Black would now have time for 12...Rac8 and 13...b6 most of his troubles would be over.

12 Na5!

No such luck! Note that the tempo saved by not having castled is exactly enough for White to establish killing pressure against Black's Queenside. Since there is no satisfactory way of protecting the b-pawn (12...Rab8 13 Bf4; 12...Bc8 13 b4 etc.) after 18 minutes thought Black decides to try his luck in "complications".

12 ... Nd5
13 Nxd5 exd5
14 Bxd5 Rac8

More in the spirit of hoping for miracles is 14...Bh3!?. White's best response probably is 15 Nc4.

15   O-O!

It is likely that the b-pawn is not a real poison and that 15 Nxb7 is O.K.. Yet after 15...Bh3! Black keeps White's King in the center and thereby has certain practical counterchances. White has already won a good clear pawn and there is no need to be greedy. The consolidating text is the sound practical approach.

15	...	b6
16	Nc4	Be6

16...Bh3 just chases White's Rook where it wants to go: 17 Rd1.

17	Ne3	Rfd8
18	Rd1	h5
19	b3	

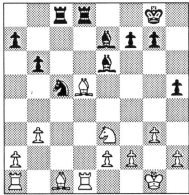

[diag. 12]

Black is a bit ahead in development, yet there is little doubt that White can successfully complete his, while retaining the extra pawn. The text seems like the obvious way to develop the QB and it is unclear why Korchnoi should feel it necessary to spend 24 minutes on it. With hindsight it would seem that he was starting to have difficulties in playing good sound moves.

19	...	Bg5
20	f4	Bf6
21	Rb1	Bh3

There is nothing of great import that Black can do on his own. He has loosened up White's Kingside pawn formation somewhat and perhaps hopes for a miracle there.

22	Bb2	Re8
23	Kf2	Bxb2
24	Rxb2	g6

25	Rbd2	Rc7

White has completed his consolidation and is ahead a sound e-pawn. On the other hand, Black has no structural weaknesses and therefore his only disadvantage is the missing pawn. Still, there is no reason why winning this position should be a difficult job for a world class GM. All that is required is the appropriate technique. For winning a won endgame, good technique involves the following principles:
- Establish and follow a clear plan.
- Don't allow counterplay.
- Avoid unclear or unnecessary complications.
- Be careful.
- Never be in a hurry, either with respect to time or number of moves.
- Hold on to material advantage.
- When ahead in material, continually try to simplify by exchanging pieces.
- Aim for the basic positions known as theoretical wins.

Yet starting around here, GM Korchnoi seems to forget that he is a pawn ahead. I think that now clearest is 26 Bf3 with the idea 27 Nd5.

26	Nc4	Ne4+
27	Bxe4	Rxe4
28	Rd8+	

The start of quite a wrong plan. Simple and correct is 28 Rd4! and if 28...Ree7, 29 e4, mobilizing the extra pawn.

28	...	Kh7
29	Rb8?!	

In playing for an attack against Black's King, White already misplaces one Rook. In effect, White is playing for complications when he should be working to make the extra pawn tell. Therefore, in order is 29 R8d4!. The fact that Black's King is on h7 rather than g8 is of no importance.

29	...	R4e7
30	Ne3	Kg7!

Black adopts a flexible defensive formation and awaits developments. Now 31 Nd5?! is harmless because of 31...Red7 32 Nxc7 Rxd1 when Black's active Rook gives excellent counterchances, e.g. 33 Rb7?! Rd2! 34 Rxa7 Bg4.

31 Rdd8?!

Continuing to chase the wind when the position requires care and attention. There was still plenty of time to undo the damage and head back with 31 Rbd8!, threatening 32 Nd5.

31	...	Be6
32	Rg8+	

32 Rd2 is better.

32	...	Kf6
33	h3??	

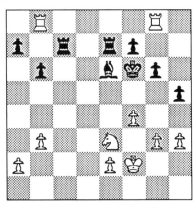

[diag. 13]

Finally throwing away the win. Rather than being careful while preempting possible Black counterplay by exchanging a pair of Rooks with 32 Rge8! Red7 34 Rbd8, Korchnoi is still transfixed by the thought of attacking Black's King. With the text he "gladly" puts a pawn en prise, while forgetting that Black's well placed pieces can also create threats.

33	...	Rc3!

Ending White's dream, since the intended 34 g4? fails to 34...hxg4 35 hxg4 (35 Nxg4+? Bxg4 36 hxg4 Rc2) 35...Rxe3! 36 Kxe3 (No better is 36 g5+ Kf5 37 Kxe3 Bxb3+) 36...Bxg4+ followed by 37...Rxe2 when, if anyone is better, it is Black. Meanwhile Black is threatening 34...Bxb3.

Being the great player that he is, Korchnoi bites his lips and heads for equality.

34	Rbe8!	Rxe8
35	Rxe8	Rc5!

With the threats of 36...Ra5 winning the a-pawn and 36...Bxh3, capturing the loose h-pawn. White can only parry one of them.

36	g4	Ra5
37	f5	gxf5
38	gxf5	

38 gxh5?! Kg7! can only be in Black's interest.

38	...	Bxf5
39	Nxf5	Draw

After 39...Kxf5 40 a4 the position is dead even.

* * * * *

Game 6

White: Lev Polugaevsky
Black: Viktor Korchnoi
Played at 1977 Semi-Final Candidates Match, Evian, France, Game 8

1	d4	Nf6
2	c4	e6
3	g3	Bb4+

GM Korchnoi is responsible for bringing this check to full respectability in international play. The ultimate point of the check is that White has no "perfect response. If White now plays 4 Nc3, then the opening has become the Nimzo-Indian with White having chosen the Romanishin Variation (4 g3). Of course, if White is interested in this, he would not be playing 3 g3, but instead 3 Nc3.

If White selects 4 Nd2, then the d-pawn is unprotected and Black achieves excellent play in the center with the thematic 4...c5. According to current theory White cannot expect any opening advantage thereafter.

The "Korchnoi Variation", 3...Bb4+, is currently a major viable alternative to the normal 3...d5. It is another important reason why more and more "Catalan players" avoid an early d4. See already the earlier Games 4 and 5 and the following Game 7.

4 Bd2

The previous discussion has made it clear that the text is the only way for Catalan players to go for an opening advantage. Black can, of course, respond with the routine 4...Bxd2+ when, after 5 Qxd2, the opening transposes into a playable yet inherently passive-for-Black variation of the Bogo-Indian Defense. Such a course of action would rob Black of the chance of demonstrating any of the sophistication behind the chosen move order. Therefore ...

4	...	Be7!
5	Bg2	d5
6	Nf3	0-0
7	0-0	

It is time to take our first look at what Black's 3rd and 4th moves have wrought. We have exactly the same position as in the main line of Game 4 after White's 6th move, except that instead of being back home on c1, the QB has been developed to d2. Therefore it can be said that White has gained one developmental tempo—yet is this really a gain? Having the Bishop on d2 so early can easily turn out to be a disadvantage for White: the opportunity to fianchetto the QB is lost, the d2 square is taken away from the QN and—less importantly—in some positions after White's Queen moves to b3 or c2 the e-pawn is unprotected and chances of play along the d-file are decreased. In addition, it can be expected that the QB will have to move again relatively soon.

> 7 ...   c6

Entering the Closed Variation is Black's only promising continuation; moreover, the ability to enter this variation under favorable conditions is the major objective behind the ...Bb4+, ...Be7 maneuver. Black should not choose 7...dxc4?! as after 8 Qc2 a6 9 Qxc4 Bb7 he is a whole tempo behind the 10 Bd2 variation given in the notes to Black's 9th move in Game 4.

> 8 Qc2

The usual and best place for the Queen in the Closed Catalan: the c-pawn is protected and support given for the important e4 advance. We have learned that in the standard Closed Variation (3...d5 4 Bg2 Be7 5 Nf3 0-0 6 0-0 c6) development of the Queen to b3 (i.e. 7 Qb3) is less effective because the potential for the central advance e4 decreases and little in turn is gained. However, in our case 8 Qb3 comes with a meaningful strategic basis: the clumsily placed QB is to be exchanged off for Black's KB via Bb4, thereby enhancing White's control over the dark squares. Therefore 8 Qb3 is a good alternative to the standard 8 Qc2.

> 8 ...   Nbd7

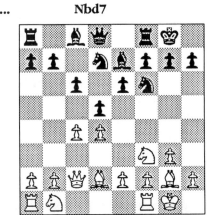

[diag. 14]

The respective strategic themes in the Closed Variation are:
BLACK needs to quickly complete the development of his QB with
...b6 and Bb7/Ba6. Because White has a slight central superiority, Black
can only hope to get full equality if he neutralizes that by getting in...c5
himself.
WHITE will build on his central superiority by aiming for e2-e4. This
advance will also enhance the scope of his KB.

9 b3

White protects the c-pawn and is ready to continue with the standard
plan of 10 Nc3 and 11 e4. Yet, as will be seen, under the circumstances
of the "Korchnoi Variation", this is difficult to execute. Therefore, White
probably does better to transpose into the "old Bf4 variation" (3...d5 4
Bg2 Be7 5 Nf3 0-0 6 0-0 c6 7 Qc2 Nbd7 8 Bf4) with 9 Bf4. Korchnoi himself
(now on the White side!) did so against GM Murray Chandler at Hastings
1988/89 and retained a slight edge after 9...Nh5 10 Bc1! f5 11 b3 Ndf6 12
e3 Bd7 13 Ba3! Bxa3 14 Nxa3, because of control of the dark squares and
the superior Bishop.

9 ...   b6
10 Rd1

The objectives of the text are to try to inhibit an early ...c5 by Black
as well as to enhance the power behind an eventual e2-e4. After the
immediate 10 Nc3, Black has 10...Ba6! with an annoying pressure on the
c-pawn.

10 ...   Ba6!

After the passive 10...Bb7, White has time for 11 Nc3 and thereby a
normal edge after both the standard 11...Rc8 12 e4 dxe4 13 Nxe4 as well
as the interesting 13 Ne5!? c5 14 Bf4, as played in Palatnik - Rashkovsky,
Palma de Mallorca 1989.
In the standard Closed Variation, the thematic placement of the QN
for White is as follows: if Black plays ...Bb7, White responds with Nc3;
if Black chooses ...Ba6, White selects the flexible Nbd2. Of course, this
is not possible here and therefore White's task is more difficult.

11 a4

With the reasonable idea of continuing with 12 a5 after 11...Rc8?!, yet
essentially amounts to loss of a developmental tempo. Only with 11 Bf4,
enabling 12 Nbd2 and hopefully 13 e4 can White hope for a slight edge.

11 ...   Ne4

Playable, yet starting with this move Black seems to forget that he is in the Catalan. Best is the thematic 11...c5!, with Black achieving comfortable equality after 12 Na3 Bb7! 13 Qb2 Rc8 14 Rac1 Ne4 15 Be1 Bf6, Yusupov - Haritonov, USSR Championship 1988.

12   Bf4   Rc8
13   Nbd2

Finally completing the harmonious development of the Queenside minor pieces. I would now expect a great fighter like Korchnoi to follow up his 11th move with 13...f5!?. However, his modest response is also thematic and sound.

13   ...   Nxd2
14   Rxd2   g5?!

Yet this is most inconsistent. What Black did not dare to do on his previous move—gaining space on the Kingside by means of pawn advances—he does now under inferior conditions. Because Black has exchanged off his most actively placed piece on the Kingside, chances for success there are considerably decreased.

In the spirit of the Closed Variation is the careful 14...Nf6 and if 15 Ne5, the thematic 15...c5!?. Black's chances for equality are then bright.

15   Be3   f5
16   Rdd1!   Bf6
17   Rac1

Finally the development of all of White's pieces is complete and he can look confidently toward the future. He has retained his original central superiority and pressure, the important e5 square is a permanent weakness and Black's g-pawn is not so secure either. White has no weaknesses and no worries. His advantage is clear.

17   ...   h6?!

Instead of being helpful, this is counterproductive because Black creates a new fundamental weakness - the h-pawn. It was imperative for Black to notice that his forces are rather scattered about and that the immediate need was to improve their coordination. Correct is 17...Rf7! and after 18 Qd2, 18...Rg7.

18   Qd2!

Lining up against the g-pawn: White now has three pieces trained against it and the h-pawn is waiting in the wings. Here was the last chance for 18...Rf7. Instead, Black makes the situation worse with ...

[diag. 15]

18 ...   Bg7?

Protecting the h-pawn and opening the way for the KR's activity along the f-file. But the key point is g5 and White immediately exploits this factor.

19   h4!!

From a purely strategic viewpoint the undermining of the g-pawn is obvious. Yet the strength of the text—even its playability—rested on the correct evaluation of the position resulting several moves hence. In hindsight the evaluation may appear easy to do, but in real life the situation is much more uncertain, because undeniably White's King position is considerably denuded.

19   ...   f4!?

The only move to worry about when considering 19 h4!!. It does hasten Black's demise, yet offers some hope for counterchances. After the routine 19...g4, White retreats 20 Ne1 and then at his leisure starts working on all the holes in Black's camp, for instance, 20...Kh7 21 Nd3 followed by 22 Nf4 etc.

20	gxf4	g4
21	Ne5	Nxe5
22	dxe5!	Qxh4
23	cxd5!	cxd5

Forced, as 23...exd5? is refuted by 24 Rxc6!. After the text, a static analysis may indicate that Black is in fine shape: material is equal, White has both doubled e- and f-pawns, whereas Black has a passed h-pawn and his Queen is poised close to White's King. However, the board dynamics show quite a different picture: White has excellent prospects of infiltrating via the c-file into Black's position and a properly timed f5 break will annihilate Black's center. Even though White's King is fairly open, it is safe enough because Black cannot readily marshal additional forces to assist the Queen in its attack.

24   Rxc8!   Bxc8

The alternative 24...Rxc8, risks the immediate break-up of Black's center with 25 f5!? when 25...Bxe5? 26 fxe6 is killing but 25...exf5 is not so clear (26 Bxd5+ Kh8 27 Bf4 Qe7; 26 Qxd5+ Kh8 27 e6 Bxe2). White, of course, has no reason to rush and can first improve his position with 25 Rc1!. Then 25...Rf8 26 Rc7 transposes into the game; 25...Rxc1+?! 26 Qxc1 Bxe2? 27 Qc8+ Kf7 28 f5! gives White a decisive attack; 25...Qd8 is necessary, with White retaining a large advantage after 26 Rxc8 Bxc8 27 Qc2 as well as 26...Qxc8 27 f5!.

25   Rc1!   g3
26   Rc7   Ba6?

Allowing White to capture on a7 with gain of time must be inherently hopeless. For better or worse, the consistent 26...h5! had to be ventured. The play then can become exceedingly complicated, with one likely continuation being 27 fxg3 Qxg3 28 b4! h4 29 Bf2 Qg4 30 Qe3 h3 31 Qxh3 Qxf4 32 Bg3! Qe3+ 33 Kh2. White not only threatens 34 Rxc8!, but his pieces also dominate the board, making Black's chances for survival poor.

27   fxg3   Qxg3
28   Rxa7   Bc8
29   b4!   Kh8

29...h5 gets the same response.

30   Bf2!

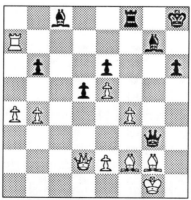

[diag. 16]

30	...	Qg4

Or 30...Qxf4 31 Qxf4 Rxf4 32 Ra8 Rc4 33 Bxb6 and the connected passed pawns will win.

31	Rc7	h5
32	Qe3	Rg8

32...Bh6 is parried by 33 Qd3! Bg7 34 Qf3 etc.

33	Qf3!	Qf5

There also are no prospects after 33...Qxf3 34 exf3.

34	Bh4!	d4
35	Bg5	Qg6
36	Qd3	**Black resigns**

The endgame after 36...Qxd3 37 exd3 is hopeless, as is the middlegame after 36...Qe8 37 Bc6 Qf8 38 Qg6.

*   *   *   *   *

Game 7

White: Edmar Mednis
Black: Josef Franzen
Played at Copenhagen International Tournament 1989

1	c4	e6
2	g3	d5
3	Bg2	dxc4

This capture usually occurs after the insertion of 3...Nf6 4 Nf3. There is no basic difference between these alternatives.

4	Qa4+	Nbd7

Usual and best. The alternatives are inferior to some degree. For instance, the solid 4...c6 is too passive since the c-pawn will have to go to c5 to give sufficient central support. On an instant evaluation basis 4...Bd7 5 Qxc4 Bc6 may appear attractive, yet it lacks long term future after 6 Nf3, because on c6 the Bishop is awkwardly placed, takes away that square from the QN, while blocking the c-pawn.

5	Qxc4	c5
6	Nf3	Ngf6

This is the normal position in the Catalan complex where White has not yet moved his d-pawn and Black has played an early ...dxc4. (The standard move order is 1 c4 Nf6 2 g3 e6 3 Bg2 d5 4 Nf3 dxc4 5 Qa4+ Nbd7 6 Qxc4 c5.) The strategic themes are:

Black's overriding need is to smoothly develop his Queenside. Because Black's c- and e-pawns give him good central influence, once his Queenside development is complete Black can expect comfortable equality.

White wants to hinder Black's Queenside development. The Queen and the KB are the key pieces in that effort. If Black's development remains delayed, White will be able to advantageously open up the position.

7   0-0   a6

This standard move is not as effective as it looks at first glance because White can inhibit Black's immediate plan. More frequent in grandmaster play is 7...b6, with the idea that 8 Nd4 can be met by 8...Ne5 when the endgame after 9 Nc6 Nxc4 10 Nxd8 Nd5 is perfectly satisfactory for Black. I think that White's best way of keeping an opening edge is with 8 Ng5! Rb8 9 Nc3, e.g. 9...Bb7 10 d4! Bxg2 11 Kxg2 Qc8 12 dxc5 Bxc5 13 Bf4 Be7! (only move) 14 Qxc8+ Rxc8 15 Nb5 with pressure in the endgame, Smyslov - Averkin, USSR 1979.

8   Qb3!

[diag. 17]

Squelching both 8...b5? and 8...b6? because of 9 Nd4 Rb8 10 Nc6. Still, Black must smoothly develop his Queenside to hope for equality. Another problem for him is that White, by omitting an early d4, has not given Black any targets for counterplay in the center. What is Black to do?

8   ...   Be7?!

The routine game plan starting with this move does not do the job. After the game IM Franzen felt that his best plan would have been

8...Ra7 followed by 9...b6. This is reasonable, yet the poor location of the QR does make Black's road to equality arduous. I think that Black's most effective set-up is 8...Bd6 followed by 9...Rb8, but White still keeps some pull.

9 d3!

Again, by keeping his central pawns back while going about his development, White prevents counterplay and keeps up pressure against the Queenside.

9 ...   0-0
10 a4

Continuing the objective of containing Black's Queenside: White prevents ...b5 while getting ready to lame Black's Queenside with a a5 advance. Nevertheless, Black must give development of his Queenside his maximum priority. Therefore 10...Nd5 with the idea 11...b6 and 10...Bd6 with the follow-up 11...Rb8 make sense.

10 ...   e5?!

Black wants to play 11...Rb8 without being bothered by 12 Bf4, but the weakening of d5 while wasting a tempo (the e-pawn has taken two moves to get to e5!) can not fail to ultimately tell against him. Even in inferior positions it is usually much better to follow the strategic themes of that position rather than voluntarily creating new problems.

11 Nbd2!

Much more in the spirit of Catalan without d4 than the routine 11 Nc3. On c3 the QN by itself "stands great", but can not help White to achieve anything else. Yet from c4 the QN will be able to attack the e-pawn, keep watch on the important b6 and d6 squares and ensure the safety and effectiveness of the a5 advance. Because White has been intentionally keeping the position closed, the extra time to reach the ideal c4 square is well worth it.

11 ...   Bd6
12 Nc4   Bc7
13 a5

A picture perfect Catalan for White: Black's Queenside is paralyzed and he has weaknesses in the center, while White's pieces are purposely and actively placed. All that White needs is a "proper" line opening to exploit these advantages.

13 ...   Re8
14 Bd2

I looked at 14 Ng5 (threatening 15 Nxf7) b ut after, for instance, 14...Qe7 there was no clear follow-up. Therefore, I decided to first complete my minor piece development. White now is ready for action. If Black does nothing, White will crack open the Queenside with 15 Qa3 and 16 b4. This will soon lead to Black's b-pawn becoming indefensible.

14   ...   Nb8?!

Aiming for 15...Nc6, but meets a tactical refutation. Also inadvisable is 14...e4?! because after 15 dxe4 Nxe4 16 Be3 followed by 17 Rfd1, the line opening can only benefit the side with superior development which obviously is White. Black has to be satisfied with 14...Rb8 or 14...Nf8.

15   Ng5!

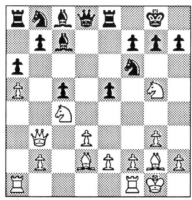

[diag. 18]

With the primary threat of 16 Nxf7! (16...Kxf7 17 Nxe5+ Ke7 18 Qf7+ Kd6 19 Nc4 Mate) and a secondary one of 16 Bxb7. Black's reply, therefore, is forced.

15   ...   Nc6
16   Nb6!

The position after 15...Nc6 is somewhat frustrating for White in the sense that "White should be winning easily," yet there is nothing that simple. Thus 16 Nxf7 Nd4 is not so clear, while Black has real chances for counterplay after 16 Bxc6 bxc6 17 Nxf7 Qd5!. Therefore, starting with the text, I decided to always go for the clearest plan.

16   ...   Bxb6
17   Qxf7+

Also good is 17 Nxf7 Be6 (17...Nd4?? 18 Nh6+ allows the smothered mate on f7.) 18 Nxd8 Bxb3 and now not 19 Nxc6?? Bc7! when White's Knight has no place to go, but instead 19 Nxb7!. Yet the resulting position seemed to be more difficult to judge than the game continuation.

17	...	Kh8
18	Qc4	Qe7
19	axb6	h6
20	Ne4	Nxe4
21	Qxe4	Nd4
22	e3!	

Continuing with the approach of choosing the clearest road. Notice how White's Q + KB battery keeps Black's QB from being developed.

22	...	Nb3
23	Rad1	Nxd2
24	Rxd2	Qd8
25	Rc1!	Qxb6
26	Qd5	

As late as move 26, the strategic theme of the undeveloped Black Queenside is clearly apparent. White is sure to remain a pawn up as Black's only choice is whether to lose the b- or c-pawn.

26	...	Bf5

"Forcing" White to capture the b-pawn since the c-pawn now is poisoned: 27 Qxc5?? Rac8 28 Qxb6 Rxc1+ 29 Bf1 Bh3 and Black mates. The alternative, 26...Qb4, loses the c-pawn after 27 Rdc2 Bf5 28 Qxc5.

27	Qxb7	Qa5
28	Rdc2	Bxd3
29	Rxc5	Qd2

[diag. 19]

Black finally seems to be getting some counterplay as he is threatening both 30...Rf8 and 30...Rab8. Yet since White has done nothing wrong, the "justice" of chess should should allow White to keep his substantial advantage. In fact there are two ways of doing it. The elegant method is 30 Be4 Bxe4 (30...Rab8? 31 Qxb8! Rxb8 32 Rc8+ Rxc8 33 Rxc8 Mate) 31 Qxe4 Qxb2 32 Rc7 when Black will not be able to defend his porous Kingside. However, I preferred a simpler way where I remain up material while retaining attacking chances.

	30	Qxa8	Rxa8
	31	Bxa8	Qxb2
	32	Bd5	

Not necessary, but I was starting to run short of time and it seemed sensible to centralize the Bishop so that it can watch both Black's Kingside and my Queenside.

32 ...   a5

Black's only hope is the passed a-pawn. After 32...e4 33 h4! Black's Bishop cannot help defend the King.

33 h4!

Clearing h2 for the King while threatening h5 to weave a mating net over Black's King. Now 33...g6 runs into mate after 34 Rc8+ Kg7 35 R1c7+ Kf6 36 Rf8, while 33...h5 is refuted by 34 Rc8+ Kh7 35 R1c6 Qa3 36 e4! followed by 37 Bg8+. Thus Black pulls back his Bishop.

33 ...   Bf5

After his move Black offered a draw. Nothing so unusual about that, but what was unusual was that after the game he apologized for it, saying that he had realized that he was lost when he did so.

34 h5!   g5

Opening up the King position, but the threat was 35 Rc8+ Bxc8 36 Rxc8+ Kh7 37 Bg8+ Kh8 38 Bf7+ Kh7 39 Bg6 Mate.

	35	hxg6	Bxg6
	36	e4	

Another "safety first" move in time pressure. Of course, the immediate 36 Rc8+ Kg7 37 Rg8+ works just as in the game. Black remains completely defenseless after the text also.

	36	...	a4
	37	Rc8+	Kg7
	38	Rg8+	Black resigns

After 38...Kf6 39 Rc6+ Black first loses his Bishop and soon the King.

Dutch Defense

Game 8

White: Ivan Farago
Black: Jens Kristiansen
Played at Copenhagen International Tournament 1989

1   d4   f5

This position is the characteristic starting point of the Dutch Defense. After more than fifty years in the wilderness as far as international play is concerned, starting in the late 1980s the Dutch Defense has swept back into favor. The primary force behind this renaissance are the young Soviet GMs and IMs, abetted by young Western GMs such as Nigel Short of England and Lars Bo Hansen of Denmark. Because so many of the currently established openings become overanalyzed so quickly, it makes sense for the energetic young generation to look for other worlds to conquer, thereby attempting to remain a step ahead of their seniors in current opening developments.

The important strategical themes of the Dutch Defense are as follows: Black's primary central interest is control of e4. By having the f-pawn accomplish this, Black also keeps open the prospect of mobilizing it for a potential Kingside attack with a later ...f4 advance.

However, Black's move also has two serious disadvantages: nothing is done to further development and there is some weakening of the King position. Moreover, the f5 pawn inhibits the development of the QB along its original diagonal and this Bishop can readily turn out to be a "bad Bishop" hemmed in by his own central pawns.

White's prospects lie with the Queenside pressure characteristic of 1 d4 openings. In addition, often a properly timed e4 advance can both enhance the pressure of White's fianchettoed Bishop against Black's Queenside and prepare for an attack against Black's fundamentally somewhat weakened Kingside.

It is foolish for White to expect to have some immediate refutation at hand. However, a perceptive understanding of the demerits that 1...f5 has should allow White to obtain a larger long term advantage out of the opening than is possible in the high quality main line openings.

The above statements clearly imply that I don't expect the Dutch to join the list of openings judged to be 100% perfect. Yet it does have good points and Whites must be well prepared to face it. In particular, White should not underestimate the Dutch, but play "the best" that is available.

2   c4   Nf6
3   Nc3

An instructive moment. White chooses a less usual continuation because he feels that Danish IM Kristiansen—as a regular Dutch player —will be well prepared for the main lines starting with 3 g3. That no doubt is true but the important point is that White retains a larger than usual strategic advantage after 3 g3. As I mentioned earlier, it is imperative for White to play "the best" against the Dutch. The best setup is the KB fianchetto starting with 3 g3 or with 3 Nf3 followed by 4 g3. There are three excellent reasons why the early KB fianchetto is best: (1) The Bishop controls the important e4 square; (2) The Bishop bears down on Black's Queenside, and (3) The Bishop can assist in a later e4 break.

3   ...   e6
4   Nf3   Bb4

[diag. 20]

This position now shows many of the features of the Nimzo-Indian Defense. In fact, the Queenside deployment is identical. The only difference is on the Kingside where Black's f-pawn is already on f5 rather than back home on f7. Black thereby has more control of e4, though at the cost of a developmental tempo and a slightly weakened Kingside. On an objective basis the pluses and minuses probably cancel each other out. Yet I believe that in real life this position is easier to handle for the expert on the Dutch Defense than for a White player who has not delved deeply into its truth.

5   g3

Unless one is World Champion Garry Kasparov, it is probably easier to handle the positions without the doubled c-pawns. Therefore 5 Qb3 or 5 Bd2 come to mind. Also interesting is to speed the mobilization of the Queenside with 5 Bg5. A good example of this is Nogueiras - Naumkin, Moscow 1990: 5...0-0 6 e3 Bxc3+ 7 bxc3 d6 8 Bd3 Qe8 9 Qc2 Qh5 10 h3 Nc6 11 0-0-0! Qf7 12 Nd2 Ne7 13 g4 with White having some advantage due to his attacking chances on the Kingside.

5	...	0-0
6	Bg2	d6
7	0-0	Bxc3
8	bxc3	

The c3-c4-d4 central pawn cluster is a frequent and important occurence in QP openings. Most commonly it occurs from the Nimzo-Indian Defense. Its characteristics are as follows:

(1) The good points are that the c4 and d4 pawns control key central squares and the c3 pawn gives excellent support to the d4 pawn. White's center has been enhanced by the fact that the b2 pawn has been turned into the c3 pawn.

(2) There are two bad points: the c4 pawn is a chronic weakness because it can not be protected by another pawn and the a-pawn is isolated. This latter factor can become a serious problem in the endgame.

In most cases the good and bad points are of approximately equal significance and do not affect the evaluation of the game position. In almost all cases the resulting position is very unbalanced and the play is dynamic. There generally are two correct ways for White to handle this central formation: (1) Leave the c4 and d4 pawns as is: (2) Aim for a properly timed c5 advance, dissolving the double pawn and opening the position for White's Bishops. We will see an excellent example of this in the note to Black's 9th move.

The Encyclopedia of Chess Openings A (1979), quoting an old analysis by Ex-World Champion Max Euwe now suggests 8...Qe8, claiming equality for Black. To me that seems overoptimistic, because White's central superiority and the potential of the Bishop pair should be good enough for the normal slight opening advantage.

| 8 | ... | Ne4 |

Thematic and good: Black activates his Knight onto the important e4 square with gain of time.

| 9 | Qc2 | Nc6 |

Via some major transpositions we have reached Kasparov - Karpov, 1985 World Championship, Match Game 19, i.e. Karpov could have gotten this position if instead of his offside 9...Na5?! he had played the sensible 9...d6. (The actual game course was 1 d4 Nf6 2 c4 e6 3 Nc3 Bb4 4 Nf3 Ne4 5 Qc2 f5 6 g3 Nc6 7 Bg2 0-0 8 0-0 Bxc3 9 bxc3 Na5?! 10 c5 d6 11 c4!! b6?! 12 Bd2! Nxd2 13 Nxd2 with a large advantage—at no cost—to White. Instead of the fearful 11...b6?! Kasparov suggests the natural 11...dxc5 when after either 12 Ba3 or 12 Rd1 White has "unpleasant pressure," but Black at least has a pawn for his sorrows.)

10 d5?

[diag. 21]

A surprising misplaying of the central pawn structure by a strong GM. The immobile doubled c-pawns will now be a permanent structural weakness and, moreover, White has given up control of e5 while getting nothing in return. The number of times that this advance is promising is very very small.

If White wants to start playing aggressively, 10 c5!, a la Kasparov, is promising. Also reasonable are 10 Ba3, 10 Rd1 and 10 Nd2.

10	...	Na5
11	Nd4	Qf6!
12	dxe6	

Worse is 12 Bxe4?! fxe4 13 Qxe4 e5 14 Nf3 Bf5 when Black will recover his pawn with a substantial advantage.

12	...	Bxe6
13	Nxf5	Bxf5
14	Bxe4	Rae8
15	Bxf5	Qxf5
16	Qd3	Qc5

The inherent disadvantage of the c3-c4-d4 pawn cluster—magnified by the erroneous 10 d5?—are now obvious. Once Black captures on c4, material will be equal but White will be handicapped by having isolated a- and c-pawns.

17 Rb1?!

To me this move shows that White is underrating his opponent in choosing to hold on to an unimportant double pawn at the cost of a very clumsy misplacing of his QR. Correct is the developmental 17 Be3, with just a slight disadvantage for White (Kristiansen).

17	...	b6
18	Rb4	Qh5!
19	Be3	Nc6
20	Ra4?!	Ne5
21	Qd5+	Kh8
22	Re1	Rf5?!

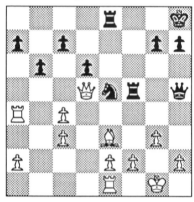

[diag. 22]

Black gets spooked by the pin on his Knight and thereby gives up most of his advantage. As Kristiansen later pointed out, correct is 22...a5!, locking in White's QR while preventing counterplay. Instead of being a threat, 23 f4? is nothing but a serious weakness: 23...Qh3! 24 fxe5 Rxe5 25 Qd2? (25 Qg2 allows a lost endgame) 25...Rh5 and Black will mate. Note how irrelevant to the scene of action White's QR is.

| 23 | Qg2 | Ng4 |

Now after 23...a5 White has time for 24 h3 followed perhaps by 25 f4 or 25 c5.

| 24 | Rxa7 | Nxe3 |

The ambitious 24...Rxe3? doesn't work because of 25 fxe3 h6 26 h4 Nxe3 27 Qe4! (Kristiansen).

| 25 | fxe3 | Qg5 |
| 26 | Qe4! | |

Taking advantage of Black's back rank weakness, thanks to the active location of the QR, White is able to prevent the immediate infiltration by Black's major pieces. White's disadvantage is now slight.

26	...	Rfe5
27	Qf4!	Qe7
28	Rf1	Kg8
29	Qf3	h6
30	Ra8	

Even though White, by arithmetic count, is up two pawns, his miserable pawn structure means that he must be the one aiming for the draw. Exchanging off one set of Rooks is the correct way since it removes a powerful Black attacking piece from the board.

30	...	Rxa8
31	Qxa8+	Kh7
32	Qf3!	Rxe3
33	Qf5+	Kg8
34	Qd5+	

After 34 Qc8+ Qe8 35 Qxe8+ White can transpose into the next note. Instead of 35 Qxe8, 35 Qxc7!? seems dangerous, yet it appears that White can survive after both 35...Rxe2 36 Qxb6 Qe4 37 Rf2 and 36...Rxa2 37 Qd4.

34	...	Qe6

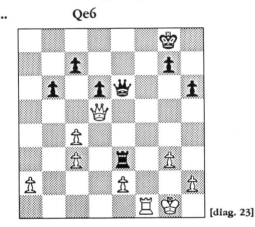

[diag. 23]

35   Rf3??

Short of time and no doubt upset at "squandering" the advantage of the White pieces against a lower rated opponent, White simply leaves his important e-pawns hanging. Necessary is 35 Qxe6+ Rxe6 36 Kf2 when after 36...Re4 Black has the advantage but with proper defense White should be able to hold.

35	...	Rxe2	
36	Qxe6+	Rxe6	
37	Kf1	Re4	
38	Rf2	Rxc4	
39	Rc2	d5	
40	Rd2	Rxc3	White resigns

White quickly played 41 Rxd5 and then immediately resigned in view of 41...Rc1+ 42 Ke2 Rc2+ when both the R & P endgame after 43 Kf3 Rxa2 and the K & P endgame after 43 Rd2 Rxd2+ are hopeless.

English Opening
Game 9

White: Edmar Mednis
Black: Igor Ivanov
Played at Brighton (England) International Tournament 1983

1   c4

Now we have the English Opening—true or false? The correct answer is "both" or another way of saying it is "it depends." About half the time the game will transpose into something else, most frequently a 1 d4 opening, yet many Reti Openings also result and there are even opportunities for some transpositions into 1 e4 openings. As a matter of fact, in a number of cases whether a variation is deemed to be English, Reti or a QP opening is simply a matter of convention or history. As a rough guideline we can say that if White delays d4 or if after White's d4, Black's c- or e-pawn captures it without a White pawn being able to recapture, then the opening variation will be considered to be English rather than QP. Obviously, to be an English White must have played a very early c4.

What White's first move makes very clear is that his focus, at least in the beginning, will be on the Queenside. Unlike 1 d4 which also controls e5, 1 c4 only looks on the left side of the board: the b5 and d5 squares, development of the QN to c3 and development of the Queen along the d1 - a4 diagonal.

1   ...   Nf6

Normal, flexible and good. Black delays making a definitive decision regarding what set-up he favors and "invites" White to transpose into a QP opening with 1 d4.

Black's most thematic, independent response is 1...e5, about which can be said that "what White didn't dare to do on his first move, Black does." As a matter of fact many GMs consider this variation to be a Sicilian Defense Reversed. (I will comment further on this a bit later.) Because they are reluctant to play "a Sicilian" even with a move in hand, these GMs "prevent" 1...e5 by first playing 1 Nf3 and only after 1...Nf6 or 1...c5 enter the potential English lines with 2 c4.

2   g3

Most common is the immediate 2 Nc3—see also Game 10. As a follow-up to 1 c4, 2 Nc3 is absolutely perfect in a theoretical sense. Yet there are two practical reasons why many GMs (including me) delay it. In the first place, Black can respond with 2...e6, "threatening" 3...d5. This leaves White with only the choices of acquiescing to a Queen's Gambit or Nimzo-Indian with 3 d4, a Queen's Gambit with 3 Nf3 d5 4 d4 or entering the strategically messy English Variation named after GM Mikenas with 3 e4.

Moreover, after 2...e5 Black can achieve a quasi-pin of the QN with ...Bb4 after either 3 g3 Bb4 or 3 Nf3 Nc6 4 g3 Bb4—see Game 10. I don't like to allow that either.

	2	...	e5
	3	Bg2	d5

Again the most demanding plan: Black opens up the position while ensuring active piece development for himself, yet at the strategic cost of exchanging off his primary central d-pawn for White's secondary central c-pawn. Note that this again parallels White's approach against the Sicilian. Because of the opportunities for active, dynamic play, this variation is currently very popular among GMs.

Black can also choose a centrally more thematic way of aiming for ...d5 by first playing 3...c6. I think that White's only way to go for an advantage then is to open up the position with 4 d4. After 4...exd4 5 Qxd4 d5 6 cxd5 Black either has to absorb an isolated d-pawn with 6...cxd5 or some central inferiority after 6...Nxd5. Of course, Black can also play 3...Nc6, aiming for Game 10 positions or 3...d6 with the primary intent of achieving King's Indian formations after ...g6, ...Bg7 etc. Of course, those welcoming King's Indians would be more likely to start off with 1...Nf6, 2...g6, 3...Bg7 etc.—see Game 11.

	4	cxd5	Nxd5
	5	Nc3	Nb6

Just about the only move played currently. Instead 5...c6 is too passive, 5...Be6 allows White to favorably open the position after 6 Nf3 Nc6 7 0-0 Be7 8 d4!, while 5...Nxc3 6 bxc3 enhances White's center while getting nothing in return.

	6	Nf3	Nc6
	7	0-0	Be7

[diag. 24]

It is time to take a deeper look into this position. The most important strategic point to note is that we have the mirror image of the Old Dragon Variation in the Sicilian Defense (1 e4 c5 2 Nf3 d6 3 d4 cxd4 4 Nxd4 Nf6 5 Nc3 g6 6 Be2 Bg7 7 0-0 Nc6 8 Nb3) if White now continues with 8 d3. The difference of course is that White is a move up on Black in the Sicilian and this is a huge difference. After all, what is the difference between White and Black at the start of the game except that White is on move? Therefore in this position also White has the normal slight opening advantage. Because of this major factor, I can not really feel that I am playing the Sicilian Defense here since in that case I would have to first go for equality.

Nevertheless, the realization that thematically Diagram 24 is a Sicilian Dragon Reversed is crucial for understanding what the strategic themes for both sides are:

- WHITE'S thematic arena of early activity will be the Queenside. The half-open c-file is the traditional route of pressure, with c5 being the key weak square on Black's Queenside. White's KB is a significant force in applying pressure against Black's Queenside, aiming at the Queenside can also make Black's e-pawn vulnerable to an attack from a White Bb2 and/or a b-pawn advance to b5. If Black is forced to undertake a clumsy defense of the e-pawn or the c5 square, then White can aim to open the position with d4, thereby taking advantage of Black's clumsily placed pieces.
- BLACK needs to make use of the central presence provided by having the only primary central pawn on the fourth rank, i.e. the e5 pawn. In general, this means that Black's attacking chances are on the Kingside. However, this attack is difficult to execute because playing the thematic ...f5 will lead to difficulties protecting the e-pawn, as well as weakness on the a2 - g8 diagonal. This is quite different from the Sicilian Defense where f4 for White is a normal and strong attacking move.

Therefore the primary use of the e5 pawn will be as support for a ...Nd4 sortie and prevention of White's d4. In case of carelessness by White, the ...e4 advance can become powerful.

8 d3

Traditional, sensible and good. This position would result if White had played d3 earlier, e.g. 1 c4 e5 2 Nc3 Nf6 3 Nf3 Nc6 4 d3 d5 (4...Bb4 5 Bd2) 5 cxd5 Nxd5 6 g3 etc.

Nevertheless, the text is not required at this moment and therefore much attention has been devoted over the past two years to delaying it in favor of quick action on the Queenside. As will be seen, the strategic themes discussed in connection with Diagram 24 remain in place. What does happen is that White rushes his immediate plans by one move. The important lines then are: 8 a3 0-0 (8...a5 is probably playable but such a voluntary weakening of the Queenside is currently unattractive to most GMs. In the game Mednis - Kozul, Palma de Mallorca 1989, White retained a slight edge after 9 d3 0-0 10 Be3 Re8 11 Rc1 Bf8 12 Nb5 a4 13 Bxb6 cxb6 14 Nc3 Nd4 15 Nd2 b5 16 e3.) 9 b4 Be6 10 Rb1! f6 11 d3:

(1) 11...Qe8?! 12 Nd2! Qf7 13 Nb3! Rab8 14 Qc2 Rfd8?! 15 Bxc6! bxc6 16 Na5 Qe8 17 Bd2! f5 18 Rfc1 Rd6 19 b5! with a won position for White, Ivanchuk - Timman, Tilburg 1990. White devastates Black's Queenside before Black can get something going on the Kingside.

(2) 11...Nd4 12 Nd2 Nd5 13 Bb2 Nxc3 14 Bxc3 c6 15 Bxd4 Qxd4 16 Nb3 Qd7 17 Nc5 Bxc5 18 bxc5 Bd5 19 Qc2 Rf7 20 Rb4 Rd8 21 Rfb1, Azmaiparashvili - Asseev, USSR 1990. White's pressure against b7 gives him a slight edge.

| 8 | ... | 0-0 |
| 9 | a3 | Be6 |

Here too Black can prevent White's next with 9...a5, but I don't think that it is worth the weakness. One example: 10 Be3 f5 (10...Re8 transposes into Mednis - Kozul, given earlier) 11 Na4! Kh8 12 Nxb6 cxb6 13 Qb3 Ra6, Mednis - J. Begovac, Sombor 1974. Now I played the immediate 14 Rfd1, after which Black had 14...Bc5 as a defense. Instead the immediate 14 Rac1 would prevent that and leave Black with a chock full of weaknesses and no compensation thereof.

| 10 | b4 | a5 |

I believe that this is the critical variation: rather than just suffering a spatial disadvantage on the Queenside in silence, Black also creates some weaknesses in White's camp there. The key alternatives are:

(1) 10...f5?! 11 Bb2 Bf6 12 Nd2! Qe8?! 13 Nb3 Rd8 14 Nc5 Bc8 15 Nb5!, Dzindzichashvili - J. Donaldson, US Open 1988. Black is defenseless against the dual threats of 16 Nxc7 and 16 Bxc6 followed by 17 Nxa7.

(2) 10...Nd4 11 Bb2 Nxf3+ 12 Bxf3 c6 13 Rc1 f6 14 Qc2 Qe8 15 Ne4, C. Hansen - Hübner, Wijk aan Zee 1988. White's initiative on the Queenside gives him a slight, yet durable edge.

| 11 | b5 | Nd4 |

[diag. 25]

Black takes advantage of White's incomplete Queenside development to engage in some tactics, i.e. 12 Nxe5? is bad because of 12...Bf6 13 Nc4 (13 f4? loses to 13...Nb3) 13...Nxc4 14 dxc4 Bxc4. Also unsatisfactory is 12 Nxd4?! exd4 13 Na4 Bd5 14 Nxb6 cxb6 15 a4 Bxg2 16 Kxg2 Qd5+ 17 Kg1 Bc5 (Romanishin) when Black's spatial advantage in the center gives him a slight edge.

Meanwhile Black is threatening a dual incursion on b3. What is White to do?

12   Bb2!?

An opening novelty when played. I was not sure how to react to Black's aggressive move 10/11 plan and therefore decided that it "can't be wrong to develop my QB to a good square." That is true: nevertheless much subsequent experience and analysis has demonstrated that only with the strategically thematic 12 Nd2 can White expect some advantage. Black cannot respond with the normal 12...Nd5? because 13 Bxd5! Bxd5 14 e3 wins a piece for White. Best seems 12...c6 to cut down on the scope of White's KB. White can respond with either 13 a4 or 13 bxc6 bxc6 (13...Nxc6 14 Rb1) 14 Bb2! threatening 15 e3 - in all cases Black still has not demonstrated equality.

12   ...   Nb3

Only this repositioning is correct. Inferior are both 12...f6?! 13 Nd2! when Black in effect is a tempo behind the 12 Nd2 variation and 12...Bb3?! 13 Qc1 when 13...Nc2 14 Rb1 f6 15 Nd2 leaves Black all tangled up while 13...Bd5 14 Nxd4 Bxg2 15 Ne6! (Adorjan) will lead to doubled e pawns for Black (15...Qd6 16 Nxc7!).

13   Rb1   f6
14   Nd2   Nxd2?!

An instructive strategic misstep: Black aims to lessen White's initiative on the Queenside by exchanging two sets of minor pieces. It does not quite work because White's thematic opportunities on the Queenside remain.

Black's correct plan can be discovered by returning to the roots of this variation as discussed after Black's 7th move: Black's prospects derive from active piece development in conjunction with the central presence provided by the e-pawn. Therefore Black needs to retain his pieces by playing 14...Nc5!. After 15 a4 Rc8! 16 Qc2 c6! 17 bxc6 bxc6 18 Ba3 Nd5!, Mednis - Geenan, Metz 1989, Black's active piece deployment and good central influence gave him sound equality.

15	Qxd2	Nc4
16	Qc1	Nxb2
17	Qxb2	Rb8
18	a4	

For White the inherent strategic themes of the opening remain: he will use the fianchettoed Bishop and the half-open c-file for pressure against Black's Queenside pawns. Helping White is the secure advanced b-pawn; hindering Black is his potentially exposed a-pawn. Therefore Black's safest defensive plan is 18...b6, safeguarding all weaknesses save for the c-pawn which then becomes a backward pawn. White does retain a pleasant advantage, but the job of getting at the c-pawn remains formidable.

18	...	Qd4?!

Instead Black prefers activity and shoots his Queen into White's part of the board. Yet the Queen has no helpers and since White's position is without fault, Black's activity is bound to fail. White, on his part, goes about establishing the thematic pressure along the c-file.

19	Qc2!	Rfd8
20	Ne4	Rbc8

20...f5? is refuted by 21 Qxc7.

21	Nd2!	c6

This weakening is not to be avoided since 21...Bd5? is met by 22 Bh3 and 21...b6? loses to 22 Bb7 Rb8 23 Qxc7 Bd6 24 Qc6 Qxa4 25 Ne4! Qa3 26 Ra1 Qb4 27 Rfb1 Qd4 28 e3! Qxd3 29 Rd1, winning a piece.

22	bxc6	bxc6
23	Rb7	Bb4
24	Rc1	c5?!

Black continues to play too optimistically. Here was the last chance to start dissolving his Queenside weaknesses with 24...Bxd2! 25 Qxd2 Qxa4 26 Qc3 c5! 27 Ra1 Qd4 28 Qxa5 c4. Nevertheless, White's active piece placement, particularly control of the seventh rank, gives him a clear initiative. Yet Black at least is rid of his structural problems and should be able to weather White's attack after, for instance, 29 dxc4 Bxc4 30 h4!.

25 Nc4!

[diag. 26]

Putting Black's KB into a permanent box. While it is true that the Bishop is "ideally" placed to protect his a- and c-pawns, it is irrelevant to anything else on the board. Black's position is unenviable, e.g. 25...Bxc4?! 26 dxc4! leaves Black defenseless on the light squares. Probably the best there is is 25...Rb8 26 Ra7 Rd7, though White's advantage is major after 27 Ra6.

25 ... h5?!

Black is in no condition to afford such a fundamental weakening of his Kingside. The refutation is swift.

26 Be4!

With the "simple" threat of 27 e3 trapping the Queen. Because now 26...Bxc4 27 dxc4 leaves Black's Kingside in shreds, the Queen has to make its ignominious retreat.

26	...	Rf8
27	e3	Qd8
28	Qe2	Bg4

After 28...h4 probably simplest is 29 Bg6 Bf7 30 Rxf7! Rxf7 31 Qh5.

29 Bf3!

The d-pawn now is unimportant; Black's weakened Kingside is what matters.

29	...	Bxf3
30	Qxf3	Qxd3
31	Rd1!!	Qg6

The Knight is poisoned: 31...Qxc4? 32 Rdd7 Qg4 (32...Rf7 33 Rxf7 Qxf7 34 Rxf7 Kxf7 35 Qb7+) 33 Qxg4 hxg4 34 Rxg7+ Kh8 35 Rh7+ Kg8 36 Rbg7 Mate.

32	Rdd7	Rcd8
33	Rxg7+!	

Black was hoping for a tactical save in case of 33 Qd5+?! Kh7 34 Rxd8? Rxd8 35 Qxd8 Qb1+ 36 Kg2 Qe4+ followed by 37...Qxb7. However, the text forces a strategically won position.

33	...	Qxg7
34	Rxg7+	Kxg7
35	Qxh5	

Strictly from a material balance Black is O.K. since two Rooks are equivalent to Queen + pawn. But positionally it is all White's: his King is completely secure while Black's is exposed; his Queen has complete mobility whereas Black's Rooks have no scope for any activity; the agile Knight is much superior to Black's petrified Bishop; Black's c-pawn is stymied, while White has a sound 4 P vs. 2 P majority on the Kingside, with, moreover, the h-pawn being a valuable passed pawn.

White's winning method will consist of using the Q + N combination, in conjunction with the judicious mobilization of his Kingside pawn(s), to infiltrate Black's position. This will lead to the capture of either Black's King or decisive material. White's strategy is bound to be successful because Black can neither prevent White's incursions nor generate counterplay.

35	...	Rd3
36	Qg4+	Kh6

The King is insecure here and should have immediately headed back to h8.

37	h4	Rdd8
38	Qf5	

More effective is the immediate 38 h5! Rg8 39 Qe6! (39...Rdf8 40 Nxe5), but my main concern was to reach the time control at move 40 while retaining all my advantages.

38	...	Kg7
39	h5	Kh8
40	Kg2	Bc3
41	Qc2	Bb4

42	Qf5	Bc3
43	h6	Rf7
44	Qe6!	Rdf8
45	Nd6	Black resigns

[diag. 27]

The game was adjourned with White sealing his 45th move and Black resigned without resuming play. The main variations are: 45...Rh7 (45...Rc7 46 Ne4) 46 Nf5! Bb4 47 Kf1! Bc3 (Black is, in effect, already in zugzwang. Thus 47...Rc7 loses to 48 Ne7! Kh7 49 Qf5+ Kh8 50 Ng6+ and if Black throws away his passed pawn with 47...c4, White gratefully plays 48 Qxc4 and then resumes the squeeze.) 48 Qd6 Kg8 (48...Rhf7 49 Nh4! Kg8 50 Ng6 Re8 51 Qd5 etc.) 49 Ne7+ Kf7 50 Qd5+ Ke8 51 Ng8! Rhf7 52 Qa8+ Kd7 53 Qxf8! Rxf8 54 h7 and White wins. Though this may appear to be a long and complicated route, in real life the situation is actually rather simple: White just keeps enhancing his domination over the position until a forced tactical solution appears.

This game won the Best Played Game prize at the tournament.

*   *   *   *   *

Game 10

White: Viktor Korchnoi
Black: Tigran Petrosian
Played at 1977 Quarter-Final Candidates Match, Il Ciocco, Italy, Game 5

1	c4	Nf6
2	Nc3	e5
3	Nf3	Nc6
4	g3	

By far the most popular and theoretically significant variation of the English Four Knights complex: The fianchettoed KB will both watch the key e4 and d5 central squares as well as press on Black's Queenside. The original variations—4 d4 exd4 5 Nxd4 Bb4 6 Bg5 as well as 4 e4—are long since obsolete since it has been learned that such "brute force" approaches are not successful in the positionally sophisticated English Opening. If White wants to vary from the text, currently well thought of alternatives are 4 a3, 4 d3 and 4 e3. All of them fit the visually unassuming but strategically logical description.

| 4 | ... | Bb4 |

Over the past 25 years this has been Black's favorite response. The reason is that complicated, strategically unbalanced positions result, yet without either side balancing on the edge of a precipice. Thus both sides obtain good winning chances, without undue risk of losing. The text is the start of a coherent plan of development and central support. Firstly, Black will quickly castle and then with ...Re8 utilize the KR for central activity and support of the e-pawn if it is advanced to e4. Secondly, the KB is ready to be exchanged off to both lessen White's control of d5 as well as to saddle him with doubled pawns. White, for his part, will then try to make use of the latent power of his Bishop pair and start undermining Black's e-pawn once it, as is usual, gets to e4.

The major alternative to 4...Bb4 is 4...d5. This, by transposition of moves, will lead to Game 9.

| 5 | Nd5!? |

[diag. 28]

At the time of this game the text was still relatively infrequent, but it has been gaining adherents continually. The concept behind the move is an interesting one: White wants to stay in the sophisticated mode of an unbalanced English, but without the permanent structural problem of having unwieldy doubled c-pawns. Even though moving the same piece twice so early in the game is against conventional opening principles, the slow moving and closed nature of this variation allows White such a "luxury."

The historically main line variation is 5 Bg2 0-0 6 0-0 and then Black either plays the immediate 6...e4 7 Ng5 Bxc3 8 bxc3 Re8 or the preparatory 6...Re8.

5 ... Bc5

Despite first appearances, the Bishop will not have much prospects along the g1 - a7 diagonal. Yet, in a sense it must be frustrating for Black that there is no ready road to equality after White's amateurish appearing Knight jump. Witness the following alternatives:

(1) Black aims for symmetry with 5...Nxd5 6 cxd5 Nd4. Yet after 7 Nxd4 exd4 8 Qc2! White winds up with the more useful KB, pressure against Black's Queenside and therefore with a normal opening advantage. One example: 8...Qe7 9 Bg2 Bc5 10 0-0 11 e3 Bb6 12 a4 dxe3 13 dxe3 a5 14 Bd2, Korchnoi - Karpov, 1978 World Championship Match, Game 27.

(2) Black tries for a refutation with 5...e4, forcing White's Knight to the edge; 6 Nh4. Nevertheless, no way exists to take advantage of that and White retains a slight edge, e.g. 6...0-0 7 Bg2 Re8 8 0-0 Bc5 9 d3! exd3 10 Qxd3 Ne5 11 Qc2 c6 12 Be3! cxd5 13 Bxc5 d6 14 Bd4 dxc4 15 Rfd1 Qe7 16 Nf3 Nc6 17 Qxc4 Qxe2 18 Qxe2 Rxe2 19 Bxf6 gxf6 20 b3, Ree - Ligterink, Amsterdam 1988. White will recover the pawn and remain with the superior pawn formation.

(3) Black tries to retain the KB on b4 with 5...a5 when 6 Nxb4 axb4 gives Black pressure along the a-file. But without White's QN on c3, Black's Bishop on b4 is of little importance. After the developmental 6 Bg2, transposing into Miles - Adams, Palma de Mallorca 1989, White has every reason to expect to retain his first move advantage. The game course showed this to be so: 6...0-0 7 0-0 Re8 8 b3 d6 9 Bb2 Bg4 10 d3 Bc5 11 h3 Bh5 12 e3! Nxd5 13 cxd5 Nb4 14 g4 Bg6 when both the game's 15 e4 and the alternative 15 d4 exd4 16 Nxd4 give White a nice spatial advantage.

6 d3!

I like this move because the threat of 7 Bg5 either forces the time losing 6...h6, as in the game, or 6...Nxd5 7 cxd5 when again White keeps more space, pressure on the Queenside and the more active KB.

Of course, the developmental 6 Bg2 0-0 7 0-0 is also good, with White slightly better after 7...Nxd5 8 cxd5 Nd4 9 Ne1 d6 10 e3 Nf5 11 Nc2 Bd7 12 b3 followed by 13 Bb2, Eingorn - Tseshkhovsky, Moscow 1985.

6	...	h6
7	Bg2	d6
8	0-0	0-0
9	e3	

Assuming control of the d4 square and being in position to play d4 at White's option. Black in response creates a retreat square for his Bishop as well as making it difficult for White to gain more Queenside space with b4.

9	...	a5
10	Nc3!	

A perceptive sophisticated retreat: the Knight on d5 has served its purpose and White does not want Black to have the opportunity to lighten his defensive load by an exchange at an opportune moment. Back home on c3 the Knight controls key central squares and is well placed for White's potential pawn advances: b4 and/or d4.

It is now time to take stock of this purely strategic position. White's slight advantage derives from the following factors:

(1) White has much better prospects of controlling d5 than Black has of controlling d4.

(2) White's KB has much more potential than Black's KB.

(3) White's thematic play on the Queenside is certain to come, whereas it is not at all clear how Black can get at White's Kingside.

10	...	Ba7
11	a3	Nh7

This somewhat clumsy retreat is to enable ...f5. Yet that idea is not a particularly promising one since Black lacks an effective follow-up. A more fruitful plan to me seems 11...Be6 (making use of 6...h6) followed by 12...Qd7. Also on next move e6 looks like a better spot for the QB.

12	Kh1	Bg4
13	Qc2	f5
14	Nb5!	Qd7?!

Better is 14...Bb6 when White has the choice between 15 Bd2 followed by 16 b4 or 15 b3 followed by 16 Bb2 and a timely d4.

15	Nxa7	Rxa7
16	b3	Raa8
17	Ng1!	

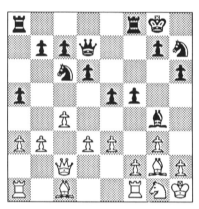

[diag. 29]

With somewhat unconventional, yet in every respect excellent play (Petrosian, the maneuverer, could well have been White in this game) Korchnoi has obtained a clear advantage out of the opening. Let us compare each side's situation.

   a) For WHITE:
- He has the Bishop pair in a position which soon will be moved up.
- He will have play against Black's Queenside after the imminent b4.
- White's KB has a marvelous diagonal.
- He has the potential d4 central advance.

   b) For BLACK:
- He has a passively placed KN.
- His QB location on g4 is more of a liability than strength.
- His attacking chances on the Kingside are rather nebulous. Advancing either the e- or f-pawn leaves weak squares in its wake and Black therefore is reluctant to touch either pawn.

17 ...   Rae8

This routine move does not improve Black's position. Since it should be rather obvious that White's Queenside play will start via b4, Black's QR should remain home to guard the a-file. A helpful plan is to get the KN back into the game by 17...Ng5 and 18...Ne6.

18 Bd2   Nf6
19 f3!?

GM Korchnoi is one of the great fighters of all time, with one of his characteristics being that periodically in strategically rather clear positions he chooses unconventional moves/plans to unbalance the position so radically that his opponent is thrown for a loop. This is such a moment. White voluntarily loosens his Kingside pawn formation and shuts off his KB from its wonderful central diagonal. What does White receive in return? He chases Black's Bishop to the edge of the board and then is able to put his KB on h3 to apply pressure against Black's f-pawn. Still, on an objective basis, these seem relatively small fruits.

The safe, sound, thematic conventional 19 b4! is riskless and perfect. After 19...axb4 20 axb4 White has no need to fear 20...e4. He activates his QB by 21 Bc3 forcing Black to start worrying about the safety of his advanced e-pawn. Then 21...d5 22 cxd5 Nxd5 (Or 22...Qxd5 23 Bxf6 Rxf6 24 dxe4 fxe4 25 Rab1, threatening 26 b5) 23 dxe4 fxe4 24 b5 leaves Black chock full of weaknesses, while 21...Ne5 22 Bxe5 Rxe5 23 Ra7 Qc6 24 d4 Re7 25 b5 Qb6 26 Qa2 yields White a riskless initiative on the Queenside.

19	...	Bh5
20	b4	b6
21	Bh3	Bf7
22	Ne2	axb4?!

Why hand the a-file over to White? More thematic are to attack by 22...g5 or defend with 22...Ra8.

23	axb4	Ne7
24	b5	Rd8

Instead, 24...Ra8 can be met by 25 Ra6. But more promising seem 24...Rc8 which defends the c-pawn and threatens 25...c6, or the violent 24...g5.

25   d4?!

In principle it is correct to open up the position for White's Bishops, but at this moment the resultant weakness of the c-pawn enables Black to create significant counterplay. The positional 25 Ra7! retains a substantial advantage (25...d5 26 Bb4 Rfe8 27 e4!).

25	...	c6!
26	bxc6	Qxc6
27	Rac1	Rc8
28	dxe5	dxe5
29	Bb4!	

[diag. 30]

This turns out to be the critical moment in the game. Black has three reasonable continuations:

(1) 29...Qb7 30 Bxe7 Rxc4 (30...Qxe7 31 Qb3 is also slightly in White's favor.) 31 Bxf8! Rxc2 32 Rxc2 Kxf8 33 Bxf5, with a slight edge for White.

(2) 29...Rfe8 30 Bxe7 Rxe7 31 Bxf5 Rcc7 (Marjanovic) when it is unclear whether White can hold on to his pawn.

(3) 29...Nfd5!? 30 cxd5 Qxc2 31 Rxc2 Rxc2 32 Bxe7 is judged unclear by GM Marjanovic.

29 ... Ned5??

Though in time trouble, Black aims to improve on the last variation, but overlooks a key point.

30 Bxf8 Nxe3
31 Qc3 Nxf1
32 Bb4!

White's marauding Bishop gets out, while Black's Knight remains trapped. Therefore Black will wind up a piece down.

32 ... Bh5
33 Rxf1 e4
34 Bg2 Qxc4

In the long run, an endgame with a piece down against a world class GM must be inherently hopeless. Theoretically no better, yet with superior swindling chances in mutual time pressure is the middlegame after 34...Bf7.

35 Qxc4 Rxc4
36 Be7 Nd5
37 Nf4! Nxf4
38 gxf4 e3

In lost positions, all tactics tend to fail, e.g. 38...exf3 39 Bxf3 Rxf4?? to 40 Bd5+.

39	Re1	e2
40	Kg1	Rxf4
41	Kf2	g5

The game was adjourned here, with White sealing his next move. Black only has two pawns for the piece, which is insufficient unless there are some extraordinary factors. They do not exist here.

42	Bd6	Rd4
43	Bc7	b5
44	Rxe2	Bf7
45	Rb2	Bc4
46	Be5	Rd1

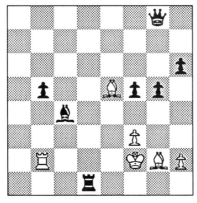

[diag. 31]

Even though obviously Black does not have sufficient compensation for the piece, the two pawns seem to be pretty effective for defensive purposes. That is, to win, White will have to get at Black's Kingside pawns. But how to achieve this is not so obvious. For instance, the direct 47 Bh3 leads nowhere after 47...Kf7! since 48 Bxf5?? fails to 48...Rd5. What is needed is a more perceptive plan.

47   f4!!

As a general principle White wouldn't want to exchange pawns. However, the overriding need for White is to open the position so that the extra Bishop can provide the necessary power to get at Black's Kingside. The text and 49 h4! help achieve this. White is favored in his plan by having the QB as the extra Bishop since it covers the h-pawn's queening square. Therefore, White does not have to be particularly concerned that the f-pawn is exchanged off.

47	...	Kf7
48	Bf3	Rd8
49	h4!	

The undermining of Black's Kingside continues. Now after 49...gxh4, White's secure f-pawn would be the winner, whereas after 49...gxf4, White's h-pawn will be decisive. Therefore the best that Black has is to get himself a protected passed pawn.

49	...	g4
50	Bc6	Kg6
51	Bxb5	

White's pawn play has loosened up Black's Kingside pawn formation while ensuring that the f-pawn is secure from being exchanged off. Therefore, White can now work to activate his Rook. The text achieves this, in the process also snipping off a pawn.

51	...	Bxb5
52	Rxb5	Rd2+
53	Ke3	

White cannot protect the h-pawn with 53 Kg3 because Black can check away by 53...Rd3+ 54 Kg2 Rd2+ etc.

53	...	Rh2
54	Rb6+	Kh5
55	Rf6!	

The correct winning technique must be to utilize the extra piece to create new advantages. The text leads to a passed f-pawn—a most important advantage. Less ambitious play may not be sufficient to win, e.g. 55 Bg7 Rh3+ 56 Kf2 Rf3+ 57 Kg2 Rg3+!! etc., or 55 Bf6 Rh3+ 56 Ke2 Rf3.

55	...	Rh3+

There are no prospects at all in 55...g3 56 Kf3 g2 57 Rxf5+ Kg6 58 Rf6+ Kh5 59 Kf2 etc.

56	Kf2	Rh2+
57	Ke3	

White's King cannot remain on the Kingside with 57 Kg3 because Black again has the stalemate motif 57...Rh3+ 58 Kg2 Rg3+!!. In any case it is logical to activate the King so that it can support the f-pawn's advance.

57	...	Rh3+
58	Kd4	Rh1

Again 58...g3 is too early: 59 Ke3 Kxh4 60 Kf3! h5 61 Rg6 g2+ 62 Kf2!, winning.

59	Rxf5+	Kxh4
60	Rf6	h5
61	Rg6!	

Placing the Rook behind Black's advanced passed pawn, while clearing the way for his own passed pawn.

61	...	Rf1
62	Ke4	Re1+
63	Kd5	Kh3
64	f5!	

Passed pawns must be pushed!

64	...	h4
65	f6	Rf1
66	Ke6	g3
67	f7	g2

The stalemate trick, 67...Rxf7 68 Kxf7 g2 69 Ke6?? g1=Q! 70 Rxg1 stalemate, is foiled by 69 Bd4.

68 Bf6

White's active King ensures the win. Black gives a few spite checks before resigning.

68	...	Re1+
69	Kd5	Rd1+
70	Ke4	Re1+
71	Kd3	Black resigns

* * * * *

Game 11

White: Edmar Mednis
Black: Heinz Lehmann
Played at Berlin International Tournament 1983

1	c4	Nf6
2	g3	g6

If Black likes playing the King's Indian Defense, then the move order used in this game is the optimum one: he retains a flexible KB fianchetto formation and "at worst" he will be playing the King's Indian, with White having chosen a variation also involving the fianchetto of his KB.

3	Bg2	Bg7
4	Nf3	0-0
5	0-0	d6

With this Black shows his true King's Indian colors. "Gruenfeld types" would play 5...d5, whereas those going for maximum solidity choose 5...c6 followed by 6...d5.

6	Nc3	e5

Signaling his interest in main line King's Indians. Devotees of the Yugoslav Variation would play the symmetrical 6...c5, when White's only prospect for an advantage is to break the symmetry by 7 d4, thereby transposing into a genuine QP opening.

7	d3

White is determined to stay in the English opening. Here was the last chance to transpose into a main line of the King's Indian with 7 d4.

7	...	Nc6

The usual move and in every sense a perfect one. Black works to develop his Queenside by placing the QN on its perfect square, thereby also giving Black control of the important d4 square. To preface the text by 7...c5 would lead to a permanent weakening of d5 and there is no reason for Black to make that concession so early in the game.

It is important to note that this position can be reached in many possible logical ways. The "true English" move order is: 1 c4 e5 2 Nc3 Nc6 3 g3 g6 4 Bg2 Bg7 5 d3 d6 6 Nf3 Nf6 7 0-0 0-0

8	Rb1

[diag. 32]

This move already sets out very well the mutual strategic themes. These are:

- WHITE, as is usual in the English, will be attacking on the Queenside. The text is the straightforward way of preparing the commencing of this action with 9 b4. Again a major role for pressing on key squares—d5, c6, b7—will be the responsibility of White's KB. Therefore, as a general principle, White should strive to prevent its exchange for Black's QB.
- BLACK'S prospects - as characteristic for King's Indian formations - are on the Kingside. Therefore, Black should aim to get in ...f5 and look for the opportune moment to execute the ...e4 or ...f4 advances. Moreover, often control of the d4 square offers Black opportunities for piece play against e2 (by the QN) or f2 (by the KB).

8 ... a5

This temporary hold-back of White's b4 advance has become during the past decade Black's most common approach. Its immediate advantage is that after the pawn exchanges on b4, Black will have control of the a-file. Yet permanent control is not guaranteed and White often is the one who ultimately winds up as the boss of the file. Moreover, the advance of the a-pawn means that Black's important b6 square can turn out to be an eventual weakness. In my opinion, the pluses and minuses of the insertion of 8...a5 9 a3 balance each other.

Therefore, Black is equally in order if he immediately chooses the respectable alternatives: 8...h6, 8...Re8, 8...Nd4, 8...Bf5, 8...Bd7.

9 a3 h6

I think that this is both Black's most flexible and best move. He ensures that the QB can be developed to its optimum e6 square from where it helps protect d5 and can still go to the Kingside later on. In addition, for a potential Kingside attack it is useful to control g5.

Viable alternatives include 9...Nd4, whereby Black aims to lighten his defense by exchanging the QN and 9...Re8 when Black is trying for simplification via the 10...e4 advance.

10	b4	axb4
11	axb4	Be6
12	b5	Ne7

Here 12...Nd4?! is inferior since after 13 Nd2! White threatens b7 and after e.g. 13...Qc8, plays 14 e3, shunting the Knight to f5 where it interferes with the scope of the QB.

13 Bb2

Completing the development of the minor pieces and being in position to challenge the a-file with a Ra1. With the QB "watching" e5, it is also more difficult for Black to get in ...d5. Strategically inferior is 13 Bd2 because the Bishop has few prospects on the c1 - h6 diagonal, while also taking away the important d2 square from the KN.

13 ... Qd7

Black's only consistent way of mobilizing forces for Kingside play. The alternative, 13...Qc8, leaves Black with problems along the a-file after 14 Ra1! Rxa1 15 Qxa1 Bh3 16 Bxh3! Qxh3 17 Qa7, forcing the retreat 17...Qc8 when after 18 c5! White's initiative on the Queenside and center is quite real, whereas Black's Kingside play has not started.

According to long standing theory, Black can equalize with the regrouping starting with 13...Nd7. But to my mind such expectations are apt to not be realized, because Black is aiming to play on White's turf. An instructive execution of White's strategy is shown from the course of Andersson - Gulko, Biel Interzonal 1976: 14 Nd2 c6 15 Ra1 Qc7 16 Qc2 Nf5 17 Rfc1! Nf6?! 18 Qd1 Qd7?! 19 Rxa8! Rxa8 20 Ra1 Qc8 21 Rxa8 Qxa8 22 Qa4! Qxa4 23 Nxa4 Bd7 24 Nb6 Be8 25 bxc6 bxc6 26 Nb3, with White successfully penetrating Black's Queenside and winning on move 32.

14 Nd2!

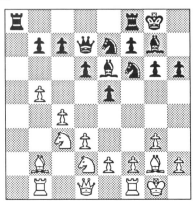

[diag. 33]

This was an important theoretical novelty when played. Instead of the insipid 14 Re1 which allows Black to smoothly cover his b7 weakness, Black now is forced to make some unpleasant choices. For instance:

(1) After 14...c6?! 15 Na4! the weakness on b6 is very apparent, e.g. 15...Nc8 16 bxc6 bxc6 17 c5! Bh3 18 Nc4! with a large advantage to White.

(2) After 14...Rfb8?! 15 Ra1! Black's problems along the a-file and in general, the Queenside remain and the absence of the KR from the Kingside makes his attacking prospects there poor.

The tactical justification of the text is a strictly strategic, long range sacrifice of the Exchange.

14   ...   Bh3?!

The German IM is being either naive or daring. After the game he told me that he did expect the coming sacrifice, but wanted to play the text, anyway. Yet his decision is wrong. To arrive at the right decision, Black must keep remembering that his chances are on the Kingside. Therefore the only correct move is 14...Rab8!. The thematic course of Mednis - Zapata, Amsterdam 1986, then was: 15 Re1 Bh3 16 Bh1 Ng4 17 Ra1 f5 18 Nd5 g5 when after the time wasting 19 Ra7?! Nc8! 20 Ra2 c6 Black had a slight advantage which the Columbian GM went on to convert into a convincing 36 move "attack on the Kingside" win.

Instead of 19 Ra7?! correct is 19 Nxe7+ Qxe7 20 e3! (GM Murey) when Black's Kingside play can be stymied and White can restart his Queenside pressure with 21 Ra7. White then has a continuing slight edge.

15   Bxb7!   Bxf1
16   Qxf1

Of course, since 16 Bxa8 Bxe2 leads to nothing for White.

White does White have for the sacrificed material? Firstly, it's important to recognize that since White has gotten a very good pawn for the Exchange, he is down only approximately one half of a pawn. As compensation he has/gets:

(1)   An enhanced powerful KB, whereas Black's superior Bishop —the QB—has left the board. This greatly decreases Black's potential chances for a meaningful Kingside attack.

(2)   White has the Bishop pair, with both Bishops to have good scope if the position gets opened. The only way that Black can hope to exploit his extra Rook is in open positions.

(3)   The fundamental weaknesses on a6, c6 and d5 give White excellent prospects to infiltrate into Black's Queenside— already the natural scene for White's opportunities.

(4)   The White minor pieces can develop good play in this congested position whereas Black would not have an easy time using his Rooks—as wonderfully put by GM Robert Byrne.

(5)   On an over-all basis, White's opportunities are clear, whereas Black's prospects are very difficult to get a handle on. Therefore, it can be said that despite his slight material sacrifice White is actually risking very little.

16   ...   Ra7

Keeping control of the a-file, though at the cost of a clumsy location for the Rook. After the passive 16...Rab8, White can, of course, retreat to g2 or go for more with 17 Qg2!?, when 17...Rfd8 is answered with 18 Ba3, while 17...Nh5 allows the centrally active 18 Nd5!.

17 Bg2

Under the changed circumstances, 17 Qg2 is not so promising as after 17...Rd8 Black gets in ...d5 when the Qg2 stands awkwardly.

17 ... d5

Looks attractive, yet by giving up the c5 square Black makes his Queenside more vulnerable to an invasion by White's forces. GM Byrne feels that Black's best bet could be a slow action on the Kingside starting with 17...Nh7, 18...Ng5, 19...Ne6 and then ...f5. Another reasonable plan is the immediate 17...c6!? because Black does not have to fear 18 b6 Ra6 19 c5 dxc5 20 Nc4 Ned5!. Instead, White could continue with 18 Nb3 or 18 bxc6 Nxc6 19 Nde4, aiming for control of d5.

18 Qc1! d4

Reopening the h1 - a8 diagonal can only be in White's interest. Therefore, also 18...dxc4 19 Nxc4 can only help White improve his piece coordination. Yet the attempt at keeping the pawn on d5 also seems fruitless, e.g. if 18...Rfa8, White plays 19 Qc2 followed by 20 Qb3.

19	Nce4	Nxe4
20	Nxe4	Nf5
21	Nc5	Qc8
22	Na6	

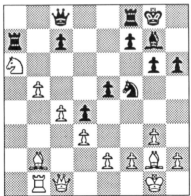

[diag. 34]

With White ready to continue his Queenside pressure/infiltration with Ba3, Ra1, Bc5, Black's position is an eyelash away from disaster; for instance, 22...Rd8? 23 Ba3 Bf8? loses to 24 Bxf8 Rxf8 25 Qa3! followed by 26 Qc5. The attempt at a blockade with 22...c5?! also fails after 23 Ra1

Rd8 24 Ra4! Bf8 25 Qa1 when White threatens both 26 b6 and 26 Nxc5. Under such threatening clouds, Black has to forget about materialism and give it back immediately with 22...Rxa6! 23 bxa6 Qxa6. Of course, White retains a clear edge after 24 Ba3 Rd8 25 Bc5.

22	...	c6?!
23	Ba3	Rd8
24	Bc5	

Perhaps even stronger is 24 Nb4 cxb5 25 Nc6!.

24	...	cxb5?!

By overlooking White's zwischenzug on move 26, Black not only loses back the Exchange, but also remains down a crucial pawn. Imperative was 24...Rxa6 25 bxa6 Qxa6, although White's Queenside pressure after 26 Ra1! Qc8 27 Qa3! is very close to decisive.

25	Bxa7	Qxa6
26	Ra1!	

As late as here the key strategic theme is White's domination of the Queenside. It is now so pervasive that Black's Queen has no square from which to protect the b-pawn.

26	...	Qe6
27	cxb5	Nd6
28	b6	

White's remaining task is clear and easy enough to execute: queen the b-pawn.

28	...	e4
29	Rb1	Rc8
30	Qb2	Qd7
31	Bxe4!	

White can win a whole piece with 31 b7 Nxb7 32 Qxb7 Rc1+ 33 Bf1 Rc7 34 Qa8+ Kh7 35 Bb8, but it seemed to me that simpler is to win the Exchange while retaining a dominating position.

31	...	Nxe4
32	b7	Nd6
33	bxc8 = Q+	Nxc8
34	Bc5	Kh7
35	Qb7	Qe6
36	Qe4	Qa2
37	Rb8	Black resigns

White's domination of the Queenside also wins the Knight, e.g. 37...Qa6 38 Qe8 or 37...Na7 38 Qb7.

Gruenfeld Defense
Game 12

White: Lev Polugaevsky
Black: Viktor Korchnoi
Played at 1977 Semi-Final Candidates Match, Evian, France, Game 10

	1	d4	Nf6
	2	c4	g6
	3	Nc3	d5

Black's last move brings about the Gruenfeld Defense, named after Austrian Grandmaster Ernst Gruenfeld, who in 1922 introduced it into international tournament play. I think that it is the most unbalancing— and therefore riskiest—of all defenses against 1 d4. Black not only allows his primary central d-pawn to be exchanged off for White's c-pawn, thus relegating him to long term central inferiority, but, moreover, allows White to follow up in safety with e4, thereby also establishing an early vast central superiority.

Why is Black engaging in such apparently suicidal endeavor? By creating successful counterplay he hopes to challenge, contain and eventually annihilate White's center. If Black is unsuccessful, the White center will smother him alive. The Gruenfeld is only suited for players who crave for and excel in active counterplay. If you don't enjoy counterattacking, while risking long term trouble, do not play the Gruenfeld.

4 cxd5

The Exchange Variation, as this simple capture is accurately called, is White's most strategically direct way of attempting to show up the Gruenfeld's inherent deficiency. In the period following World War II, this variation was considered to be too naive to offer chances for an advantage. Currently it is by far the most popular method against the Gruenfeld.

	4	...	Nxd5
	5	e4	Nxc3

Only so, even though it seems to enhance White's center some more by turning his b-pawn into a c-pawn. There are three important reasons why the text is the only correct move:

  (1) A crucial tempo is saved for the start of counterplay,
  (2) In case of retreat to b6 or f6, White's Nc3 would be more active than Black's retreating KN,
  (3) In positions of central inferiority, it is important for the inferior side to exchange off at least one of its minor pieces. Otherwise, the presence of four minor pieces on its part of the board will cause breathing difficulties, since by defini-

tion an inferior central situation means that one's space is cramped.

6   bxc3   c5

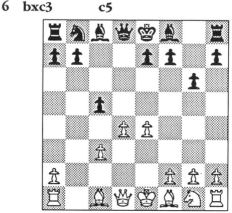

[diag. 35]

This is the basic starting point of the Exchange Variation complex. Black can first play the "flexible" 6...Bg7, yet all the main line variations still call for ...c5 on the next move.

Already the strategic themes for each side have been set:

White must safeguard his superior center. This will only be possible if his development is sound and efficient. The realization of the central superiority will be the primary objective of the middlegame, with the most likely spheres of action being the center and the Kingside.

Black must create counterplay against White's center—the sooner, the better. His primary target is the d-pawn, with the e-pawn becoming a secondary target in some variations.

7   Bc4

In conjunction with 8 Ne2 this was considered to be the only correct piece deployment for White at the time of this match: the KB is rapidly developed to an active diagonal and the Knight can fully participate in the protection of the d-pawn since it is immune from an annoying pin by Black's QB. This method is still alive and well, but now must be referred to as the Old Exchange Variation. During the past ten years the Modern Exchange Variation, featuring the KN development of f3, has been born. Even though this makes the Knight subject to a real pin after a ...Bg4, the Knight's more active location on f3 compared to that on e2, is a full counterweight. At the start of the 1990s both exchange variations are theoretically viable and popular in practice.

7   ...   Bg7
6   Ne2   0-0

9	0-0	Nc6
10	Be3	

White's initial development has been successfully completed.

It is now up to Black to decide how to continue challenging White's center. In the second half of the 1960s GM Robert J. Fischer did much to popularize the following method of increasing pressure on d4: 10...Qc7 11 Rc1 Rd8. By far the most common variations are those involving the early development of the QB to g4: 10...cxd4 11 cxd4 Bg4 12 f3 Na5 or the immediate 10...Bg4 11 f3 Na5. Characteristically, GM Korchnoi selects an even more ambitious plan.

10	...	Na5
11	Bd3	b6

Black plans to apply pressure on the e-pawn with 12...Bb7, while continuing to challenge the d-pawn. There are two reasons why he refrains from the central exchange ...cxd4: (1) White's central dominance is enhanced since Black's c-pawn on its fourth rank is exchanged for White's c-pawn on the third, (2) White's QR will find good prospects for action along the opened c-file. Yet also in chess it is difficult to get something for nothing and keeping the central tension exposes Black to the following potential negatives: (1) his c-pawn may go lost (as happens in the game), and (2) White has the option of the d5 advance since his QR will not be en prise to Black's KB.

12 Rc1!

White improves both the offensive potential and defensive situation of his QR. At this moment the c-pawn is at least partially poisoned since after 12 dxc5?! bxc5 13 Bxc5 Qc7 14 Bd4 e5 15 Be3 Black gets excellent compensation for the pawn with either 15...Rd8 or the immediate 15...Nc4.

12	...	e6?!

Black thinks only of himself and is surprised by an "elementary" capture. He wants to continue with ...Bb7 without being "bothered" by d5, as after 12...Bb7 13 d5! c4 14 Bb1 e6 15 dxe6 fxe6 16 Qxd8 Rfxd8 17 Nd4 with a small endgame edge for White in Knaak - Smejkal, Halle 1974. Black can also first exchange on d4, 12...cxd4 13 cxd4, and then play 13...e6, again in security and with White retaining the typical slight opening advantage.

13 dxc5!

GM Polugaevsky needed 54 minutes to make this correct capture, whereas a top computer would have saved its time without pondering over whether Black gets some intangible compensation for the pawn.

Unlike the situation discussed one move earlier, 13...dxc5 14 Bxc5 is clearly advantageous for White since the attack on the KR gains one tempo, while another developmental tempo has been cashiered by the insertion of Rc1 by White and ...e6 by Black.

13	...	Qc7
14	cxb6	axb6
15	c4!	

Since White's objective in the Exchange Variation is to build and safeguard a strong center, the last thing that he wants to allow is a bind on the center and Queenside, such as after 15 Rb1?! Nc4!. After the text White retains the clearly superior center and if Black wants to recapture the lost/sacrificed c-pawn he will have to risk a nasty pin along the c-file.

| 15 | ... | Ba6 |

This direct approach does not work out too well. More promising is to play a purely strategic game a pawn down with 15...Nb7!? followed by ...Nc5, as suggested by GM Keene. Black's QR then has good pressure along the a-file and it would be difficult for White under tournament conditions to discover the best deployment of his forces to try to capitalize on his extra pawn.

| 16 | Nd4! | Nxc4 |

After 62 minutes of thought Black decides to brave the rapids, though that was hardly his intention when playing 12...e6?!. Yet the normal alternatives are patently unsatisfactory: after 16...Rfd8 White seals off all potential threats by 17 Nb5! Qd7 18 Be2, while 16...Bxd4 17 Bxd4 Rfd8 is zwischenzuged with 18 Bf6.

| 17 | Qe2 | Rfc8 |
| 18 | a4! | |

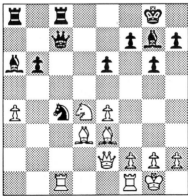

[diag. 36]

A new danger has appeared for Black: the threatened 19 Nb5 would break the communication between the QB and the Knight and lead to the unavoidable loss of the latter. Therefore White's Knight must be removed from the board ...

18	...	Bxd4
19	Bxd4	

... which, however, still leaves the pin along the c-file in existence, and, moreover, Black's Kingside is now permanently weakened because of the absence of the KB.

19	...	e5
20	Ba1!	

Premature is 20 Bxe5?! Qxe5 21 Bxc4 as after 21...Bb7! the double attack on the a- and e-pawns reestablishes material equality. White has no need to rush matters since Black remains in an unenviable bind.

20	...	b5

Trying to eliminate the Queenside pawns while also getting the QR into the game is Black's only hope.

21	axb5	Bxb5
22	h4?!	

White of course wants to double on the c-file, but the immediate 22 Rc2?! is parried by 22...Qa5! when after 23 Bxc4 Bxc4 24 Rxc4 Rxc4 25 Qxc4, 25...Qxa1! reestablishes material equality by exploiting the back rank weakness. Therefore it is quite in order for White to "make air" for his King.

The important question then becomes: should White play 22 h3 or 22 h4 ? It seems to me that in too many cases in master practice the "active" h4 (or ...h5 for Black) is played. Unless there are very clear prospects for an attack with an early follow-up h5, the pawn on h4 (...h5 for Black) can easily turn out to be an annoying weakness in the middlegame. This is what happens in this game also. After the safer 22 h3! Black would have had much greater difficulties in drawing the game.

22	...	Ra6!

Black plans to close off the c-file with 23...Rc6. White therefore must hurry to win something.

23	Rb1!	Be8
24	Bxe5	

White can aim for an attack by playing 24 h5, yet can also very easily wind up with nothing after 24...Rc6. With the text White wins a "good pawn," yet because of Black's accurate defense—helped by the fact that all pawns are on the same side—will have to reconcile himself to the draw, after fifty moves of effort.

24	...	Qxe5
25	Bxc4	Rac6
26	Bd5	R6c7
27	Qe3	Bc6!

While it is generally true that when down material one should try to exchange pawns and not pieces—the situation is often quite different when all the remaining pawns are on the same side. For example, in our specific case the only theoretically won endgame is the King & pawn one. All others: pure Bishop, pure Queen, pure Rook(s) are drawn. The great value of the extra pawn in this type of middlegame position is that the pawn can be utilized for attacking purposes. Therefore it is in Black's interest to exchange sufficient pieces to bring about a single piece endgame. Because at this moment White's Bishop is much more active than Black's, it is quite logical for Black to aim for the Bishop exchange first.

28	Rbd1	Bxd5
29	Rxd5	Qf6
30	Qg3	

Already it is apparent that the weakness of the h-pawn cramps "White's style."

30	...	Rc4!
31	f3	Rc1
32	Rdd1	R1c2
33	Kh2	Qa6

GM Keene draws attention to the possible 33...R8c5 with the idea ...Rh5—another indication of the inappropriateness of 22 h4?!.

34	Rf2

This proposed Rook exchange brings Black closer to a theoretically drawn endgame, yet because White's major pieces are so modestly placed, it is difficult to come up with an attractive active plan.

34	...	Rxf2
35	Qxf2	Qf6
36	Qg3	Rc5

Black now threatens to go after the exposed h-pawn with 37...Rh5. Since 37 Rd5 is dangerous because of 37...Rc1!, threatening 38...Qa1, White has nothing better than to allow the coming R & P endgame.

37	Rd6	Qe5!
38	Qxe5	Rxe5
39	Rd5	Re6

[diag. 37]

Endgames of R + 4P vs. R + 3P, with all pawns on the same side and a "normal" type position are known as theoretical draws. As long as the defender does not voluntarily acquiesce to a passive situation where White's K + R + pawns dominate the board, the draw is relatively easy to hold. There is no reason why Korchnoi should not have felt secure here.

40 h5

Advancing the h-pawn will lead to the inevitable—and for Black desirable—exchange of it. On the other hand, if White immediately activates his King, Black sets up a firm defensive pawn formation with 40...h5!. Therefore White's best practical try is 40 g4! followed by 41 Kg3.

40	...	Kg7
41	Kg3	Ra6

Black is satisfied to keep the status quo. He definitely does not want to allow isolated pawns by capturing on h5 himself.

42	f4	Ra4
43	Kf3	Rb4
44	Re5	Ra4

Here the game was adjourned and White sealed his next move. GM Polugaevsky was reconciled to the inevitability of the draw and upon resumption of play played the rest of the game in virtual blitz tempo. GM Korchnoi, however, took plenty of time on the clock to ensure that he is not overlooking anything.

45	Rd5	Ra3+
46	Kg4	

White can try 46 Ke2 Ra2+ 47 Rd2 Ra5 48 e5!?, but Black is safe enough after 48...gxh5 49 Rd7 Kg6 50 Rd6+ Kg7.

46	...	Ra2
47	g3	Rh2!
48	hxg6	

The pressure on the h-pawn means that this exchange is necessary to activate the Rook. Yet the exchange puts Black another step closer to the draw.

48	...	hxg6
49	Rd7	Re2
50	e5	

Because White's extra pawn is the e-pawn, rather than say the h-pawn, he does have some modicum of chances and Black must watch that the possible further advance of it does no harm to him.

50	...	Re3
51	Kh4	Kf8
52	Rd8+	Kg7
53	Re8	Ra3!
54	g4	

Instead 54 e6 fxe6 55 Rxe6 just simplifies further down to a R + 2P vs. R + P endgame.

54	...	Ra4
55	Kg5	Ra5!

[diag. 38]

The simplest defensive plan: Black prevents the further advance 56 f5 because of 56...Rxe5!—see move 71. Nothing of significance happens over the next sixteen moves, with White moving back and forth rapidly and with Black doing the same at a more measured pace.

56	Re7	Rb5
57	Rd7	Ra5
58	Kh4	Kf8
59	Rd4	Rb5
60	Re4	Ra5
61	Re3	Rb5
62	Kg3	Ke7
63	Kh4	Kf8!
64	Rd3	Ra5
65	Rd7	Rb5
66	Ra7	Rc5
67	Ra6	Kg7
68	Ra8	Rb5
69	Re8	Rb4
70	Kg5	Rb5
71	f5	

By now the circle has been completed and White puts Black to the final small test.

71	...	Rxe5
72	Rxe5	f6+
73	Kf4	fxe5+
74	Kxe5	gxf5 Draw

Black keeps the opposition after 75 Kxf5 Kf7 76 Kg5 Kg7! and thereby the certain draw.

* * * * *

Game 13

White: William Martz
Black: Craig Chellstorp
Played at Houston International Tournament 1974

1	d4	Nf6
2	c4	g6
3	Nc3	d5
4	Nf3	

A flexible and perfect developmental move. After the thematic 4...Bg7 response, White can choose to enter the Modern Exchange Variation with 5 cxd5, the Russian System with 5 Qb3, as well as currently less popular lines.

4   ...   Bg7
5   Bf4

White selects the Classical Variation, so named because in the early years of the Gruenfeld it was by far the most popular line. Its logic is impeccable: White will aim for early pressure against Black's Queenside with the QB bearing down on c7 and White's QR will be developed to c1 for action along the c-file. Nevertheless, White's prospects for retaining an opening advantage are currently not rated too highly. The reason is that Black's counterplay generally succeeds in eliminating White's central superiority.

5   ...   0-0

Black smoothly completes Kingside development prior to initiating central action. Black does not have to worry about losing the c-pawn after 6 cxd5?! Nxd5 7 Nxd5 Qxd5 8 Bxc7, because he gets a huge jump in development after the normal 8...Nc6 and thereby the superior chances, e.g. 9 e3 Bf5 10 Be2 Rac8 11 Bg3 Qa5+ 12 Qd2 Nb4 13 0-0 Rc2, Anikaev - T. Georgadze, USSR 1973.

The immediate 5...c5 is also fully satisfactory, as demonstrated by Garry Kasparov in the first game of his 1986 World Championship Match against Anatoly Karpov.

6   Rc1

Recently this formerly main line move has been largely replaced by the more flexible 6 e3 because we have learned that White can't do without the safeguarding of d4 and Kingside development, whereas the early development of the QR neither forestalls counterplay nor creates imminent threats.

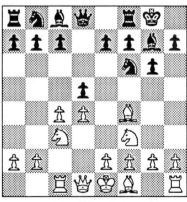

[diag. 39]

Black does have a practical problem here: how to respond to White's early mobilization of Queenside forces? Should he take advantage of the unprotected status of White's c-pawn by capturing on c4? Should he initiate immediate counterplay with 6...c5? How about 6...c6, securing the center and closing off the c-file?

I believe that the key to making the right decisions is to remember the over-all theme of the Gruenfeld Defense:

Black must aim to challenge White's center, primarily by pressure on d4.

White needs to safeguard his inherently superior center.

6   ...   c6?!

The safest response and, according to theory, quite playable. Therefore my attaching the dubious mark is not based on theoretical considerations but on factors based on style and experience, i.e. personal items. If a player's only defense to 1 d4 is the Gruenfeld, then he is steeped in the various thematic methods of applying pressure to White's center and, therefore, will feel uncomfortable in the passive protection of his own center. However, if you have a mix of defenses to 1 d4, including in particular the Slav, then the text is fine. In such a case you will simply be wearing your solid hat. Practitioners of the Slav will recognize the resulting position as a Semi-Slav where Black has chosen to fianchetto his KB and thereby kept the diagonal open for his QB.

However, it is my strong opinion that "Gruenfeld types" should select either 6...dxc4 or perhaps preferably 6...c5. Characteristic main line play for each variation then is:

(1) 6...dxc4: 7 e3 Be6 8 Ng5 Bd5 9 e4 h6 10 exd5 hxg5 11 Bxg5 Nxd5 12 Bxc4 Nb6 13 Bb3 Nc6 14 d5 Nd4 15 0-0 Qd7 with approximately equal chances, I. Rogers - Ftacnik, Biel 1984.

(2) 6...c5: 7 dxc5 Be6 8 e3 Nc6 9 Be2 Ne4 10 0-0 Nxc3 11 bxc3 dxc4 12 Ng5 Bd7 13 Bxc4 Na5 14 Bd5 Rc8 15 Qd3 e6 16 Bf3 e5 17 Bg3 Rxc5 18 Rfd1 Rc7, Farago - W. Schmidt, Polanica Zdroj 1981. White's superior center has disappeared and Black has full equality.

7   e3   Qa5

Black's most active plan, setting up a pin and applying some pressure on the Queenside. Theory also rates highly 7...Bg4, getting rid of the "bad Bishop" after 8 h3 Bxf3 9 Qxf3 and then safeguarding the center by 9...e6. However, I must again caution impatient Gruenfeld players that they will feel very uncomfortable in the resulting solid, yet inherently passive positions.

8   Qb3

Applying pressure on both d5 and b7, yet the Queen is exposed here to a potential counterplay action. The more modest 8 Qd2!, breaking the pin and opening the option for 9 cxd5 as a follow-up is more suited for a slight opening advantage.

8   ...   dxc4?

This move and the immediate follow-up shows the great danger of mixing up strategic themes. Here Black first ensures the retention of the d5 central point by playing the passive, defensive 6...c6 and then two moves later negates the whole approach by giving up the center. It is not that the concept of ...dxc4 is so bad as a way of gaining developmental time, but the execution requires more patience and preparatory development. Therefore, Black should first play 8...Nbd7!. Then Black is "threatening" 9...dxc4 10 Bxc4 Nb6 and its prevention by 9 cxd5 allows Black smooth development by 9...Nxd5 10 Bg3 N7b6 to be followed by 11...Be6 and equal chances. As a way of trying to retain some advantage after 8...Nbd7!, GM Korchnoi in Korchnoi - Martz, Chicago International 1982, played the high class waiting move 9 h3 and after 9...dxc4 10 Bxc4 Nb6 continued with 11 Bc7! Ne8 12 Be5 Nxc4 13 Qxc4 Be6 14 Qe2. Then, instead of the game's 14...Nd6?! 15 Bxg7 Bc4 16 Qc2 Kxg7 17 Ne5 Be6 18 0-0 and a slight advantage to White because of his superior center, GM Hort recommends 14...Bxe5 15 Nxe5 Nf6! 16 0-0 c5, when with the elimination of White's central edge Black reaches full equality.

9   Bxc4   b5?

Of course, this was the point of Black's previous move: he plans to chase away the KB and then continue with 10...Be6. Yet note the inherent fault lines of Black's non-traditional attempt at counterplay: he creates new weaknesses (c6, b5) while leaving his Queenside undeveloped. Punishment is swift and severe.

If Black had seen what was coming he would have hunkered down with 9...e6. Already it is too late for 9...Nbd7?! because of 10 Ng5 e6 11 Bxe6 fxe6 12 Nxe6! and a clear advantage to White.

10   Bxf7+!!   Rxf7

[diag. 40]

Black hopes for 11 Ne5?! which is made rather harmless by 11...e6. But White has a nice finesse which exposes all the self-created holes in Black's position.

11	Bxb8!	Rxb8
12	Ne5	e6
13	Nxc6	Qb6
14	Nxb8	Qxb8
15	Qxb5!	Rb7
16	Qa5	

The previous moves were more or less forced for both sides. The immediate slugfest is over and a survey of the damage shows that with a Rook and three pawns for two Bishops White has a clear material advantage. Because his pawn configuration is compact and his piece deployment good, as soon as he gets castled White can expect to reach a winning position.

16	...	Rxb2!

By far Black's best practical chance, as he gets back a pawn and activates his Rook. Inherently hopeless is 16...Bd7?! 17 b3 Bc6 18 Qg5!, Navarovsky - Sehlstedt, Reykjavik 1957, and White won on move 26.

17	Qd8+?!

White scores brilliantly with the idea behind this check, yet it is not the best. What he is committing here is the frequent error of playing an attack with just some of the pieces and not all. Stronger is 17 Na4! when 17...Rb1? loses to 18 0-0! Rxc1 19 Qd8+ followed by 20 Rxc1. Therefore necessary is 17...Rb7, but White's advantage is close to decisive after 18 0-0 Bd7 19 Nc5.

17	...	Kf7

18   Ne4

The point of the previous move, with White having a multitude of threats: 19 Ng5 Mate, 19 Nd6+, 19 Rc7+. Yet could not White's uncastled King turn out to be a problem? Black's next two checks are obvious and forced.

18	...	Qb4+
19	Kf1	Ba6+
20	Kg1	

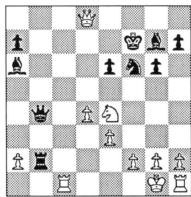

[diag. 41]

White has escaped the checks and renews all his threats. What now, Black?

20	...	g5?

Black allows the following combination and a quick end. Also 20...Ne8? leads to a forced loss: 21 Ng5+ Kf8 22 Nxe6+ Kf7 23 Rc7+!! Kxe6 (23...Nxc7 24 Ng5 Mate) 24 Qxe8+ Kf5 25 Rf7+ Kg5 26 Qd8+ Kh5 27 g4+! Kxg4 28 Rf4+ Kh5 29 Qh4 Mate (Analysis by GM Robert Byrne).

However, there is a defense: 20...Qf8!!. In fact, in the game Kluger - Molnar, Hungary 1955, Black even achieved good counterplay.

21	Rc7+	Kg6
22	Rxg7+!	Kxg7
23	Qxf6+	Kg8
24	Qxg5+	Kh8
25	Qe5+	Kg8
26	h4	**Black resigns**

White threatens a mating attack of his own with 27 Rh3 and 28 Rg3+. The attempt to parry this by 26...Rb1+ 27 Kh2 Rxh1+ 28 Kxh1 Qb1+ 29 Kh2 Qxa2 leaves Black three pawns down after 30 Qb8+ Kg7 31 Qxa7+.

King's Indian Defense
Game 14

White: Pia Cramling
Black: Aldo Haik
Played at Metz, France International Tournament 1989

1	d4	g6
2	e4	Bg7

By choosing the move order for the Modern Defense, Black signals his willingness to turn the opening from a closed type to a semi-open one, i.e. into the Pirc or Modern Defense. This would be the likely happening if White now plays 3 Nc3 or 3 Nf3. Her response, however, clearly demonstrates that she prefers to remain in a more or less conventional closed system. As currently used, the name Modern Defense refers to systems where Black fianchettoes his KB and delays playing ...Nf6. If White does not play c4, the opening has the character of a semi-open system; if White plays c4, then the opening is considered to be part of closed systems.

3	c4	d6
4	Nc3	Nd7

White has chosen the Averbakh Variation against the Modern Defense and Black responds with what is presently considered to be the soundest method of remaining within the Modern Defense complex. The formerly preferred way, 4...e5, has left the stage because after 5 dxe5! dxe5 6 Qxd8+ Kxd8 7 f4! White achieves very annoying pressure against Black's in-the-center King.

Instead of the text Black can immediately transpose into the King;s Indian Defense with 4...Nf6. However, the White has a large number of choices as to how to proceed, e.g. the Sämisch Variation with 5 f3, the Averbakh with 5 Be2 and 6 Bg5 or the Classical with 5 Nf3.

5	Nf3	e5

This advance is without fault now since 6 dxe5 dxe5 just decreases White's central superiority (she is exchanging the d-pawn on the 4th rank for Black's d-pawn on the third) while gaining nothing in turn.

6	Be2	Ngf6

Finally, by transposition, reaching the King's Indian Defense.

7	0-0	0-0

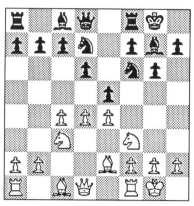

[diag. 42]

After some rather major transpositions, the Positional Variation within the Main Line has arisen. The normal move order (and what you would have to look up in reference books on the openings) is: 1 d4 Nf6 2 c4 g6 3 Nc3 Bg7 4 e4 d6 5 Nf3 0-0 6 Be2 e5 7 0-0 Nbd7. It is important to realize that the move order used in this game is a rather frequent guest in international tournaments. There are two major advantages associated with it: (1) A number of White variations against the King's Indian are eliminated, and (2) Black does not have to worry about defending the slightly inferior endgame resulting after 7 dxe5 dxe5 8 Qxd8 Rxd8 9 Bg5, but instead is assured of reaching a characteristic King's Indian middlegame. Of course, these plusses are not obtained for nothing: Black risks winding up in the Pirc Defense or the semi-open variations of the Modern Defense and therefore has to be theoretically ready for them.

It is time now to look at the characteristics of the King's Indian. The basic pawn structure is that occurring after Black's 4th move in the Main Line (1 d4 Nf6 2 c4 g6 3 Nc3 Bg7 4 e4 d6).

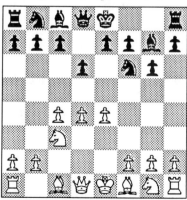

[diag. 43]

The King's Indian in a simplified comparison can be looked upon as a more modest and patient half-brother of the Gruenfeld. Witness these characteristics:

- Black allows White to build a strong center (pawns on c4, d4, e4), but then with 4...d6 restrains any incursion into Black's part of the board.
- In early opening play Black keeps the position closed so that there is less risk of being run over than in the Gruenfeld.
- Black's usual counterplay objective also is d4. This can be started via a ...c5 or ...e5 advance. We have learned that in a majority of variations, ...e5 is more effective because it makes use of a primary central pawn.

Let us return to the position before Black's 7th move in the normal move order, i.e. Black's Knight is still on b8. He has three choices: (1) 7...exd4 gives up the center and is not considered to be 100% sound, (2) 7...Nc6 applies thematic pressure on d4. Called the "Mar del Plata Variation" it is a high risk/potential variation coming back into popularity, (3) 7...Nbd7 is called the Positional Variation and has been a mainstay in the King's Indian since World War II.

The Positional Variation traces its popularity to an inherent flexibility. Even though the QN seems to be ignoring d4, pressure can be quickly applied with a sequence involving ...c6, ...exd4, ...Qb6, ...Ng4. Black can also aim for counterplay against e4 with ...exd4, ...Re8, ...Nc5.

The important strategic themes in this variation are:

Black will aim for counterplay against either d4 or e4, depending on White's choice of sub-variations. If White keeps the center closed by playing d5, Black will try to undermine the d-pawn with ...c6 and/or attack the e4 base with ...f5. In all cases, Black's maneuvering must be extremely accurate and sophisticated because if Black is not successful in his counterplay efforts, White's significant central superiority will leave Black uncomfortably cramped.

White needs to prevent effective counterplay by Black against d4 and e4. If White is successful in this, his superior center will allow him to exert strong pressure against Black's position. Positions where White chooses to eliminate the central tension by playing either d5 or dxe5 (with ...dxe5 as Black's response) have the following spheres of action: White will look for his prospects on the a- through d-files; Black's chances are on the Kingside.

8 Qc2

The text and 8 Be3 have become increasingly popular in the 1990s. Formerly the rather exclusive main line had been 8 Re1 and after 8...c6, 9 Bf1 with the idea of early on negating counterplay against e4.

8 Qc2 is a more flexible way of trying to achieve the same end since the Queen protects e4 and the KR can go to d1 to protect d4 or apply pressure along the d-file.

8   ...   a5?!

An instructive opening inaccuracy/error. The move is a standard method of ensuring stable access to c5 for the QN. Yet the execution of it must be most exact because it carries with it a permanent structural liability: the weakening of the Queenside. Even though at the moment only b5 appears weakened, the long term consequences are worse than that because if Black will need to play ...c6 to safeguard the d5 square, then d6 and b6 are permanently weakened also and therefore the important c5 square becomes vulnerable as well.

The correct move order is the careful 8...c6 9 Rd1 Qe7. If then 10 Rb1, 10...a5 as in J. Lautier - V. Hort, Novi Sad Olympiad 1990, seems quite playable.

9   dxe5!

A decision never to be taken lightly since after the thematic recapture with the d-pawn, White's primary central superiority has vanished because she, in effect, has exchanged the d-pawn on the fourth rank for Black's d-pawn on the third rank. The exchange is effective here because White can start exploiting the pawn weaknesses on the Queenside described in the previous note.

However, please note that if instead of having played 8...a5?!, Black plays 8...c6, then 9 dxe5 dxe5 is ineffective for White because she gains nothing in return for having enhanced Black's center. Often such unmotivated exchanges even boomerang because on a fundamental basis White's d4 square can become vulnerable while d5 is securely in Black's hand forevermore.

9   ...   dxe5

There is no choice because 9...Nxe5?! leaves White with the superior center, while Black is left with a permanent weakness on b5 and can be even vulnerable to a later c5 advance once White places a Rook on the d-file.

After the text another long term deficiency in Black's position appears: the KB's central diagonal has been closed. Under normal conditions this problem can be overcome readily enough; here it is another stone around Black's neck.

10   Be3   c6

Unfortunately Black can't do without guarding the key d5 square in this way. For instance, 10...Qe7?! 11 Nd5! Nxd5?! 12 cxd5 leaves Black's c-pawn defenseless.

11	Rad1	Re8?!

According to IM Cramling, this is a further inaccuracy. Because Black must remove the Queen from the d-file in any case (White's threat is 12 Nxe5), he should do so immediately with 11...Qe7. After the text White can establish a complete grip on the weak dark squares in Black's Queenside (b6, c5, d6).

12	Na4!	Qe7
13	Nd2!	

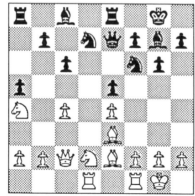

[diag. 44]

Threatening 14 c5 followed by 15 Nc4 when White can continue squeezing Black with 16 Nd6 or aim at capturing the a-pawn. Notice that in such positions there are no positive features from 8...a5?!—there are only negatives.

13	...	Nf8

Otherwise Black cannot develop the Queenside but now White's QB infiltrates via the vulnerable c5 square onto the undefended d6 square. Again the problems caused by 8...a5?! are apparent, because with the a-pawn back on a7, Black could play 13...b6 followed by 14...Bb7.

14	Bc5	Qc7
15	Nf3!	

So that after 16 Bd6 the e-pawn goes lost. This forces Black to again deactivate a piece—this time the KN.

15	...	N6d7
16	Bd6	Qd8
17	c5	Qf6
18	Rfe1!	

Black is in such a crouch that he cannot improve his position in any meaningful way. Therefore White uses the well-known strategem first formulated by former World Champion Mikhail Botvinnik: in situations where the defender cannot improve his position the stronger side should make some good waiting moves and wait for further self-weakening by the opponent. It works immediately.

18   ...   h5?!

Weakens the important g5 square. If 18...Ne6, then 19 Nb6!—as occurs a move later. The best that Black has is 18...h6, followed by 19...Nh7 and 20...Ng5—though Black's position remains drab.

19   h4!   Ne6

If Black does nothing White will continue with 20 Bc4 and 21 Ng5, but the text allows the following tactical trick.

20   Nb6!   Nxb6
21   Bxe5   Qe7
22   Bxg7   Nd7?

This example of crass materialism leads Black into a hopeless situation as his Kingside will now be indefensible. White's QB had to be recaptured, when after 23 cxb6 White's advantages are manifest: the extra (though doubled) pawn, superior center and development, Black's weakened Kingside. Still Black's chances are immeasurably better than in the game, because he has some swindling power. In the game he simply won't be able to do a thing.

23   Bc3   Ndxc5
24   Bf1   Ng7
25   Qd2!

[diag. 45]

White is ready to take advantage of Black's chronically weakened Kingside with 26 Qh6 followed by 27 Ng5. Black prevents this for the immediate future but at the cost of additional loss of time.

25	...	Kh7
26	Ng5+	Kg8
27	Bc4	Be6
28	Nxe6	Ncxe6
29	Qh6	Qf8
30	a4!	

After preventing any hoped-for counterplay on the Queenside, White is ready to begin penetrating with his Rooks along the d-file, starting with 31 Rd7. Black cannot prevent this with 30...Rad8? because of 31 Rxd8 when 31...Rxd8 loses to 32 Bxe6 and 31...Nxd8 is refuted by 32 Qxg6.

Therefore Black throws a Queenside pawn into the wind as a way of hoping to prolong the game. The play through move 40 took place in mutual time trouble. Under these circumstances, White's only practical goal becomes to hold on to what she has gained until the security of time control is reached.

30	...	b5
31	axb5	cxb5
32	Bxb5	Rec8
33	Bf6	

Immediately decisive is 33 Bd7! followed by 34 Bxe6.

33	...	Rc7
34	Rc1	Qb4
35	Bf1	Rac8
36	Rxc7	Rxc7
37	Rd1	Rc8

37...Qxe4?? loses instantaneously to 38 Rd8+!.

38	Qe3	Ne8
39	Bc3	Qb3
40	Ra1	

Undoubtedly stronger is 40 Rd7!.

40	...	a4
41	Be2	Rd8
42	Kh2	

As is customary in the 1990s, the play continues for the second session of 20 moves in one hour. White's position is theoretically completely won: a good extra pawn, the superior center, attacking chances against

Black's Kingside. Nevertheless, the won position must be turned into a full point. White's approach is most instructive throughout: she takes plenty of time on her moves, prevents any whiff of counterplay and makes progress, slowly yet surely.

42	...	N8g7
43	g3	Kh7
44	Qf3	f5
45	exf5	Nxf5
46	Qe4	Qb6
47	Kg2	Rf8
48	Rf1	Rf7
49	Qxa4	

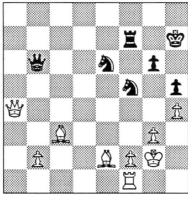

[diag. 46]

White now is two pawns up, still has the Bishop pair in an open position, while Black's Kingside remains fundamentally weak. IM Cramling continues in the proper mode for winning a won position: enhancing her position while preventing Black's opportunities.

49	...	Ned4
50	Qa6!	Qd8
51	Qc4	Re7
52	Bd1	Qa8+
53	Kh3	Qa7
54	Qd5!	

Recentralizing the Queen after the pawn capture excursion of 49 Qxa4.

54	...	Qa6
55	Kg2	Qf6
56	Bb3	Re2
57	Kg1	Re8
58	Qf7+	Qxf7

59	Bxf7	Ne2+
60	Kg2	Re7

60...Rf8 61 Ba2! Nexg3 is parried by 62 Re1!.

61	Ba2	Rc7

61...Nxc3 62 bxc3 Re2 fails to 63 Bb1 (63...Ne3+ 64 Kf3).

62	Bf6	Nexg3
63	Re1!	

Of course, 63 fxg3 Ne3+ 64 Kg1 also wins easily, but the text is even stronger since the straying Knight on g3 remains en prise, while White engineers a mating attack.

63	...	Rc2
64	Re8	g5
65	hxg5	Black resigns

If 65...h4, the end comes after 66 Bf7 Ng7 67 g6+ Kh6 68 Rh8.

♦   ♦   ♦   ♦   ♦

Game 15

White: Anatoly Karpov
Black: Garry Kasparov
Played at 1990 World Championship Match, New York, Game 19

1	d4	Nf6
2	c4	g6
3	Nc3	Bg7
4	e4	d6
5	Nf3	0-0
6	Be2	e5

GM Kasparov must use the normal move order in aiming for the King's Indian because against the Classical/Normal/Main Line Variation (5 Nf3, 6 Be2 7 0-0) he plays the unbalancing Mar del Plata Variation (7...Nc6). Moreover, there is little risk that Karpov will choose to enter the endgame with 7 dxe5 since his winning chances are slight against a player of Kasparov's caliber. In a match for the World Championship, the challenger must go all out to play for the win with the White pieces. This does not mean taking stupid risks, but does require the need to continuously set up challenges for the opponent. The well known, slightly superior endgame after 7 dxe5 dxe5 8 Qxd8 Rxd8 9 Bg5 would not be expected to be enough of a challenge to Kasparov.

7   Be3

Prior to this match GM Karpov played exclusively the standard 7 0-0. Most likely he avoided it in the match because of GM Kasparov's outstanding recent results with 7...Nc6. Seemingly the Karpov team had not found weak chinks in Kasparov's armor of the Mar del Plata Variation.

The text forms the Gligoric Variation, named after Yugoslav GM Svetozar Gligoric who, with his successes, brought it into prominence in the early 1960s. It is an ambiguous, flexible variation. The immediate point is that the attempt at refutation with 7...Ng4 is parried easily by 8 Bg5. In fact this is a main line variation within the Gligoric, but mutually playable for both sides. The strategic ideas of 7 Be3 are twofold: (1) White keeps open the question of what to do with his King: castle on the Kingside, castle on the Queenside, or leave it in the center (as in this game), (2) In case of a ...exd4 by Black, White has the option of recapturing with the Bishop. Yet in a sense the Gligoric Variation is mostly a challenge to Black: how should he try to "refute" it, i.e. at various moments Black can play ...Ng4, attacking the QB. When is this advisable and when is it a serious loss of time?

These considerations make the Gligoric just a bit unsuitable for Karpov. His unique talent is the understanding of strategically clear variations at a greater depth and with deeper sophistication than anyone else. The ambiguous Gligoric Variation does not allow the full flowering of this talent.

7   ...   c6

The inherent viability of the Gligoric is well illustrated by the fact that even after some thirty years of playing at the grandmaster level, theory is far from deciding which is Black's most effective response. Just in this match alone, a different method was used in each of the five games. In Game 3 Black played 7...Qe7; Games 5 and 7 saw 7...Na6 8 0-0 c6 and 7...Na6 8 0-0 Ng4, respectively; in Game 11 Kasparov preferred the immediate 7...exd4; 7...c6 is chosen here.

The immediate point of the text is to safeguard d5; the sophisticated insight is to accomplish this while keeping all other options open. We have something like a variant of the cat-and-mouse theme: White's flexibility/ambiguity is countered by Black's flexibility/ambiguity.

8   d5

[diag. 47]

The most principled response. Alternatives are:

(1) 8 dxe5 dxe5 9 Qxd8 Rxd8 10 Nxe5 Re8 11 f4 Nbd7! 12 Nxd7 Nxe4! with endgame equality (GM Azmayparashvili).

(2) 8 0-0, when 8...Na6 transposes into Match Game 5; 8...exd4 9 Nxd4 could well transpose into Game 11, and 8...exd4 9 Bxd4 is considered to give Black excellent prospects for equality after both 9...Qe7 and 9...Re8.

(3) 8 Qd2, when after 8...Nbd7 9 0-0 Re8 or 8...Re8, White must play d5 and the Queen's location on d2 gets in the way of the possible repositioning of the KN or QB.

By closing the center White prevents a ...exd4, ensures a substantial spatial advantage and brings about the most thematic strategic confrontation of the King's Indian:

Because his spatial advantage is on the Queenside, White's prospects are there:

(a) If Black plays ...cxd5, then after cxd5, White's primary incursion file is the open c-file and the vulnerable points to aim at are d6 and c7:

(b) If Black closes the c-file with ...c5, White will work to open the b-file with a b4 advance.

Black's thematic counterplay starts with the ...f5 advance. Then depending on White's deployment, he will:

(a) advance further with f4, or

(b) apply additional pressure on e4 with ...Nf6, trying to force White's exf5, when ...gxf5 will lead to enhanced central influence for Black, or

(c) play ...fxe4 at a moment when White has to recapture with the f-pawn and Black can exploit the opened f-file. This last approach is the one that calls for the most delicate timing.

8 ... Ng4

I believe that this is more effective than 8...cxd5 9 cxd5 when White will have the clearly defined use of the open c-file. There is no hurry for Black to capture on d5. Keeping that option open makes it harder for White to formulate a clear course of action. White on his part does not want to play a premature dxc6 as after ...bxc6 White has lost control over d5.

9   Bg5   f6!

It is important to force White to make an early decision regarding which diagonal the QB will be on. Then Black can concentrate on trying to exploit that factor. The obvious 9...Qb6?! is ineffective since after 10 0-0 Qxb2?! 11 Na4 Qa3 12 Bc1 Qb4 13 Bd2 Qa3 14 Rb1! Black's Queen is in serious trouble.

10   Bh4

Slows down Black's plan of playing ...f5, but at the cost of otherwise having the Bishop passively placed. White will have to spend time to have it gainfully redeployed. The retreats, 10 Bc1 and 10 Bd2, allow the immediate 10...f5!?. Starting with the text, both sides will have to show great sophistication in their maneuvers to get the most out of their potential.

10   ...   Na6!

This flexible developmental move is apparently a novelty. Black correctly wants to have as much development as is reasonably possible before undertaking definitive action. An immediate standard approach has been 10...h5, but with White as yet not castled on the Kingside, it seems imprudent to weaken one's own King safety.

11   Nd2   Nh6
12   a3

Because Black has avoided playing ...cxd5, White's most effective plan against Black's Queenside is not so easy to ascertain. The text prepares to expand on that side with b4, though a more efficient preparation would be 12 Rb1. White avoids that in case Black still plays ...cxd5 when the QR is placed best on c1. Such a hope, however, seems somewhat naive in light of Black's continuing refusal to capture on d5.

12   ...   Nf7
13   f3

There seems to be nothing wrong with the consistent 13 b4. Instead, White prepares the coming voluntary retreat of the QB which has the disadvantage of allowing Black's Kingside play to develop rapidly. GM Karpov must have felt at least somewhat uncomfortable in the ambiguous Gligoric of this game since in later games of the match he switched to the Sämisch Variation.

13	...	**Bh6**
14	**Bf2**	**f5**
15	**Qc2**	

Black's thematic play on the Kingside has started, but White is still keeping open all his options. Again, there is nothing wrong with the thematic 15 b4 (15...Qg5 16 g3). Or White could castle Kingside, since after 15...Qg5 16 Nb3 c5 17 Na5! (GM Seirawan) White's minor pieces on the Queenside are much more effectively placed than Black's Queen on the Kingside.

15 ...   Bd7!

Completing the minor piece development, rather than rushing in with 15...Qg5 which leads to nothing after 16 g3. Black shows complete understanding of classical principles as well as demonstrating the proper level of patience. It is the play of a World Champion at full maturity though only 27 years old.

16 b4   c5

With White's b-pawn finally mobilized he was threatening 17 dxc6 bxc6 18 c5, with serious problems for Black's center. Therefore Black puts a stop to such "nonsense" by closing off the c5 square. Obviously 17 bxc5?! Nxc5 18 Bxc5?! dxc5 is bad for White since his dark squares have been weakened and Black's KN gets a fantastic blockading square on d6. On the other hand, White's gain, a protected passed d-pawn, could only be of value in an endgame and White would have to navigate many miles of an arduous middlegame before he could hope to reach an endgame.

17	**Rb1**	**b6**
18	**Nf1**	

[diag. 48]

Preparing to exert pressure on f5 by means of 19 Ne3. After 25 minutes of thought the World Champion finds a perceptive parry.

18   ...   Bf4!!

So that after 19 Ne3?! Qg5 20 Ncd1 Black has 20...Bxe3 21 Nxe3 f4. White therefore decides to chase the annoying Bishop back, but at the cost of a fundamental weakening of the Kingside.

19   g3   Bh6
20   h4

Otherwise a ...Ng5, taking a bead on the f3 and h3 squares can be unpleasant. After the text Black starts bringing his do-nothing-on-the-Queenside Knight towards the Kingside, aiming to place it on f6 to apply pressure on White's e-pawn.

20   ...   Nc7
21   g4?!

Much too much of a good thing: after advancing his pawns in the center and on the Queenside, White follows suit on the Kingside. Yet this leaves weak squares in its wake and, considering that the Kingside is Black's normal trump, is an unjustifiably optimistic tack. As GM Polugaevsky suggested, in order is 21 Bd3! followed by 22 Nh2, thus keeping all squares on White's side under control. The delicately balanced position then offers equal chances.

21   ...   fxg4!
22   fxg4   Bf4!

Of course, Black is not going to allow his KB to be buried alive after 23 g5. On f4 the Bishop is secure and active—a rare opportunity for Black's KB in positions where White has closed the center with d5.

23   Ne3   Ne8
24   Ncd1   h6!

Preventing an eventual g5 by White, as well as having the thematic ...g5 response after White's h5, thereby preventing line openings against Black's King. But, of course, the f5 square will go into White's hands after the h5, ...g5 sequence so that it is hardly an obvious move to play. After 22 minutes thought GM Kasparov arrives at the ultimate truth of the situation on the Kingside.

25   h5   g5!

Such a Kingside pawn formation (e5, g5, h6) is normally quite bad for Black because his KB, being stuck behind the pawns on e.g. g7, has no scope at all. Yet here the situation is just as different as day is from night:

the KB on f4 is secure outside its pawn chain and is in fact the best Bishop on the board. Black's position is the easier one to play and he already enjoys a slight advantage. Of course, this is clearer in hindsight than during the actual nerve-racking play.

26 Rg1

White's prospective attack on the Queenside has become stillborn and he now prepares to shift his King to safety on the Kingside. Black meanwhile uses this time to increase the pressure on g4 as well as to improve the placement of his Queen and Knights.

26	...	Nf6
27	Rg2	Qc8
28	Kf1	Nd8!

Since on f7 the Knight obviously has no prospects, its heads for b7 to be in position for a line opening on the Queenside.

29	Kg1	Nb7
30	Kh1?	

[diag. 49]

White seems oblivious to Black's chances on the Queenside. One of the important principles of middlegame strategy is that if the side with an advantage on a part of the board refuses to try to build on it, the opponent often via a properly timed counteraction can turn things around in that sector. This is what will happen here.

If White had realized the seriousness of the situation, he would have hurried to keep the Queenside as closed as possible after 30 b5! a6 31 a4 axb5 32 axb5. GM Azmayparashvili considers this position equal whereas GM W. Watson calls White's position "most uncomfortable" after 32...Ra3. It seems rather safe to say that Black must have at least some advantage after 32...Ra3: the Bf4 and Nf6 are wonderfully active and he has control of the only open file.

30	...	cxb4!
31	axb4	a5!

The undermining of White's formerly superior Queenside is now complete. White can not afford 32 bxa5? bxa5 since Black then has a viable passed a-pawn, whereas White's extra pawn—the c-pawn—is blockaded manifold.

32	Nf5	Bxf5
33	exf5	

White hardly had any choice than to get some breathing room with the above exchange, yet that also can only be favorable for Black since his protected passed pawn is the central e-pawn and that is much more powerful in the middlegame than White's completely blockaded passed protected f-pawn.

33	...	axb4
34	Rxb4	Nc5!!

Heading for domination of the central squares. With White's c-pawn securely blockaded, Black's b-pawn becomes irrelevant in the larger scheme of things: getting at White's King.

Instead after the tactically sound but strategically faulty 34...Nxd5?, White plays 35 Rb2 followed by 36 Bf3 and his pieces start living again. White's chances then probably are about equal to Black's.

35	Rxb6	Nce4
36	Rc6	

The Rook only stands optically well here, because it now is missing from protection of his Queenside. But good advice is scarce, e.g. 36 Bf3 Nxf2+ 37 Nxf2 Qc5 38 Rb1 Ra3 gives Black a powerful initiative; 36 Bg1 Ra3 is most unappetizing for White; after 36 Be1 Black can play either 36...Qc5 37 Rb5 Qd4 or perhaps even take back his pawn with 36...Nxd5.

36	...	Qb7
37	Be1	Ra1

Good, but probably even better is 37...Ra3!, especially considering White's serious time trouble. One major point is that the logical appearing 38 Bd3?! (38 Nc3? Qb4!) leaves White defenseless after 38...Qa7!, threatening 39...Qd4. White therefore needs to play the immediate 38 c5! to gain some time for establishing a defensive formation and that is a hard move to play in time pressure.

38	Bf3	Nc5

39 Bc3   Rc1 Draw

[diag. 50]

What an unexpected ending! After playing his move GM Kasparov offered the draw which Karpov, having only two minutes for his last move, quickly accepted. Kasparov at this moment still had ten minutes on his clock. It is a very tough goal to achieve confident and accurate evaluations of unbalanced positions during the torrid heat of battle. GM Kasparov later commented that it was only during the post-mortem with GM Karpov that he started realizing how bad White's position was.

White's next move, 40 Qb2, is forced, but then Black must decide on how to continue. A number of moves seem reasonable, including 40...Qxb2, 40...Qa7 and 40...Qa8. Of these, 40...Qa8! is strongest, threatening 41...Qa4. Then 41 Rc2?! is met powerfully by 41...Rb8. The only defense is 41 Qa2!, though after 41...Nfe4 42 Qxa8 Rxa8 43 Bb2 Rb1 White remains under severe pressure. A forced win is difficult to prove, but the problems clearly are all White's.

This game is a picture perfect demonstration by the World Champion of how to handle the King's Indian when White has closed the center with an early d5 in the Normal Variation. Black's only imperfect "move" was the draw offer. Yet from the standpoint of the match score at that point—Black was one point ahead—his decision was fully justifiable on practical grounds.

Nimzo - Indian Defense
Game 16

White: Svetozar Gligoric
Black: Julio Kaplan
Played at Los Angeles International Tournament 1974

1	d4	Nf6
2	c4	e6
3	Nc3	Bb4

After Black's last move the Nimzo-Indian Defense has been reached, named after the genius GM Aron Nimzovitch who in the 1920s illuminated Black's potential with it. Though at first glance the Nimzo-Indian looks like a tactical opening, i.e. Black pins White's QN and can try to exploit the pin by immediate follow-ups such as ...Ne4 or ...c5, Qa5, Ne4, Nimzovitch gave it the required strategic underpinning to make it last in GM play. His primary approach was to combine control of e4, achieved by fianchettoing the QB, with play against White's doubled c-pawns. Modern master practice has added a dynamic element to Nimzovitch's original concept: taking advantage of the active location of the KB Black starts early active central counterplay with ...c5 or ...d5 or a combination of both.

4 e3

The text, introduced by Akiba Rubinstein, has been White's steadiest response during the past 70 years. White ignores both the pin and the "threat" of doubling his pawns in favor of safeguarding d4 while starting Kingside development. The Rubinstein variation has stood the test of time and I have every expectation that it will continue to do so.

Capablanca's 4 Qc2, preventing the doubled pawns at the cost of developmental time and support of d4, has blown hot and cold and in the early 1990s is hot again. Other important move 4 alternatives where important work will also continue are 4 a3, 4 Bg5, 4 Nf3 and 4 f3.

4	...	b6

[diag. 51]

The immediate fianchetto was Nimzovitch's way. It's strategic pluses are obvious and real: the QB will have an excellent central diagonal controlling e4 and bearing down on White's Kingside. Yet there also are two small sophisticated disadvantages and these have caused a marked decrease in the popularity of this variation:

(1) Because of neglecting to take an early central stand with his c- and/or d-pawn, Black can easily wind up with an unpleasant spatial inferiority, and

(2) Because White has not committed himself yet to any definitive plan of Kingside development he can select one which is most effective against Black's fianchetto. It should be remarked that the idea of fianchettoing the QB is a high class one. It is just that Black is generally better off if he chooses variations where he first castles, takes a central stand with ...c5 or ...d5 or both and then at the proper moment fianchettoes.

The most flexible move in the 1990s is 4...0-0, since Black will not be able to start any kind of meaningful play in the center with the King still there. For those who like immediate central counterplay 4...c5 is faultless. This will be discussed in Game 17.

To summarize the strategic themes after 4...b6:

Black will fianchetto the QB to achieve control over e4. If Black loses control of e4, without obtaining compensation thereof, he will be clearly worse.

White wants to exploit his natural central superiority while working to neutralize the effectiveness of Black's QB along the h1 - a8 diagonal.

5   Bd3

Just as on the previous move, so here too White ignores Black's "thing" in favor of his own normal development. The text is sound enough, yet if White wants to make life more difficult for Black, then he should play 5 Nge2!, with the idea that after 5...Bb7 6 a3 Black has an unpleasant choice to make. If 6...Bxc3+, then after 7 Nxc3 White has the Bishop pair in a comfortable position; if 6...Be7, then after 7 d5 White has a pleasant space advantage.

Therefore Black does better with 5...Ba6, but he then is playing for specific "tactics" rather than sound Nimzovitchan strategy. The result: after either 6 Ng3 or 6 a3 White can hope for a somewhat larger advantage than in the other current main line variations. Of course, the difference is not large, yet the modern master does not want to voluntarily part with any ground at all.

| 5 | ... | Bb7 |
| 6 | Nf3 | 0-0 |

The present day way of handling this variation: Black combines the QB fianchetto with the dynamics of early central play. The original Nimzovitch approach (also used successfully by Bobby Fischer) was to immediately take advantage of the control of e4 by playing 6...Ne4. This works well after the insipid 7 Qc2?! f5! 8 0-0 Bxc3 9 bxc3 0-0; however White can do better with 7 0-0!, when both 7...Nxc3 8 bxc3 Bxc3 9 Rb1 and 7...Bxc3 8 bxc3 Nxc3 9 Qc2 (9...Bxf3 10 gxf3 Qg5+ 11 Kh1 Qh5 12 Rg1!) give White too much compensation for the sacrificed material. And otherwise Black is a significant tempo behind the variations possible after 7 Qc2?!—therefore not surprisingly White is assured a sound opening superiority.

| 7 | 0-0 | c5! |
| 8 | Bd2 | |

White can not expect an advantage if he fails to challenge Black's ambitious play. While his first developmental move against the Nimzo-Indian (4 e3) was perfect and the second (5 Bd3) inherently sound, the modest text is just too modest. The disadvantage of combining the early QB fianchetto with a later ...c5 is that Black risks leaving his KB out on a limb on b4. To exploit this factor White should play 8 Na4!. The threatened 9 a3 forces 8...exd4 when after 9 exd4 Black must maneuver most accurately to achieve eventually equality. Currently Black's most promising response is considered to be 9...Re8 so that after 10 a3 the Bishop can retreat all the way to f8.

| 8 | ... | d6 |

Getting ready to develop the QN while leaving the diagonal of the QB open is fully in the spirit of Nimzovitch. According to theory Black can also equalize with the "more modern" approach of 8...cxd4 9 exd4 d5.

9	a3	Bxc3
10	Bxc3	Ne4!
11	Bxe4	

There is no reason why such an exchange should lead to any advantage. White's hopes for that must rest on a slight central superiority and the two Bishops. Therefore 11 Be1 makes sense. However, Black's control of e4 gives him dynamic equality, e.g. 11...Nd7 12 Nd2 f5 13 Qc2 Nxd2 14 Bxd2 Qh4, Donner - Spassky, Beverwijk 1967.

11	...	Bxe4
12	Nd2	Bb7!

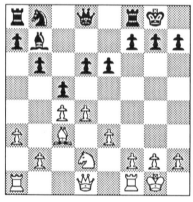

[diag. 52]

Instead in Gligoric - Smyslov, Havana 1967 Black played 12...Bg6 and achieved approximate equality after 13 dxc5 dxc5 14 Qf3 Nd7. Perhaps GM Gligoric had prepared an improvement for White.

In any case, IM Kaplan's move is more logical and better. Why should the Bishop voluntarily leave his thematic central diagonal? After the text Black has full dynamic equality with his more active Bishop compensating the slight central inferiority. In the coming play White either does not realize it or doesn't want to believe this and as a result his position starts to steadily go downhill.

13   Qg4

There just are no preconditions for a successful attack on Black's King. Equally unproductive in this regard is 13 dxc5 (13...dxc5?! 14 Qg4) because of 13...Qg5! 14 Nf3 Qxc5. In the spirit of the position is 13 Qe2 followed by expansion on the Queenside with 14 b4.

13	...	f5
14	Qg3	Qe7
15	Rfe1	

With White's Queen on g3, more logical is 15 Rae1.

15	...	Nd7
16	f3	Rae8

Mobilizing his forces on the center/Kingside - where Black's chances are apt to be. Black is playing in full accordance with the theme of the position.

17 Rad1

The Rook has no future here. The immediate 17 e4 is better.

17	...	e5!
18	d5?!	

Strategically dubious since Black has excellent prospects of undermining the pawn's support and, as will be seen, tactically faulty. Correct is the modest 18 dxe5, with only a slight advantage to Black after 18...dxe5.

18	...	b5!
19	cxb5?	

Leads to a strategically lost position. Only with 19 e4! was there hope for a successful defense.

19	...	Bxd5
20	e4	Be6!

Overlooked by White when playing his 18th and 19th moves: Black prevents Nc4, thereby leaving White with no compensation for the inferior pawn formation, misplaced pieces and lack of meaningful counterplay. Black, on the other hand, has the pawn center and excellent prospects for a Kingside attack.

IM Kaplan's play continues to be exemplary and I have no further improvements to suggest for White.

21	b3	f4!
22	Qf2	Rf6
23	Ba5	

The immediate 23 Nc4 will cost White a pawn after 23 ...Bxc4 24 bxc4 Nb6. The text prevents ...Nb6 and reestablishes the Nc4 plan. Black immediately prevents that and does so with a gain of time by attacking the b-pawn.

23	...	Qf7
24	Rb1	g5!

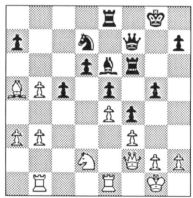

[diag. 53]

The pawn structure on the Kingside is now characteristic of the attacking positions arising from King's Indian formations with the important difference that Black is not handicapped by having a blocked in KB. Despite having a time advantage on the clock of about an hour, White could not find a way to stem Black's attack.

| 25 | Qe2 | g4! |
| 26 | Nc4 | Qh5! |

In spite of the impending time trouble, Black correctly judges that his attack must be decisive. White's scattered pieces cannot be mobilized for a satisfactory long term defense and therefore he hopes that the counterplay with the Knight will give some practical chances.

27	Nxd6	Rh6
28	h3	gxh3!
29	Nxe8	hxg2

With the threat of 30...Qh2+ 31 Kf2 g1=Q Mate, while 30 Kf2 Qh4+ also leads to mate. Therefore White is forced to give up the Queen, but this keeps the attack back for only a little while.

| 30 | Qxg2+ | Rg6 |
| 31 | Rb2 | |

Also 31 Nc7 fails to the decisive 31...Bh3!.

31	...	Bh3
32	Qxg6+	Qxg6+
33	Kh1	

Or 33 Kh2 Qg3+ 34 Kh1 Qxf3+ 35 Kg1 Qg3+ 36 Kh1 Kf8!, threatening both 37...Kxe8 and 37...f3. Around here the only practical question remaining was whether Black would make the time limit on move 40.

| 33 | ... | Qxe8 |

34	Rg1+	Kf8
35	Rh2	Qh5
36	Rf1	Nf6
37	Bc7	Ke7
38	Rff2	

Prevents the threatened 38...Bxf1 39 Rxh5 Nxh5 with Black a piece up. But now comes a bit of final tactics.

38	...	Nxe4!

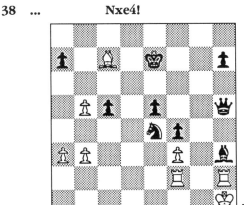

[diag. 54]

Planning mate after 39 fxe4 Qd1+ 40 Rf1 Qxf1.

39	Re2	Ng3+
40	Kg1	Nxe2+
41	Rxe2	Qg5+
42	Kh1	Be6 White Resigns

* * * * *

Game 17

White: Leon Pliester
Black: Edmar Mednis
Played at Amsterdam (OHRA) International Tournament 1986

1	d4	Nf6
2	c4	e6
3	Nc3	Bb4
4	e3	c5

Black issues a principled challenge to White's d-pawn and stakes his ground in the center. He delays castling so as to start earlier action in the center. Moreover, the delay in castling leads to certain sophisticated possibilities not appreciated as recently as twenty years ago. It may seem that White can continue with normal development but the definition of what is "normal" has changed significantly.

White's normal appearing choices now surely include 5 a3 which transposes into the Sämisch Variation (4 a3) after 5...Bxc3+, 5 Bd3 and 5 Nf3. But how about 5 Nge2—is this also a "normal" move?

5   Bd3

This sound and flexible developmental move is rapidly losing popularity—for reasons discussed a bit later on. The equally "sound" 5 Nf3 has almost disappeared from international play because after 5...Nc6! White's options are unattractive: 6 Bd3 transposes into the game and 6 d5 Ne7! causes big trouble for White's d-pawn, since 7 d6?! (Necessary is 7 dxe6 with approximate equality) 7...Nf5! 8 Qd3 b5! 9 cxb5 Bb7 is already better for Black, Christiansen - Browne, USA Championship 1981.

However, it is the unnatural looking 5 Nge2 that is making giant strides in popularity. Its major point is similar to that in the 4...b6 5 Nge2 positions: White gets ready to break the pin on his QN with 6 a3, without risking the doubled pawns. In a sense we are returning to one of the roots of the early Nimzo-Indians: the doubling of the c-pawns can be a major problem for White in many variations. In other words, White's compensation must be very clear as otherwise he will have troubles. Black's most common response is 5...cxd4 and after 6 exd4 he can either continue his central play with 6...d5 giving White the choice between 7 a3 or 7 c5 or prefer 6...0-0 7 a3 Be7 when White has the ambitious 8 d5 at his disposal. In all cases White has excellent prospects for a normal opening advantage.

5   ...   Nc6
6   Nf3

Though a perfect move, according to conventional opening principles, the text has markedly lost popularity in GM play over the past ten years. The reason is a specific sophisticated point which I will get to in my next comment. At present Whites are preferring the alternative KN development with 6 Nge2. Yet, compared to the positions after the immediate 5 Nge2, here Black is a developmental tempo ahead and his chances are bright for equality after either 6...cxd4 7 exd4 d5 or the immediate 6...d5.

6   ...   Bxc3+
7   bxc3   d6

[diag. 55]

Black's 6th and 7th moves establish the Hübner Variation, named after German GM Hübner who in the 1970s was the first person to accurately demonstrate its potential. Black will now follow up with 8...e5, thereby gaining good central influence. This, in conjunction with potential play against the doubled c-pawns, gives Black excellent prospects for playing for a win without any particular increase in the risk of losing. Such a combination of features is exactly what the modern master is looking for.

The potential of the Hübner Variation can best be seen when comparing it to the following main line of the Sämisch Variation: 4 a3 Bxc3+ 5 bxc3 c5 6 e3 b6 7 Bd3, followed by Ne2. There White is able to build a harmonious center because the f-pawn is free to advance. By comparison, in our position the Nf3 blocks the f-pawn, has no offensive prospects and even makes Black's 8...e5 a more powerful move because of the threatened pincer 9...e4. The strength of the Hübner variation is based on the very poor location of the KN on f3. This factor more than justifies Black's entering a Sämisch type position a whole tempo down.

Thematic play for both sides in the Hübner Variation is as follows:

Black hopes to eventually get at the doubled c-pawns. He will look to dissolve any existing pawn chain in such a way that he is left with a superior Knight vs. Bishop situation. Black must prevent any routine opening of the position which allows White's Bishops powerful scope.

White wants to retain his spatial advantage in the center in such a way that effective coordination of Black's pieces is prevented. He should always be on the lookout to activate his Bishop pair. Usually this will require an opening of the position—often at the cost of sacrificing a central pawn.

8   0-0

The flexible text has pretty much replaced the formerly "obligatory" 8 e4 e5 9 d5. What we have learned is that White's imposing center is more unwieldy than powerful. The key game in bringing home this point is Spassky - Fischer, 1972 World Championship Match, Game 5: 9...Ne7 10 Nh4 h6! 11 f4 Ng6! 12 Nxg6 fxg6 13 fxe5 dxe5 14 Be3 b6 15 0-0 0-0, with White—at best—having unattractive equality. His Bishops have so little scope that the protected passed d-pawn is just an ornament rather than a treasure. Bobby's execution of Black's potential is picture perfect: 16 a4?! a5! 17 Rb1 Bd7 18 Rb2 Rb8 19 Rbf2?! Qe7 20 Bc2 g5! 21 Bd2 Qe8! 22 Be1 Qg6 23 Qd3 Nh5! 24 Rxf8+ Rxf8 25 Rxf8+ Kxf8 26 Bd1 Nf4! 27 Qc2? Bxa4! White resigns (28 Qxa4 Qxe4).

8   ...   e5
9   Ng5

In conjunction with the next move this is by far White's sharpest way of trying to open up the position. The alternative Knight move, 9 Nd2, leads to more strategic positions, e.g. 9...0-0 10 d5 Ne7 11 e4 h6 12 Re1 Nh7! 13 Nf1 f5! 14 exf5 Bxf5 15 Ng3 Bxd3 16 Qxd3 Qd7, Balashov - Vaganian, 1989 USSR Championship. White's Bishop is the inferior minor piece since its offensive potential is so small and White's compensation for the doubled pawns is not to be seen. Again, at best, White has equality. In the game Black went on to win in good style on move 41.

9   ...   0-0
10 f4   exd4

It seems pretty clear that Black should prevent White from opening the f-file. Therefore, wrong must be 10...exf4?! because after 11 Rxf4 h6 12 Rxf6 Qxf6 13 Nh7 Qh4 14 Nxf8 Bg4 15 Qf1 Rxf8 16 Bd2, Knaak - Grunberg, Leipzig 1983, White has the advantages: his superior center is secure, the Bishop pair has potential because White has prospects for establishing pressure along the f-file against Black's Kingside, Black has no compensation for his central inferiority and no prospects for counterplay.

11 cxd4   h6!?

Blacks have usually been first playing 11...cxd4 when after 12 exd4 there are three possibilities:
   (1) 12...h6 transposes into the game.
   (2) 12...d5?! looks dubious to me since after 13 Ba3 Re8 14 cxd5 White's Knight on g5 seems fantastically placed for the attack.

(3) 12...Nxd4?! just seems reckless as Black is voluntarily
opening up diagonals for White's Bishops. A likely continuation then is 13 Bb2 Nf5 14 Qc2! Ne3 15 Bxh7+ Kh8 16 Qd3
Nxf1 17 Rxf1 when White's attack must be close to decisive.
A reference is Kuuskmaa - Uogele, Correspondence 1983—
see Chess Informant 37/612.

| 12 | Nf3 | cxd4 |
| 13 | exd4 | d5! |

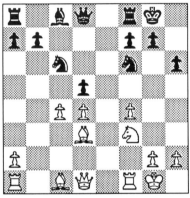

[diag. 56]

An important theoretical novelty. Earlier Black played 13...Bg4,
but I didn't trust that because after 14 d5! the position opens up.
The key game here is Benjamin - Browne, 1983 USA Championship:
14...Nd4 15 Bb2 Nxf3+ 16 gxf3 Bh3 17 Rf2 Nh5 18 Qd2 Qh4 19 Kh1
Nxf4 20 Rg1 f6 21 Bb1, with an exciting draw on move 41. Encyclopedia of Chess Openings "E" (Revised) considers that after 21 Bb1
White has compensation for the sacrificed pawn. I agree—but the
important point as far as I am concerned is that White has realized
the goal of this sub-variation: his Bishop pair has open lines against
Black's King.

My reasoning in selecting 13...d5! was as follows: since Black
with his 10th and 12th moves has made White's central pawn
formation whole, the least that he should now do is to prevent both
of White's Bishops from getting in position to attack Black's King.
The text, of course, chokes off White's QB from the a1 - h8 central
diagonal.

14 Ba3?

A poor move, though coming after considerable thinking. After
the game IM Pliester told me that he couldn't quite remember this
exact position (not surprising!) but did recall that in a "similar"

position (which as discussed in the note to Black's 11th move is 11...cxd4 12 exd4 d5?! 13 Ba3) this move is good for White. Here the opposite is true as White simply chases Black's KR to an ideal location—while misplacing his own QB.

White's only correct move is 14 Ne5!. The Swedish IM (now GM) Ferdinand Hellers and I spent some time in going over the game.

Hellers' suggestion was that Black should then play similarly to the game: 14...dxc4 15 Bxc4 Be6! 16 Bxe6 fxe6. Black has full equality since Black's Knight is superior to White's Bishop which is blocked in by the pawns on d4 and f4. This is an excellent example of Black's strategic theme of dissolving a central pawn chain so as to leave White with an inferior Bishop.

14	...	Re8
15	Ne5	

One move too late, but White has nothing better since apart from 15...dxc4 16 Bxc4 Be6, Black also was threatening 15...Bg4.

15	...	dxc4!
16	Bxc4	Be6
17	Bxe6	Rxe6

Compared to the variation given after 14 Ne5!, here Black has a much improved version of it since instead of having an isolated pawn on e6, he has a Rook ready to assume control of the e-file. Another important factor in Black's favor is that White's Bishop on a3 is just whistling in the wind along the a3 - f8 diagonal. It neither does anything on the offense, nor helps defend White's most vulnerable point: the isolated d-pawn. Here we see the second instance where Black has successfully dissolved the central pawn structure to leave himself with the superior Knight vs. Bishop relationship.

18	f5	Re8
19	Bb2?!	

Of course 19 Nxc6 bxc6 leaves Black unchallenged with the superior minor piece, but that was White's minor evil. Retreating the Bishop just accentuates Black's initiative.

19	...	Qb6!
20	Nc4	

There is nothing else. 20 Rf2 is refuted by 20...Ne4; 20 Nxc6 loses to 20...Qxb2 21 Rb1 (Or 21 Ne5 Rad8) 21...Qxa2 22 Rxb7 Re2.

20	...	Qb5
21	Rc1	

A bit better is 21 Qc2 when Black also continues with 21...Rad8.

21	...	Rad8
22	Qd3	Qd5

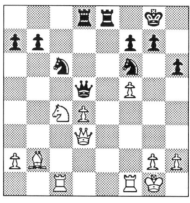

[diag. 57]

Black's consistent execution of the strategic themes of the Hübner variation has led to a complete domination of the board. White has pawn weaknesses on f5, d4 and a2, as well as locked-in Bishop—with no compensation anywhere. By now it is more than obvious that Black has the superior minor piece.

23	Rcd1	b5!
24	Ne3	

Equally unsatisfactory is 24 Na3 a6 when 25 Nc2 is refuted by 25...Qxa2 26 Ra1 Qxb2 27 Rfb1 Nxd4! 28 Rxb2 Ne2+.

24	...	Qxa2
25	Bc3	

Even worse is 25 Ba1 Nb4! when Black will blockade the d-pawn by the Knight and start mobilizing the connected passed pawns at his convenience. The text prevents the ...Nb4, ...Nbd5 maneuver, but trouble now comes from another angle.

25	...	b4
26	Ba1	Ne5!

Giving White the unappetizing choices of a hopeless endgame after 27 Qc2 Qxc2 28 Nxc2 Nc6, a hopeless endgame after 27 Qb5 Rb8 28 Qc5 Ned7 29 Qc4 Qxc4 30 Nxc4 Nd5 or sacrificing the Queen for clearly insufficient compensation. White decides on the latter course.

27	dxe5	Rxd3
28	Rxd3	Ne4

I suppose that if Black becomes careless White then has a few swindling chances. With his next move White opens up his Bishop's diagonal, but obviously it is much too late. Black's coming play is easy to understand: he aims to simplify the position by exchanging pieces.

29	e6	fxe6
30	fxe6	Qxe6
31	Nf5	Nc3
32	Bxc3	bxc3
33	Rxc3	

After 33 Rg3 Black can even play for a decisive attack with 33...Qb6+ 34 Kh1 Qf2! etc.

33	...	Rf8
34	Rcf3	Qb6+
35	Kh1	Kh7
36	h4	g6
37	Ne3	Rxf3
38	Rxf3	Qd4!

[diag. 58]

Domination! White plays on until the time control before resigning.

| 39 | g4 | a5 |
| 40 | Kg2 | a4 | **White resigns** |

Queen's Gambit Declined, Botvinnik Variation
Game 18

White: Yaacov Murey
Black: Edmar Mednis
Played at Amsterdam (OHRA) International Tournament 1986

1	c4	Nf6
2	Nc3	e6
3	Nf3	d5

White's move order (1 c4, 2 Nc3, 3 Nf3) has "tricked" Black into playing the Queen's Gambit Declined because neither is the attempt at a Queen's Indian formation with 3...b6?! fully satisfactory after 4 e4! Bb7 5 Bd3, nor does striving for a Nimzo-Indian with 3...Bb4 reach its aim after 4 Qc2!.

4 d4

After the text quite a normal position within the very broad Queen's Gambit Declined complex has arisen. The most common response— 4...Be7—leads to the Orthodox Defense variations—see Game 21. Black can also play the thematic 4...c5 when after 5 cxd5, 5...Nxd5 brings about the Semi-Tarrasch Variation (see Game 22), whereas 5...exd5 transposes into the "pure" Tarrasch Defense (see Games 24, 25, 26).

Black also has a simple way of forcing White to make a major thematic decision:

4 ...   c6

First, a note on nomenclature is in order. This position is often referred to as a "Slav Defense" because the position can (and part of the time does) arise from the move order 1 d4 d5 2 c4 c6 3 Nc3 Nf6 4 Nf3 e6. Yet since the inherent concept behind the Slav is to protect d5 while leaving the c8 - h3 diagonal open for the QB, the early "unnecessary" ...e6 takes away from the idea behind 2...c6 and therefore in my mind removes the opening from a "Slav" category.

Back to chess: by protecting the b5 square, Black now "threatens" to take on c4 and then to hold on to the captured pawn with ...b5. White's choices are either to do something about Black's threat or to ignore it. The most common "safe move" is 5 e3, leading to the Meran Variation after 5...Nbd7—see Games 19 and 20. White can also transpose into the Exchange Variation of the QGD with 5 cxd5 exd5 or protect the c-pawn directly by 5 Qb3.

Or White can try to call Black's bluff with the counter-challenging ...

5   Bg5!?

Playing the QB to g5 in the QGD is hardly unusual but in this specific position it is a major decision as White thereby risks the sequence 5...dxc4 6 e4 b5 7 e5 h6 8 Bh4 g5 9 Nxg5 hxg5 10 Bxg5 Nbd7 (see Diagram 59). The positions that result are extremely

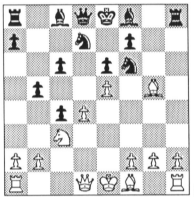

[diag. 59]

unclear—as a matter of fact, they are strategically the least clear of the whole 1 d4 complex. To play this variation successfully—for either side—you must love complicated "messy" positions, like doing extensive original research, have the time and interest to follow chess theory developments world wide and possess a fantastic memory, since variations that easily stretch into the early thirties are more common than rare.

Until 1945 the variation was thought to be theoretically slightly superior for White. Then in the game Denker - Botvinnik, 1945 USA - USSR Match, the Soviet GM scored an impressive quick victory. The evaluation then changed to equal chances/unclear and remained so until the 1981 USSR Championship. There Garry Kasparov demonstrated that with his extensive preparation and fantastic intuition in attacking positions, White (i.e. Kasparov!) does retain chances for an opening advantage. The key games were Kasparov - Timoshchenko

[diag. 60]

(Position after 30 Ba7)

in Round 13 and Kasparov - Dorfman in Round 14. Each of them had the same course through White's 30th move: 11 exf6 Bb7 12 g3 c5 13 d5 Qb6 14 Bg2 0-0-0 15 0-0 b4 16 Na4 Qb5 17 a3 Nb8 18 axb4 cxb4 19 Be3 Bxd5 20 Bxd5 Rxd5 21 Qe2 Nc6 22 Rfc1 Na5 23 b3 c3   24 Nxc3 bxc3 25 Rxc3+ Kd7 26 Qc2 Bd6

27 Rc1 Qb7 28 b4 Qxb4 29 Rb1 Qg4 30 Bxa7—see [diag. 60].

Only now did the games diverge:
  (1) Kasparov - Timoshchenko: 30...e5 31 Qa2! Rd1+ 32 Rxd1
      Qxd1+ 33 Kg2 Qh5 34 Qa4+ Ke6 35 h4! Qe2 36 Qxa5 Ra8
      37 Qa4! Kxf6 38 Qd7 Kg7 39 Rf3 Qc4 40 Qxd6 Rxa7 41 Qxe5+
      Kh7 42 Rf5 Qc6+ 43 Kh2 Black resigns
  (2) Kasparov - Dorfman: 30...Be5 31 Rc5! Rxc5 32 Bxc5! Nc6 33
      Qd3+ Kc8 34 Rd1 Nb8 35 Rc1! Qa4 36 Bd6+ Nc6 37 Bxe5 Rd8
      38 Qb1! Rd5 39 Qb8+ Kd7 40 Qc7+ Ke8 41 Qxc6+ Qxc6 42
      Rxc6 Rxe5 43 Rc8+ Black resigns

The evaluation of Diagram 59 remains as it was after the above
games: White can expect a normal opening advantage. However,
each side better play perfectly as just one misstep is all that is
required for instant death.

5   ...   h6

With the primary purpose of avoiding the unfathomable variations
resulting after 5...dxc4. Black prefers to have a purely strategic
situation, where he will, however, be handicapped by an awkwardly
placed Queen.

Still, the determined "complicator" can go for continued messiness
with 6 Bh4 dxc4 7 e4 g5 8 Bg3. Nevertheless, with either 8...Bb4 or 8...b5
Black achieves positions which are strategically considerably clearer
than those after 5...dxc4. Moreover, Black can expect approximately
equal chances.

6   Bxf6   Qxf6

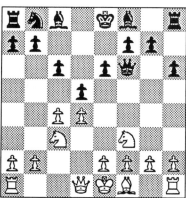

[diag. 61]

It is instructive to compare this position with a "sister" case which can
result from the following QGD, Orthodox Defense Variation: 1 d4 d5 2
c4 e6 3 Nc3 Nf6 4 Nf3 Be7 5 Bg5 0-0 6 e3 h6 7 Bxf6 Bxf6. Here Black has

recaptured on f6 with the KB, leaving it well placed and has saved a potential developmental tempo by omitting the early ...c6 in favor of the useful castling. The tempo saved also allows Black in certain variations to achieve smoothly the thematic ...c5 advance. Both from actual experience and theoretical considerations Black's prospects for eventual comfortable equality are very bright in the above variation.

In our diagram Black's task is considerably tougher. Not only is the Queen on f6 subject to a potential attack from a White Knight on e4 or a White pawn on e5, but also the misplacement of the Queen to f6 has cost Black a developmental tempo. Nevertheless, Black's position is a far from unpleasant: his d5 point is well protected and there are no fundamental weaknesses.

Thematic strategy on both sides will require the following considerations:

Black needs to complete the development of the Kingside by finding a good spot for the KB and then castling. He will have to free his cramped position by aiming for the thematic ...c5 or ...e5 central advances. Usually this will require as preparation ...dxc4 or if White has played e4, perhaps ...dxe4. With the position opening up, Black will look for opportunities to achieve active play for his Bishops.

White will try to demonstrate that he has a superior form of the Orthodox QGD. The most common method is to aim for the e4 advance, either as quickly as possible or after castling. This advance will further enhance White's central spatial superiority. "Safe" players will castle Kingside; more adventurous types will prefer castling Queenside.

7   Qc2

The text is White's most ambitious plan and is considered by Encyclopedia of Chess Openings "D" (Revised) as White's strongest continuation. White plans 8 e4 and will recapture with the Queen after 8...dxe4. (The immediate 7 e4?! dxe4 8 Nxe4 is uncomfortable for White after 8...Bb4+.)

White's most common method has historically been 7 e3 to be followed by 8 Bd3 and 9 0-0. Other good moves are 7 Qb3, 7 g3 and 7 a3.

7   ...   Nd7

Black develops while preventing the threatened 8 cxd5 exd5 9 Nxd5. More ambitious is 7...dxc4 8 e3 b5, though I don't trust Black's position after 9 a4. White recovers the pawn and Black is left with Queenside weaknesses, e.g. 9...Bb7 10 axb5 cxb5 11 Nxb5 Bb4+ 12 Nc3 0-0 13 Be2 Nd7 14 0-0 Rfd8 15 Nd2 e5 16 Bf3! Bxf3 17 Nxf3, Stohl - Sveshnikov, Leningrad 1984.

8   e4   dxe4
9   Qxe4

Black's near term needs are to remove the Queen from its awkward location and to develop the KB. The two most common plans have been 9...Qd8 and 9...Bd6, but I didn't feel confident of playing either. The former is a very substantial loss of time, while the placement of the Bishop on d6 makes it susceptible to a Ne4 "fork." Nevertheless, 9...Bd6, carefully followed up, is playable, with the main line being: 10 Bd3 c5 11 d5 Ne5 12 Nxe5 Bxe5 13 0-0 Qf4! 14 Qxf4 Bxf4 15 Rad1 and now instead of 15...0-0?! 16 Rfe1! with a clear advantage to White since Black has major problems in completing Queenside development, G. Agzamov - Gorelov, USSR 1982, correct is 15...Be5 16 Rfe1 Bxc3! 17 bxc3 Bd7! 18 dxe6 Bxe6 19 Bf5 Ke7 20 Rd5 Rac8 21 f4 with only a slight advantage for White (GM Sveshnikov).

9   ...   Bb4!?

Played in accordance with the strategic theme outlined after Black's 6th move: the Bishop is developed to a square which has more advantages than disadvantages (White's QN is pinned, a ...Bxc3 can lead to the uncomfortable double pawns), then the Queen will retreat to the comfortable e7 location, thereby freeing the good f6 square for the Knight.

10   Bd3

White prevents Black from castling. As an alternative, 10 Rc1 comes into view, though at this moment it is not clear that the QR is best placed on the c-file. In the game Vaiser - Lukacs, East Berlin 1982, Black erred with 10...c5? and stood poorly after 11 d5 Nb6 12 Bd3 g6 13 0-0 0-0 14 d6! Bxc3 15 Rxc3 Rd8 16 Qe3! Na4 17 Ra3 Nxb2 18 Be2 Rxd6 19 Qxc5 Rc6 20 Qb5 a6 21 Qb3 Bd7 22 Qxb7. Of course, Black's consistent plan is 10...Qe7. If White then tries to force the Bishop exchange with 11 a3, Black can either play 11...Bxc3+ 12 Rxc3 c5! and be close to equality or 11...Bd6, because White's Rc1 is probably a wasted move in this position. Therefore the normal 11 Bd3 is better when Black can play the immediate 11...c5 or first 11...Nf6 12 Qe2 and then 12...c5!. In either case Black should in due course equalize. Instead, in Plisecky - Lukjanov, Moscow 1982, he remained in a cramp after 12...0-0 13 0-0 b6?! 14 Ne4! Bb7 15 Nxf6+ Qxf6 16 c5!, with a clear advantage to White.

10   ...   Qe7
11   0-0

Of course, with 11 Rc1 White could transpose into the above line, but it should be clear that a Rac1 move cannot be an effective use of a tempo in this position.

11   ...   Nf6

[diag. 62]

12   Qh4

Black's position is too sound for this active looking move to be effective. After the game, GM Murey suggested 12 Qe1!? as better when after the consistent 12...c5 13 a3 Ba5 14 dxc5 Bxc3 15 Qxc3 Qxc5 White does have a sound Queenside pawn majority. However, Black's position is sufficiently free and thus he can cope with White's Queenside play well enough. White's advantage is only a small one, e.g. 16 b4 Qc7 17 c5 0-0 18 b5 Rd8, followed by 19...Bd7.

12   ...   c5!

As already discussed earlier, in positions of this type Black must free himself with either ...e5 or ...c5. Since the former is not feasible, the later must be played.

13   Ne4

Obviously here 13 dxc5? Bxc3 leads to busted pawns for White.

13   ...   cxd4
14   Nxd4   0-0

Black has successfully completed the initial phases of his thematic plans: the KB and Queen have been developed/regrouped, the King gotten to safety by castling, White's central superiority neutralized with ...c5 and ...cxd4. Now Black is ready to start active play along the d-file with 15...Rd8. White therefore decides to look for an advantage in the endgame.

15   Nxf6+   Qxf6

16	Qxf6	gxf6
17	Rfd1	

White is banking on his edge in development and the Queenside pawn majority. Moreover, Black's Kingside majority is somewhat devalued because of the doubled pawns. Black has every right to expect eventual equality. Yet to achieve this he will have to prevent the activation of White's pieces while working to complete the development of his Queenside.

Black must understand that his primary goal in the variation after 5...h6 6 Bxf6 Qxf6 is to obtain sound equality. Only after that is reached should Black look for winning opportunities.

17	...	f5!

Controlling e4 and freeing f6 for the KB.

18	Rac1	Rd8
19	Be2	Be7!

Otherwise 20 c5 can become unpleasant, but now Black has the comfortable response 20...Bf6 21 Nb5 Bd7 22 Nd6 Bc6 23 b4 a6.

20	Nb3	b6

Black is working to try to develop his QB, while holding back White's Queenside pawns. He is on the verge of equality.

21	Rxd8+	Bxd8
22	Bf3	Rb8
23	Rd1	

Neither is there anything in 23 Nd4 Bf6 24 Nc6 Rb7.

23	...	Bf6
24	Nd4	Bb7!

[diag. 63]

Successfully completing his Queenside development. White cannot play the obvious 25 Bxb7? because after 25...Rxb7 he loses his b-pawn (26 b3?? Rd7).

25   b3   Rd8

Instead foolish is 25...Bxd4?! 26 Rxd4 Bxf3 27 gxf3 since White's active Rook and Queenside majority easily outweigh the Kingside pawn weaknesses. After the text dangerous for White is 26 Nb5?! Bxf3 27 Rxd8+ Bxd8 28 gxf3 because the doubled f-pawns can become vulnerable. Therefore White brings about an equal opposite color Bishop endgame.

26   Bxb7   Draw

After 26...Rxd4 27 Rxd4 Bxd4 neither side has the slightest winning chances.

Queen's Gambit Declined, Meran Variation
Game 19

White: Viktor Korchnoi
Black: Lev Polugaevsky
Played at 1977 Semi-Final Candidates Match, Evian, France, Game 3

	1	c4	Nf6
	2	Nc3	e6
	3	Nf3	d5
	4	d4	c6

The same position has arisen as in the previous game and via the same "less than usual" move order. Here White takes the threat to the c-pawn seriously and protects it the most straightforward way with ...

5 e3

Though at first glance the text seems to rob White of his chances for an opening advantage because now his QB cannot put pressure on Black's center, there is a countervailing feature in this position. Though Black's central position is solid after 4...c6, he will be in a cramp unless he can get in the freeing ...c5 or ...e5 advances. Of these, the ...c5 advance is the easier one to achieve. Yet, because Black has already played ...c6, a later ...c5 will mean that Black has taken two moves to get there, rather than one. One tempo in a normal opening scheme is a significant item and therefore White can still expect an advantage after 5 e3—as long as he understands the theme of the resulting positions. However, because White does have the handicap of a blocked-in QB, to achieve this advantage White will need a higher level of perceptiveness than in positions where his QB is actively developed.

5 ...   Nbd7

Unless Black now follows up with the "orthodox" and insipid 6...Be7, the opening is called the Meran Variation. The name derives from the town in Italy where an international tournament was held in 1924 and the game Gruenfeld - Rubinstein continued: 6 Bd3 dxc4 7 Bxc4 b5 8 Bd3 a6 9 0-0 c5 10 a4 b4 11 Ne4 Bb7 12 Ned2 Be7 13 Qe2 0-0, with approximately equality. Because Black's concept was creative, revolutionary and sound, GM Rubinstein deserved to have his name associated with the opening. Meran's claim to chess fame should only be acknowledged from hosting the 1981 World Championship Match between Anatoly Karpov and Viktor Korchnoi.

The Meran has appeared frequently in GM Polugaevsky's games, both for White and Black, and somewhat less frequently, also in GM Korchnoi's games. Each is an acknowledged expert on it.

6   Bd3

By far White's most active plan ever since the first game, cited above. His approach will be simplicity itself: 7 0-0 and 8 e4, opening up the position and applying strong pressure against Black's center. No routine methods have been found that give Black sufficient prospects for equality, e.g. 6...Bd6 7 0-0 0-0 8 e4 dxc4 9 Bxc4 e5 10 Bg5 h6 11 Bh4 Qe7 12 Re1 Nb6 13 Bb3 Bg4 14 h3 Bxf3 15 Qxf3 Nbd7 (15...exd4? 16 e5!) 16 d5 when White has a nice spatial advantage, the Bishop pair and active piece deployment. In the 1990s very few Blacks have the interest in voluntarily choosing to defend such positions.

However, after 6 Bd3 Black can also play actively, using Rubinstein's approach which, of course, remains the "reason for living" for the Meran. Therefore, those who prefer a more strategic, slower start for White choose systems with 6 Qc2—see Game 20. Moreover, it is very clear that White should not play 6 cxd5?! because after 6...exd5 he will find himself in an inferior variation of the Exchange Variation of the QGD: Black's center influence has been increased while White is left with an inferior QB.

6	...	dxc4
7	Bxc4	b5

[diag. 64]

From the standpoint of fundamentals Black is choosing a very risky course: he is absorbing weaknesses on the Queenside and allowing White an undisputed central advantage. It is done in that hope of gaining opportunities for dynamic counterplay and is based on the circumstance that to recapture on c4 took White's KB two moves (In the Queen's Gambit Accepted White's KB can recapture in one move from f1). Black hopes to make use of this tempo to get sufficient counterplay.

Though some specifics will be different for each sub-variation, the important strategic themes for each side are unvarying:

Black must aim for an early ...c5 to both challenge White's center and rid himself of a vulnerable backward c-pawn.

White has two fundamental early choices: to mobilize his center as quickly as possible by playing e4 or to first delay Black's freeing ...c5 advance.

8 Bd3

Thematic, usual and best. White overguards the e4 square, thus enabling the e4 advance as well as placement of the Bishop on e4 after a Ne4, Nxe4 sequence. The Bishop is also well placed, once Black castles, to bear down on Black's Kingside.

Periodically, however, Whites choose two different retreats:

(1) 8 Be2, so that potential activity along the d-file is not impeded and/or after a ...c5, dxc5, Nxc5 sequence, the Bishop on d3 is not under attack. Yet the inherent passivity of the move should allow Black relatively easy equality. One example: 8...a6 9 e4 b4 10 e5 bxc3 11 exf6 Nxf6 12 bxc3 Bd6 13 0-0 0-0 14 Ne5 Qc7 15 Bf3 Bb7 =, Commons - Mednis, Houston International 1974.

(2) 8 Bb3, bearing down on e6 but if Black is careful enough to prevent any successful attacks on that point, then White's pieces will not be harmoniously placed. For example, 8...b4 9 Ne2 Bb7 10 0-0 Bd6 11 Nf4 0-0 12 Ng5 Nd5! 13 Ne4 Be7 14 Nd3 Ba6! 15 Re1 Qb6 16 Qc2 Bxd3 17 Qxd3 c5, with equality, T. Petrosian - Pomar, Palma de Mallorca 1968.

8 ...   Bb7

Black's historically most common move has been 8...a6, because with the b-pawn protected, Black is immediately ready to play ...c5. The two main line variations then are 9 e4 c5 10 d5 and 10 e5 cxd4 11 Nxb5. In each case the play is both dynamic and unclear. Over the past five years 8...a6 has again come into fashion. There is still a tremendous amount of work to do before we can form a definitive conclusion about the relative merits of the above variations as well as the 8...a6 move itself.

However, the inherent strategic deficiency of these variations for Black is that he is engaging in lots of aggressive pawn play, without being anywhere close to having completed his development. To mitigate this problem, in the middle 1960s Danish GM Bent Larsen successfully brought back into tournament play the developmental text. The QB is well placed along the h1-a8 diagonal and in particular is ready to watch the key e4 square. Again Black's freeing plan must be to play ...c5 and in this case the safety of the b-pawn is provided for by advancing it to b4. There it is not as secure as on b5 (after 8...a6) but as compensation Black gains the development of the QB to b7. For some twenty years the Larsen Variation was Black's favorite method in the Meran, but recently it has had to share its prominence with 8...a6.

9   0-0

Of course, the most dangerous challenge to Black is the immediate 9 e4. Then Black must counter by 9...b4 10 Na4 c5, with the key position resulting after 11 e5 Nd5. Black now threatens to capture on d4; therefore at first White felt obliged to capture on c5 himself either with the Knight or the pawn. But this did not lead to much because Black regains the pawn while furthering his development. Therefore for well over ten years White's "normal" move has become 12 0-0. Yet during the past three years, after the obvious 12...cxd4, Whites have been experimenting with the pawn sacrifice 13 Nxd4 (instead of the earlier 13 Re1). The variations become exceedingly complicated after 13...Nxe5 14 Bb5+ Nd7 15 Re1 Rc8 16 Qh5 g6 17 Qe2 or 17 Qe5. My best guess is that Black will be able to demonstrate that he can come through the complications with approximate equality.

The simple text carries a sophisticated strategic insight: since Kingside castling is a highly desirable "move" for White in all of the most important variations of the 6 Bd3 lines, White plays that immediately and looks forward to following up with 10 e4 under favorable conditions. For instance, 9...Bd6? 10 e4! when 11 e5 threatens to win a piece or 9...Be7?! 10 e4 b4 11 Na4 c5 12 e5 Nd5 13 Nxc5 because after Black recaptures on c5 he will be a whole tempo down compared to the normal 9 e4 b4 10 Na4 c5 11 e5 Nd5 12 Nxc5 situation. It is also patently inconsistent to play 9...a6 here since at the very best Black will transposing into the 8...a6 variation.

9   ...   b4

The only move that makes sense after 8...Bb7: Black prevents 10 e4 by forcing the QN onto that square, since 10 Na4 c5 11 dxc5 Qa5 should lead to ready equality.

10   Ne4

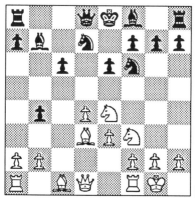

[diag. 65]

The threat of an immediate e4 by White has passed and the major fight now resolves around whether Black can get in the liberating ...c5 under satisfactory conditions. He cannot afford the immediate 10...c5? since after 11 Nxf6+! gxf6 (11...Nxf6? loses after 12 Bb5+ Nd7 13 Ne5; 11...Qxf6?! 12 Ne5! is also most unpleasant) 12 e4 cxd4 13 Nxd4 Bc5 14 Bb5 Rc8 15 Be3 Bxe4 16 Qg4 Bd5 17 Rfe1 White has a virulent attack, Peshina - Bagirov, USSR 1979.

10   ...   Be7

In the early years of this variation, 10...Nxe4 11 Bxe4 Be7 was considered to be the equalizing line until in Portisch - Polugaevsky, Portoroz Play-off 1973 White showed that 12 Nd2! 0-0 13 b3! is clearly favorable for him because the ensured retention of his KB on the h1 - a8 diagonal impedes Black's chances for the necessary ...c5 break. Nor can Black transpose into our main line by playing 11...Nf6, because after 12 Bc2! White's Queen gets in front of the Bishop in one move: 12...Be7 13 e4 0-0 14 e5 Nd7 15 Qd3 g6 16 Bh6 Re8 17 Qe4, Chernin - Borkowski, Polonica Zdroj 1988, with a very strong attack by White.

11   Nxf6+

In conjunction with the next move, White's only consistent plan. Theory also rates highly the attempt to start immediate play on the Queenside with 11 a3. However, in the game Fucak - Mednis, Cannes 1988, Black was able to show that it amounts to mostly a loss of time after 11...0-0!: 12 Nxf6+ Nxf6 13 axb4 Bxb4 14 e4 h6 15 Qe2 c5! 16 e5 Nd7 17 Be4 Qb6 18 Rd1 Rfd8 with full equality.

11	...	Nxf6
12	e4	0-0

There is little point in dithering with 12...Rc8?! as in Korchnoi - Polugaevsky, 1977 Match, Game 5, when instead of the harmless 13 Qa4, strong is 13 a3!, threatening to win a pawn by 14 axb4, while 13...bxa3 14 b4! (Korchnoi) will lead to major trouble for Black's Queenside, e.g. 14...Bxb4 15 Qa4!.

13   e5

Why not? White can't successfully play this position without gaining space in the center and freeing the e4 square for his Bishop. The immediate point of the text is that the centrally attractive 13...Nd5?! works out poorly after 14 Qc2!: (1) 14...h6 15 Qe2! with the horrible threat 16 Qe4 when the response 16...g6 leaves the h-pawn hanging, (2) 14...g6 15 Bh6 Re8 when Black has no compensation for the serious weaknesses on the dark squares after, e.g. 16 Rac1 or 16 Nd2 followed by 17 Ne4 or 17 Nb3.

White cannot expect an advantage by doing "nothing." For instance, 13 Qc2 h6 14 Be3 Rc8 15 Rfd1 c5 16 dxc5 Ng4!? 17 Bd4 e5 18 h3 exd4 19 hxg4 Rxc5 20 Qd2 a5 21 Rac1, so far Korchnoi - Polugaevsky, 1977 Match, Game 7 and now 21...Rxc1 22 Rxc1 Bc8 would have been satisfactory for Black.

13   ...   Nd7
14   Qc2

A normal move. However, since the game Polugaevsky - Mednis, Riga Interzonal 1979, the critical line is considered to be 14 Be4!?. After the game Polugaevsky told me that he had discovered this while preparing for his 1977 match against Korchnoi and had been surprised that Korchnoi had not used it. Thus I turned out to be the guinea pig. After the reasonable 14...Qb6 (by smoothly protecting the QB Black is ready for the equalizing 15...c5), White showed the fine tactical point of his previous strategic move by playing 15 Bg5 with the idea that the obvious 15...Bxg5 allows 16 Bxh7+! Kxh7 17 Nxg5+ Kg6 (17...Kg8?? 18 Qh5 is hopeless) 18 Qg4. I decided to trust Polugaevsky on this. Later analysis by me and IM Dobosz showed that White's attack is indeed very dangerous, but that with the accurate defense 18...f5! 19 Qg3 c5!, Black winds up only slightly inferior after 20 Nxe6+ Kf7 21 Nxf8 Rxf8 22 dxc5 Nxc5.

In any case, Black must allow that, since my "safe" 15...Rfe8?! 16 Bxe7 Rxe7 led to chronic weaknesses of the Queenside after 17 Qc2 h6 18 a3! b3 19 Qc3. Not wanting to be squeezed to death along the c-file, I broke loose with 19...c5!? 20 Bxb7 Qxb7 and equalized after the subsequent 21 dxc5 Rc8 22 Qb4! Nxc5 23 Rac1 Qc6 24 Rc3?! Rec7 25 Rfc1 Qd5 26 Qb5 Ne4! because if 27 Qxd5?!, Black has the zwischenzug

27...Nxc3 (28 Qd2 Ne2+). However, the next day Polugaevsky showed me that instead of 24 Rc3?!, with the correct 24 Rc4! Rec7 25 Rfc1 Qd5 26 Qb5 White keeps a clear advantage since Black lacks the tactical shot of the game.

14   ...   h6
15   Bh7+

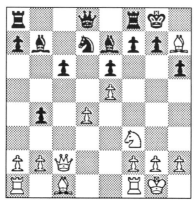

[diag. 66]

A well known maneuver: Black's King is first drawn away from protecting the KR and f-pawn and only then White's KB positions itself on the active e4 square. Of course, here 15 Qe2?! is harmless since after the thematic 15...c5 Black's QB covers e4.

15   ...   Kh8
16   Be4   Qb6
17   Be3   c5

Despite White's strenuous counter efforts, Black has finally succeeded in getting in this thematic freeing advance and should be on the verge of equality. Yet as will soon become apparent, there are still "tricks" remaining.

18   dxc5   Bxc5?

Polugaevsky played this recapture instantly, demonstrating that he is fully familiar with existing theory - BUT the theory was wrong. In his analysis in ECO D (Revised - 1987), Korchnoi gives as correct 18...Bxe4 19 Qxe4 Nxc5, with only a slight advantage for White after 20 Qc4..

The most accurate capture, however, is 18...Nxc5!, as pointed out by GM Robert Byrne. Then Black is fine, after either 19 Bxb7 Qxb7 20 Bxc5 Rfc8 or 19 Bxc5 Bxe4.

19   Rad1!

[diag. 67]

The refutation. In the first edition (1976) of ECO D appear the variations 19 Bxb7 Qxb7 20 Bxc5 Rfc8 with equality and 19 Bxc5 Bxe4 20 Bxb6 Bxc2 21 Bc7 Rfc8 22 Bd6 a5, Polugaevsky - Larsen, Palma de Mallorca Interzonal 1970, with a slight advantage to Black. The author is Korchnoi himself. Obviously, as part of his preparation for this match, he had revisited the known theory to look for dynamic ways to improve White's prospects. By searching for the truth he had discovered the text; Polugaevsky trusted "the book" and paid the price.

19 ... Bxe3

After 34 minutes of thought Black selects the best of the bad lot. Alternatives are:

(1) 19...Rad8? 20 Rxd7! Bxe4 21 Qxc5!, winning a piece (one of the points of White's 15th move).

(2) 19...Rfd8? 20 Rxd7 Bxe4 21 Rxd8+, winning a piece.

(3) 19...Bxe4?! 20 Qxe4 Rad8 (20...Bxe3 21 Rxd7 Bc5 22 Rxf7! and White wins a pawn—another one of the points of White's 15th) 21 Bg5!! f6 (21...hxg5? 22 Nxg5 and White mates—a third point of 15 Bh7+.) 22 Bh4! and White has a crushing position. For instance, 22...g5?! is refuted by 23 Qg6 gxh4 24 Qxh6+ Kg8 25 Qg6+ Kh8 26 Rde1! threatening 27 Re4, and 22...Nxe5? fails to the simple 23 Nxe5 Rxd1 24 Ng6+.

20 Rxd7 Rac8

Once more 20...Bxe4?! 21 Qxe4 Bc5 allows 22 Rxf7!.

21 Rxb7 Rxc2

Black's best chance is to get to the endgame since the middlegame after 21...Qxb7?! 22 Qb1! is hopeless, because Black's King is too vulnerable to a coordinated attack by the four White pieces.

22	Rxb6	Rxf2!
23	Rxf2	Bxb6
24	Kf1	Bxf2
25	Kxf2	

All the previous slaughter has directly led to a very important basic endgame: B + N vs. R + P. White has the material advantage of approximately 1/2 pawn and the dynamic advantage of having more pieces. With the Queenside pawns off, the position is a clear draw.

Here, however, White has genuine chances of capturing a Queenside pawn and therefore excellent prospects for the win. The task is, however, extremely difficult and is partly complicated by the potential weakness of White's isolated e-pawn. GM Korchnoi's execution of the required combination of deep strategy and accurate tactics is so exemplary that it is tempting to consider the endgame a forced win.

25	...	Rc8
26	Nd4	Rc1

Worse is 26...Rc5?! 27 Nc6 a5 28 Ke3. Black's best hope is an active Rook.

27 Nb3!

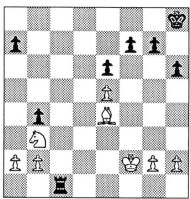

[diag. 68]

From here the Knight controls many important squares (a1, c1, c5 etc), thereby decreasing the Rook's activity.

27	...	Rh1
28	h3	Kg8
29	a3!!	

A most perceptive concept. Normally the last thing that White would want to do is to exchange off any Queenside pawns as that decreases his chances for capturing Black's pawns there. Yet in this situation the vulnerability of White's Queenside pawns ties down his pieces, thus preventing them from active operations. Therefore, Korchnoi decreases his vulnerability by in effect exchanging off the b-pawns.

29	...	bxa3
30	bxa3	Kf8
31	a4	

To win White will have to capture Black's a-pawn, retain his own a-pawn, while also preventing any potential counterplay in the center and on the Kingside. This is a very tall order and the technical difficulties in achieving it are huge. What is clear enough is that to capture the Black a-pawn White's King will have to head for the Queenside. Yet it is far from obvious where White's own a-pawn should stand. After 40 minutes thinking Korchnoi decides to advance it to the 5th rank.

31	...	Ke8
32	a5	Kd7
33	Ke2	Kc7
34	Kd2	Rf1
35	Ke2	Rh1
36	Kd2	Rf1
37	Kc3	Re1

Black's King has an optimal defensive location and moving the pawns would only lead to weakening them. Therefore Black's Rook is used for moving.

38	Nc5	Ra1
39	Kb4	Re1
40	Kb5	Kb8
41	Ka6	

The game was adjourned here with Korchnoi sealing his 41st move. After 15 minutes of thought he decides to go directly for the a-pawn. If home analysis shows that it is not yet time for this, then the King can always return to b5. Therefore what is important is to leave the options open and not use up too much scarce time on sealing.

White's strongest move is 41 Kc6!, playing on both sides of the board. If then 41...Kc8, White has 42 Nb7!.

41	...	h5?!

Makes White's job easier. Apparently Polugaevsky's team had spent the bulk of their time analyzing 41 Kc6 and were unprepared for 41 Ka6. Black's move has nothing to do with the needs of the position. Imperative is 41...Rc1! as then 42 Nb7 Re1 43 Nd6 f5! 44 exf6 gxf6 45 Bf3 e5 leads to a position where, compared to the game, Black is a tempo ahead and this gives him drawing chances. Therefore White does best to retrace the steps with 42 Kb5!.

42 Bf3!

Because the e-pawn is taboo (42...Rxe5?? 43 Nd7+), White now has time to effectively redeploy his Knight.

42	...	h4
43	Ne4!	Re3
44	Nd6!	f6

About equivalent is 44...Rxe5 45 Nxf7 Re1 when 46 Nd8! followed by 47 Nc6+ wins the a-pawn under conditions similar to the game.

45	exf6	gxf6
46	Nb5	e5
47	Nxa7	e4
48	Bg4	Kc7

The only chance to keep the game going. After 48...Rg3?! 49 Nb5, followed by 50 Kb6 and advancing the a-pawn, Black would be quickly extinguished.

49	Nb5+	Kc6
50	Nd4+	Kc5
51	Nf5	Ra3
52	Nxh4	Kb4
53	Kb6	Rxa5
54	Nf5	

[diag. 69]

The previous forced play has followed one of the major thematic scenarios of winning a won endgame: while the weaker side must worry about problems on one side, the stronger side gains a decisive superiority on the other. White's material advantage has increased to approximately 1.5 pawns and the h-pawn is a powerful passer. All that is required for the win is to pay the necessary attention to Black's e-pawn. Korchnoi was in complete control of the position and played the rest of the game quite quickly.

54	...	Re5
55	Kc6!	Kc3

There is nothing in 55...e3 56 Ng3 f5 57 Bf3 f4?! 58 Ne2.

56	Ng3	Kd2
57	Kd6!	Ke1

Or 57...Ke3 58 Nh5 followed by 59 Nxf6. Prospectless also is 57...e3 when Black has no follow-up and White plays 58 h4! followed by 59 Bf3 etc.

58	Nh5	e3
59	Nxf6	Ra5
60	Ne4	e2
61	Bf3!	

Protecting the g-pawn. The e-pawn won't run away since 61...Kd1 loses to 62 Nc3+ and 61...Kf1 to 62 Ng3+. In the meanwhile White threatens 62 Ng3 capturing the pawn. Black gives a couple of spite checks and then resigns.

61	...	Ra6+
62	Kc5	Ra5+
63	Kb4	Black resigns

* * * * *

Game 20

White: Kenneth Rogoff
Black: Edmar Mednis
Played at 1978 U.S. Championship

1	c4	Nf6
2	Nc3	e6
3	Nf3	d5
4	d4	c6
5	e3	Nbd7
6	Qc2	

The text is White's major alternative to the "standard" 6 Bd3. White avoids the complications that often result thereafter, in favor of choosing his own moment and method of aiming for an opening advantage. In many variations within the Orthodox Defense of the QGD, White's Queen is well placed on c2 since it guards the e4 square, is ready for pressure along the c-file and allows a Rook placement on d1 (including Queenside castling!). What gives independent meaning to this variation is that the Queen decides so early that c2 is the square to be on.

In the early 1990s 6 Qc2 has achieved approximate parity in popularity with 6 Bd3. For example, Chess Informant # 51, in publishing the most theoretically important games of the first five months of 1991, has selected seven games with 6 Qc2 and six with 6 Bd3. The inherent flexibility of 6 Qc2 is its major attraction. Moreover, Black's attempt at immediate counterplay with 6...dxc4?! 7 Bxc4 b5 8 Bd3 Bb7, works out badly after 9 e4 b4 10 Na4 Rc8 11 Be3! because he is a tempo behind the variations possible after 6 Bd3. In Zajchik - Bronstein, Tbilisi 1980, White gained a decisive advantage after 11...Ng4 12 Bg5 Qa5 13 0-0 c5 14 Rac1 h6 15 Bh4 g5 16 Bg3 h5 17 h4! gxh4 18 Bxh4 Bc6 19 Nxc5 Nxc5 20 dxc5 Bd7 21 c6! Rxc6 22 Qxc6! Bxc6 23 Rxc6.

6   ...   Bd6

With White's dark square Bishop locked in behind the e-pawn, there is no reason why his counterpart should not enjoy this active location. The KB not only is in position to menace White's King in case of castling on the Kingside, but more importantly from the strategic side, Black has excellent prospects of getting in the freeing ...e5 advance.

7   b3

[diag. 70]

By far White's most strategic build-up: in case of ...dxc4, White will recapture with the b-pawn, thereby enhancing the center. The slight demerit of the approach is that White will remain a tempo behind in developing the Kingside.

Therefore continuing attempts have been made to obtain an opening advantage by immediately completing Kingside development with 7 Be2 0-0 8 0-0. Yet Black is achieving eventual equality with the more radical 8...e5 9 cxd5 cxd5 10 dxe5 Nxe5 11 Rd1 Nxf3+ 12 Bxf3 Qc7! 13 h3 Bh2+ 14 Kh1 Be5 15 Bd2 Be6, Karpov - Kasparov, Linares 1991, or by the recent promising plan 8...dxc4 9 Bxc4 Qe7 10 h3 c5!? 11 dxc5 Bxc5 12 e4 Bd6 13 Nd4 Ne5 14 Bb3 Bd7, Karpov - Anand, Semi - Final Candidates Match 1991, Game 6 or 13 Nb5 Ne5 14 Nxe5 Bxe5 15 f4 Qc5+ 16 Kh2 Bd7!, Korchnoi - Timman, Semi-Final Candidates Match 1991, Game 6.

White has also two more radical approaches to try to capitalize on 6 Qc2:

(1) Immediate central advance by 7 e4 with the idea that White will have a superior center after 7...dxe4 8 Nxe4 Nxe4 9 Qxe4. In my opinion, Black has an easier route to equality after the symmetrical 7...e5!, e.g. 8 cxd5 cxd5 9 exd5 exd4 10 Nxd4 0-0 11 Be2 Nb6, Karpov - Kasparov, World Championship Match 1984 - 85, Game 33.

(2) Queenside castling with 7 Bd2 0-0 8 0-0-0. White's prospects for a Kingside attack must not be underestimated; therefore Black does best in starting immediately active counteraction by 8...c5!, e.g. 9 cxd5 exd5 10 Kb1 c4 11 Bc1 a6! 12 g4! Nb6 13 h3 Re8 14 Bg2 Bb4 with equal chances, Taimanov - Botvinnik, USSR Championship Match 1953.

| 7 | ... | 0-0 |
| 8 | Be2 | dxc4 |

Black's counterplay in the center in this sub-variation must come via ...e5. Since the immediate 8...e5 leads to an isolated d-pawn after 9 cxd5 Nxd5 (or 9...cxd5 10 Nb5 Bb4+ 11 Bd2 Bxd2+ 12 Nxd2 e4 13 Rc1 with advantage for White, Knezevic - Velikov, Athens 1981) 10 Nxd5 cxd5 11 dxe5 Nxe5 12 Bb2! Bb4+ 13 Kf1! Nxf3 14 Bxf3 Be6 15 Qd3 Be7 16 Ke2! Qa5 17 Rhc1, with a pleasant advantage for White in Portisch - Hübner, Brussels 1986, prefacing the advance by exchanging off the d-pawn eliminates this disadvantage. Of course, there is some cost—White's center is strengthened—but, nevertheless, I believe that Black's position is easier to handle after the text move.

9	bxc4	e5
10	0-0	Re8!

Black's Rook gets mobilized to either support the ...e4 advance or to have control of the e-file after the exchanging sequence ...exd4, exd4. The immediate 10...exd4 11 exd4 could well work out to be in White's favor because he has not yet fianchettoed the QB (as for instance with 8 Bb2) and therefore has the possibility of the pinning Bg5. In any case, the text is a high class waiting move, with no disadvantages whatsoever.

Of course, the two possible Black plans—...exd4 or ...e4—are completely different from each other. The idea behind the former is to have active piece play compensate for White's superior center. (It is obvious that after ...exd4 White will recapture with the e-pawn.) On the other hand, ...e4 is a long term strategic plan: by positioning itself in White's part of the board, the e-pawn will be used as a cover for Black to start mobilizing his pieces for an attack against White's Kingside.

11   a4

The point of this and the next move is to establish some Queenside pressure while waiting for the "inevitable" ...e4.

The most common move is 11 Bb2. (This position often arises as a result of the early QB fianchetto.) Black then has the two choices indicated above:

(1)   11...exd4 12 exd4 Nf8 13 Rad1 Bg4 14 Ne5 Bxe2 15 Nxe2 Qc7. In Ligterink - Ree, Wijk aan Zee 1985, White now sacrificed a pawn by 16 c5 Bxe5 17 dxe5 Ng4 18 Ng3 Nxe5 and probably got sufficient compensation after 19 Nf5 f6 20 Nd6.

(2)   11...e4 12 Nd2 Qe7 when 13 Rfe1 Nf8 14 f3 exf3 15 Bxf3 Ng4 16 Nf1 Qh4! 17 g3 Qg5 gave Black at least equality in Taimanov - Barbero, Montpellier 1986. However, a more logical preparation for f3 is 13 Rae1. This position is as yet unclear, but I would expect that "dynamic balance" is the most likely correct evaluation.

Also possible is 11 Rd1, but Black has no problems after 11...Qe7! 12 h3 e4 13 Nd2 Nf8 14 Nf1, Knezevic - Mednis, Kragujevac 1977, when the players agreed on a "strategic" draw.

11   ...   Qe7

With this Black signals that he will be choosing the play using the ...e4 advance. White cannot prevent that with 12 dxe5?! as after

12...Nxe5 White has no compensation for the isolated a- and c-pawns.

12	Rb1	e4
13	Nd2	Nf8
14	f3	

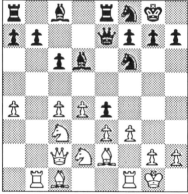

[diag. 71]

Black's central outpost must be liquidated because otherwise it can serve as the support for a strong Kingside attack.

The pawn exchange that results after the text leads to the following dynamic strategic themes:

White must try to mobilize his central pawn mass (only White will have d- and e-pawns) so as to prevent Black's pieces from being able to obtain pressure against the various loose points (e.g. a4, b4, e3, g4) in White's position.

Black must be able to hold back the advance of the d- and e-pawns in unison, while continuing to probe for vulnerable spots in White's position. Black's play must combine the attributes of care, patience and vigilance in looking for opportunities.

14	...	exf3
15	Nxf3	c5!

As already mentioned above, White's potentially strong central pawn mass must be prevented from an uninterrupted advance. With the tension inducing text move Black establishes dynamic equality. Even if White will now be able to play e4, ...cxd4 will destroy the coherence of White's center. On the other hand, the d5 advance (e.g. 16 d5) will give Black full control of the important e5 square and stamp White's e-pawn a backward pawn.

16	Bd3	Ng6
17	Kh1	a6!

With moves 16 - 19 Black, thematically though quietly, completes his development and then will be able to confidently face any potential middlegame action.

18   Bd2   Rb8
19   a5

There is nothing wrong with this move as such, but if White wants to play Nd5 he should do so immediately: 19 Nd5!? Nxd5 20 cxd5 Bg4! with equal chances.

19   ...   Bd7!

Instead faulty is the active appearing 19...Be6?! because White gets in 20 Ne4! Nxe4 21 Bxe4 with definite pressure both against Black's Queenside and Kingside.

20   Nd5?!

White has an interesting active plan in mind, but Black can successfully neutralize it and then White's pawn weaknesses will start to tell. White also is not able to play the active 20 Ng5? because of 20...Bxh2! (21 Kxh2 Ng4+). The best that White can do is to keep the dynamic balance with moves such as 20 Na4 or 20 Rbe1.

20   ...   Nxd5
21   cxd5   exd4
22   exd4

All part of White's plan. In any case, 22 Nxd4? is bad because Black wins a pawn after 22...Qe5 23 Nf3 Qxd5 since 24 Bc4 Qh5 25 Qd3 (25 Bxf7+? Kxf7 26 Ng5+ Kg8 27 Qc4+ Be6) is met by 25...Be6!.

22   ...   Rec8!
23   Qb3   f6!

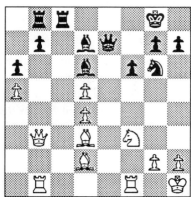

[diag. 72]

White was hoping that the d-pawns and open lines would lead to strong pressure against Black's position, but with his last two moves Black has foiled any meaningful play that White could have had.

24   Bb4?!

The Bishop has no real prospects here because exchanging it would only accentuate White's pawn weaknesses. White also gets nowhere with 24 Rbe1?! Qd8 25 Qb1 Be8! 26 Bf5 Rc4! as it is Black who gets meaningful squares for his pieces. Post game analysis showed that White's best is the defensive 24 Rbc1!, with Black's chances still somewhat superior as White has no real compensation for having isolated doubled d-pawns.

24   ...   Nf4!

Black moves in on the squares that White has vacated.

25   Rfe1   Qf8
26   Bc4   Kh8!

Carefully preventing any likely tactics as a result of the possibility of a discovered check along the a2 - g8 diagonal.

If now 27 Bxd6 Qxd6 28 Qb4, Black starts working on White's d-pawn with 28...Qxb4 29 Rxb4 Rd8!, e.g. 30 Re7 Bb5! 31 Bxb5 Nxd5.

27   Bd2   Qf7!

White was understandably loath to exchange off his QB, but now Black's Queen finds a powerful location on the Kingside. With four Black pieces then pointing at White's vulnerable King, Black will have a significant advantage. Notice how throughout Black has been able to combine the prevention of White's theme of utilizing his central superiority, with achieving his own prospects of taking advantage of weaknesses on both of White's flanks.

28   Rbc1   Qh5
29   Re4?

In trying to drive the annoying Knight away White overlooks a tactical shot. The attempt to overprotect the vulnerable g2 point by 29 Rc2? is refuted by 29...Nxd5! 30 Bxd5 Rxc2 31 Bf7 Qf5 32 Nh4 Qf2. Immediate disaster could only have been averted with 29 Bxf4 Bxf4 30 Rc2, though White's future is bleak after 30...Bg4.

29   ...   Nxg2!

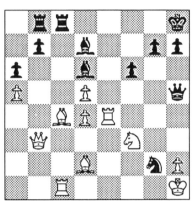

[diag. 73]

The Knight is safe enough here and has captured a most important pawn. Of course, 30 Kxg2 loses to 30...Qg6+, while 30 Rg1 allows, for instance, 30...Rxc4 31 Qxc4 Qxf3.

30   Bd3? and White resigns

Not finding any satisfactory move, White blundered with the text and resigned without awaiting the response 30...Rxc1+ 31 Bxc1 Qxf3.

Queen's Gambit Declined, Orthodox Defense, Tartakower Variation
Game 21

White: Yasser Seirawan
Black: Anatoly Karpov
Played at Brussels (SWIFT) International Tournament 1988

1	Nf3	Nf6
2	c4	e6
3	Nc3	d5
4	d4	

The same position has arisen as in Games 18 - 20, again via a move order quite different from that of the standard QGD sequence (1 d4, 2 c4, 3 Nc3, 4 Nf3) as well as different from that of the previous games. This time the transposition was from the Reti Opening into the QGD. Instead of the 4...c6 of Games 18 - 20, Black now plays the "standard" ...

4	...	Be7

By far Black's most solid continuation, leading to the various variations of the Orthodox Defense complex. Black develops his KB to a modest though faultless location and will follow up with Kingside castling. That will complete his Kingside development and bring the King to safety. Only after these two important steps have been concluded will Black look at what to do regarding his Queenside posture.

Valid alternatives, apart from 4...c6, are 4...Nbd7, 4...Bb4 which is called the Ragozin Variation and is something like a cross between the Nimzo-Indian Defense and the Queen's Gambit Declined, and 4...c5. Then after 5 cxd5, the Tarrasch Defense is reached if Black plays 5...exd5 (see Games 24 - 26) and if Black prefers 5...Nxd5, the opening is called Semi-Tarrasch Defense (see Game 22).

5	Bg5

[diag. 74]

Historically White's most common move, from the very beginnings of the Orthodox Defense to the present day. White completes the development of the Queenside minor pieces and applies implied pressure on the d-pawn. Of course, White is not naive enough to think that he has real chances of capturing that pawn "just like that"—among other factors, Black can readily protect d5 with ...c6. No, 5 Bg5 is played primarily as a high class preventive move. As already discussed in connection with Games 18 - 20, in the QGD Black's chances for central equality rest with successfully challenging White's somewhat superior center by the thematic ...e5 or, more commonly, ...c5 advance. Note that after a ...c5 advance, the vulnerability of Black's d-pawn increases considerably as a result of the quasi-pin on the Nf6. The text has always been considered as White's strongest continuation.

Also good are the Exchange Variation, 5 cxd5 exd5 6 Bg5, and 5 Bf4. White's QB is well developed on f4 as far as bearing down on Black Queenside is concerned, but Black can (as a matter of fact, he should) play in relative comfort an early ...c5. The popularity of 5 Bf4 has waxed and waned over the decades and in the early 1990s is on the decline again; 5 Bg5 just goes on and on like Old Man River.

| 5 | ... | h6 |

In a majority of the variations of the Orthodox Defense, it is useful for Black to insert the moves ...h6, Bh4. There are three reasons for this: (1) Black guards the important g5 square, (2) Black does not have to worry about an attack on the h-pawn after White's Qc2, Bd3 line-up, (3) With White's QB on h4, Black can be sure that later on, an opportune ...Ne4 will cause the QB to be exchanged. Since for Black there are neither practical nor theoretical disadvantages of inserting ...h6, Bh4 in these variations, Black does so.

What has changed, however, is the exact point where ...h6 is played.

As recently as ten years ago, Blacks tended to play it on move 6, i.e. after 5...0-0 6 e3. Lately the overwhelming number of GMs play it immediately. The reason: no disadvantage and retention of maximum flexibility for making later decisions.

6   Bh4

Of course, the thematic "normal" response. Yet the current international chess scene is extensive, diverse, and rich.. Therefore it is not surprising that since 6 Bxf6 can be played, it is played part of the time. However, the fundamental strategic demerit of that move is that the exchange does not saddle Black with any kind of a long term structural problem. It does gain one developmental tempo, though in a basically closed opening system. But the crux of the matter with this is that there is no particular way of taking advantage of this tempo gain, because the direct attempt at exploitation (after 6 Bxf6 Bxf6) by means of 7 e4 dxe4 8 Nxe4 leads to effective counterplay for Black after 8...Nc6!. This forces 9 Nxf6+ Qxf6 when no way has been found to safeguard White's central plus, e.g. 10 Qd2 Bd7 11 Qe3 0-0-0 12 Be2 Rhe8 13 0-0 Kb8. Now 14...e5 is threatened and if 14 Ne5 Nxe5 15 dxe5 Qg5, with full equality and a draw agreed in Vladimirov - Holmov, Leningrad 1967.

6   ...   0-0
7   e3

This position is the starting point for a number of possible variations within the Orthodox Defense to the Queen's Gambit Declined. A comparison of the development of each side leads to the following evaluation: White, as a result of having his c-pawn in safety on the fourth rank, has more central influence and his three developed minor pieces work on important central squares. White's Kingside development has lagged but the still closed nature of the position means that his King is in no immediate danger. Black, for his part, has—as mentioned earlier—completed Kingside development and brought his King to safety by castling. Moreover, his central bastion on d5 is quite secure.

White's short term plan is clear: he wants to complete his Kingside development. But what should Black aim for now? In fact, Black has three reasonable approaches:

(1) Lasker's freeing maneuver: 7...Ne4

Black's position is somewhat cramped, of course, and the standard technique for freeing cramped positions is to exchange pieces. The most common sequence now is 8 Bxe7 Qxe7 9 cxd5 Nxc3 10 bxc3 exd5. However, the previous exchanges have led to a strengthening of White's center since his b-pawn has been transformed into a c-pawn. This factor allows White to obtain a slight advantage as follows: 11 Qb3! Rd8 12 c4! dxc4 13 Bxc4 Nc6 14 Be2. Whether Black now exchanges Queens or not, White will castle Kingside and his central superiority will offer him the characteristic slight edge at the start of the middlegame.

(2) The delayed classical 7...Nbd7

After the usual 8 Rc1 c6 9 Bd3 dxc4 10 Bxc4, Black goes for counterplay with 10...b5!? 11 Bd3 a6 and aims to challenge White's center with ...c5, e.g. 12 0-0 c5. Again, Black's disadvantage is just the normal slight one.

By far the most popular alternative for almost seventy years is the Tartakower Variation:

7 ...   b6

If we look again at Black's position after White's 7th move, it is easy to recognize that Black's only real strategic problem is the lack of scope for his QB. Black's e-pawn hems in this Bishop and unless White voluntarily plays cxd5, thus enabling Black to recapture with the e-pawn, the Bishop will remain locked in for a long time to come. During the London 1922 tournament, the Polish-French Grandmaster Dr. Savielly G. Tartakower hit on the idea of trying to do something about the "QB problem" immediately by fianchettoing it. In his game against J.R. Capablanca he played the text move.

Black's idea is disarmingly simple and completely sound: he will follow up with the centrally logical 8...Bb7 and the supposedly permanent problem of the QB will have been solved in an instant! Even since its introduction, the Tartakower Variation has been Black's most popular way of defending the Orthodox QGD. All the recent world champions have employed it successfully: Boris Spassky, Robert J. Fischer, Anatoly Karpov and Garry Kasparov. The special practical attraction of the variation is that it combines strategic soundness with an unbalanced position. This means that not only does Black have excellent prospects for equality, but also if White does not play well he can very easily get the worst of the position.

8 Be2

This deceptively modest move can have a lot of venom behind it—as we will see very shortly. There are also three independent alternatives:

(1) 8 cxd5, with the idea of closing off the QB's diagonal from b7 before it gets there. For some forty years this was the start of the main line in the Tartakower: 8...Nxd5 9 Bxe7 Qxe7 10 Nxd5 exd5 11 Rc1 Be6, with Black playing 12...c5 next.

While White has some chances for a slight edge, the resulting positions are currently thought to be without especial challenges for Black and thus going out of GM play.

(2) 8 Rc1 Bb7 9 Bd3 (or 9 Be2) allows Black to achieve his opening objectives after 9...dxc4! 10 Bxc4 Nbd7 11 0-0 c5! and rather certain equality in the not-so-far future, e.g. 12 Qe2 a6 13 a4 cxd4 14 exd4 (14 Nxd4 Nc5 15 Rfd1 Qe8 16 Bg3 Nfe4 also is equal.) 14...Nh5! 15 Bxe7 Qxe7 16 d5 Nf4 17 Qe3 Qf6 18 Ne4 Qf5 19 Ng3 Qf6 20 Ne4 Qf5, Draw, G. Kasparov - A. Karpov, World Championship Match 1984-85, Game 34.

(3) 8 Bd3 Bb7 9 0-0 also is too routine to cope with Black's plan. After 9...Nbd7 10 Qe2 c5 Black has realized his objectives and is on the verge of equality, e.g. 11 Rfd1 Ne4! 12 Bg3 cxd4 13 Nxd4 Nxg3 14 hxg3 Nf6, I. Novikov - S. Lputjan, USSR Championship 1984.

It is fair to ask: why not the immediate 8 Bxf6 Bxf6 9 cxd5? In fact this was the early move order used, with GM Viktor Korchnoi being the creative inventor. Yet this move order gives Black the flexibility of developing the QB to e6. To prevent this, the "latest modern" practice is to wait until Black has fianchettoed the QB before starting the captures.

8	...	Bb7
9	Bxf6	Bxf6
10	cxd5	

It is now considered to be out of question to recapture with the QB, i.e. 10...Bxd5?!, as that would give White too great a superiority in the center. The revised edition of Encyclopedia of Chess Openings "D" does not even give a single example of it.

10	...	exd5

[diag. 75]

This is the basic starting point of the refined "Korchnoi method." In delaying the Bxf6 capture White has lost one whole tempo compared to the possible 6 Bxf6. In turn, what has been gained is that as a result of 7...b6, Black has fundamentally weakened the c6 square and White now hopes to take advantage of that. White has voluntarily given Black the "two Bishop advantage," but is unworried because the soundness of White's pawn chain means that there is nothing vulnerable in White's position for Black's Bishops to aim at. On the other hand, White's KN can be maneuvered to attack Black's d-pawn and this in conjunction with attacks on that pawn by White's QN, KB and Queen will force Black to play ...c6. White will then try to work directly against this vulnerable pawn or will open advantageously the center via the e4 advance.

The major thematic strategic themes for the position after 10...exd5 are:

White will try to force Black to play ...c6, thereby both creating a vulnerable pawn on c6 as well as shortening the scope of Black's QB. White then has a choice of two radically different approaches:

(1) Either going directly at c6 by piece pressure or by undermining it with b5 at a moment when Black cannot afford to respond by ...c5. If White succeeds in exchanging his b-pawn for Black's c-pawn, then Black's isolated d-pawn will become an intolerable weakness.

(2) With Black's QB passively placed on b7, White will, after due preparation, break open the center with e4. White will then try to take advantage of having the superior center by applying active piece pressure along the board.

Black has two needs:
(1) To prevent White from effectively carrying out either of the two above plans.
(2) To try to open up the position for his two Bishops by a properly timed ...c5 advance.

11   b4

By far White's most ambitious plan: he gets ready to fix Black's c-pawn on c7 by playing b5. Moreover, White is ready to minimize the effectiveness of Black's ...c5 advance by being able to exchange off his b-pawn for the c-pawn. However, because White's development is not yet complete Black can start active counterplay.

Also normal and good is 11 0-0 whereby White delays any Queenside action until his King is safe. Black's most common responses are: (1) 11...Qe7, preventing b4 but leaving his d-pawn

less protected which factor White can start exploiting with 12 Qb3!,
and (2) 11...Re8, helping guard the e4 and e5 squares. A thematic
game course then is Pr. Nikolic - N. Short, Manila Interzonal 1990: 12
b4 c6 13 Qb3 Qd6 14 a4 Nd7 15 a5 (15 b5 can be well met with
15...c5!.) 15...Rad8 16 axb6 axb6 17 Ra7 Qb8 18 Ra2! b5 19 Ne1 Be7
20 Nd3 Bd6 21 g3 Nb6 22 Bf3 Bc8 23 Rfa1 Bf5 24 Nc5 Nc4 25 Ne2.
White has a continuing slight advantage because the fixed pawn
formation is more suitable for his Knights than Black's Bishops.

11   ...   c5

Encroachment of the c6 square by 12 b5 must be prevented. The
two accepted methods are the text and 11...c6. The idea behind the
text move is clear and good: Black takes advantage of the looseness of
the Nc3 to immediately execute this thematic advance. There is no
question that tactically there is no problem with it. The important
question revolves around the long term strategic consequences. As we
will shortly see, Black will be left with an isolated d-pawn. This pawn
will be defensible yet will not provide any particular counterchances.
The net result is that high quality Black defenders have excellent
prospects for a draw but rather minimal chances for a win. This kind
of a scorecard does not appeal to all GMs. Moreover, lower rated
players can very easily wind up in a most unattractive defensive
situation.

Therefore, the 11...c6 alternative is finding more adherents with its
chief champion being English GM Nigel Short. Black does not have to
worry about the immediate 12 b5 because 12...c5! is a fully satisfactory
response. Black's approach will be to prevent an effective b5 or e4
central advance while looking for counterplay opportunities wherever
they can be found. A model example of this is A. Karpov - N. Short,
Amsterdam 1991: 12 0-0 Re8 13 Qb3 a5!? 14 a3 (Again 14 b5 c5 is O.K.
for Black.) 14...Nd7 15 b5 c5! (Only strategically correct move.) 16
Nxd5 Bxd4! 17 Rad1 Ne5! 18 Nxe5 Bxd5 19 Nc4 Qg5 20 g3 Qf5! 21
Rfe1 Qe4! 22 f3 Qxe3+! 23 Qxe3 Rxe3 24 Nxe3 Bxe3+ 25 Kf1 Bd4.
Black has full compensation for the slight material disadvantage and
the game was drawn after 26 Rxd4 cxd4 27 Rd1 Rc8 28 Rxd4 Rc5 29 f4
Kf8 30 Bd3 Ke7.

12   bxc5   bxc5
13   Rb1

[diag. 76]

This strategically very interesting position was explored at length in the 1984/1985 World Championship with Karpov and Kasparov regularly being on both sides of it. White has prospects along the open b-file and against the isolated d-pawn; Black has chances against White's denuded Queenside and particularly the a-pawn.

The only logical alternative is 13 Qb3 and GM Seirawan had prepared it as a novelty worth trying. Yet as he tells the story in Inside Chess magazine, a half hour at the board rechecking the move convinced him that after 13...Bc6 14 dxc5, Black has 14...Qa5! and is equal after 15 Rc1 Nd7 16 Nd4 Nxc5 17 Nxc6 Nxb3 18 Nxa5 Nxc1.

13   ...   Qa5!?

This thematic method of aiming for counterplay is, when properly executed, Black's most promising plan. At the time of this game the move was considered to be inferior but now we know better.

The passive 13...Bc6 was the "reliable" move of the 1984/1985 match and "official theory" (e.g. ECO D Revised) rates it best and the positions resulting after it equal, e.g. 14 0-0 Nd7 15 Bb5 Qc7 16 Qc2 Rfc8 17 Rfc1 Bxb5 18 Nxb5 Qc6 19 dxc5 Nxc5, Kasparov - Karpov, 1984/85 Match, Game 42. Yet Black's need to grovel for a draw is sufficiently unpleasant for GMs to start losing confidence in it.

14   0-0

A novelty when played. Instead Kasparov - Karpov, 1984/85 Match, Game 40, had gone 14 Qd2 cxd4 15 Nxd4 Bxd4 16 exd4 Bc6 17 Nb5 Qd8 18 0-0 with a slight edge for White because of having the superior Bishop, more active pieces and the "better" isolated d-pawn. However, in A. Yusupov - A. Belyavsky, Linares 1988, Black improved on the above game by achieving a more active piece placement as follows: 16...Ba6! (instead of 16...Bc6) 17 Nb5 Qd8 18 0-0 Nc6! 19 Rfd1 Qf6 20 Bf3 Rab8

21 a4 Rfd8 22 Qc3 Bc8 23 Rbc1 a6 24 Qxc6 Qxc6 25 Rxc6 axb5 26 axb5, Draw.

| 14 | ... | cxd4 |
| 15 | Nxd4 | Nc6! |

It is just absolutely necessary for Black to press his counterplay on the Queenside. Now White achieves nothing with 16 Rxb7 Nxd4 17 exd4 Qxc3, with total equality.

16 Ndb5

White tries to keep the position as complicated as possible.

In commenting on this game, GM Seirawan pointed out the important alternative 16 Nxd5 Qxd5 17 Bf3 Qxa2! 18 Nxc6 Bxc6 19 Bxc6 Rad8 20 Qh5 "and White has the smallest of advantages." This conclusion was subsequently tested in Seirawan - A. Belyavsky, Barcelona 1989, where White decided to play 20 Qf3 (instead of 20 Qh5). After 20...Rd6! 21 g3 a5 22 Rfd1 Rfd8 23 Kg2 Rxd1 24 Rxd1 Rxd1 25 Qxd1 Qe6 26 Qa4?! g5! whatever advantage there was belonged to Black who won in 83 moves. Instead of the decentralizing 26 Qa4?!, 26 Qd5 retains complete equality.

16 ...   Ne7

Surely the sensible move: Black protects his pawn and leaves the Bishop pair on the board for future potential. Inferior is 16...Bxc3?! 17 Nxc3 Qxc3 18 Rxb7 d4 because of 19 Rb3 Qa5 20 Bf3 Rac8 21 Bxc6 Rxc6 22 Qxd4 (22...Qxa2 23 Rb7) when White's active and secure position is ready to stamp Black's a-pawn more of a weakness than strength. I agree completely with GM Seirawan's evaluation of this position as giving White the superior chances.

17 Qa4!

With Black having the active Queen it is quite logical to exchange it off and look forward to exploiting the vulnerability of the d-pawn in the endgame. Black must exchange since 17...Bxc3? 18 Nxc3 Qxc3 19 Rxb7 puts Black at least one tempo behind the previous variation.

| 17 | ... | Qxa4 |
| 18 | Nxa4 | |

A position which looks superior for White, yet how superior is difficult to guess without a substantial amount of analysis. White's pieces seem to be actively placed but are not properly situated to menace the two potentially vulnerable points in Black's position, the a- and d-pawns. Moreover, Black's Bishops have good diagonals. Black's objective should be to eliminate the isolated d-pawn. Of course, this is easier said then done.

	18	...	Bc6
	19	Nc5	Rfc8
	20	Rfc1	Bxb5!

Making the way clear for the d-pawn's advance.

21   Bxb5

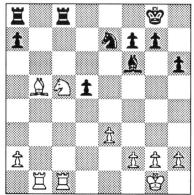

[diag. 77]

21   ...   Rc7?!

Surprisingly, when Black is on the verge of executing his plan, he gets cold feet and selects a purely defensive mode with all the tribulations that this entails.

About a month later, in J. Timman - A. Karpov, Amsterdam 1988, GM Karpov demonstrated the correct way: 21...d4! 22 Nd7 (22 e4 Bg5) 22...dxe3 23 Nxf6+ gxf6 24 fxe3 Rab8 25 Ba4 Kg7! 26 Rxb8 Rxc1+ 27 Kf2 Rc7, Draw. By preventing the incursion of White's Rook on the 7th rank, Black has safeguarded his position on both flanks. Since Black's doubled f-pawns are no more vulnerable than the corresponding White e- and g-pawns and Black's Knight is fully equal to White's Bishop in potential activity, the position is indeed completely equal.

	22	Nd7!	Bc3
	23	Rb3	Ba5
	24	Rxc7	Bxc7

The legacy of the "careful" 21...Rc7?! is that White is left with the active Rook, whereas Black is left with the weak d-pawn.

25   g3?!

GM Seirawan calls this "a waste of time." Indeed the immediate King centralization (25 Kf1 etc.) would put White a valuable tempo ahead of the game continuation.

25	...	Rc8?!

Black also loses time. Better is 25...Bd6, followed by ...f6, Kf7, Ke6 (Seirawan), with a continuing comfortable edge for White.

26	Ba6	Ra8

Forced since 26...Rd8? loses to 27 Rb7! Rxd7 28 Bb5.

27	Rb7	Bd6
28	Bb5!	

White has gotten exactly the type of endgame that he would wish to have from the position after 13 Rb1: active pieces, play against the d5 isolani and no problems for oneself. The text prepares to bring the Bishop to b3 for an attack on the d-pawn.

28	...	a5
29	Ba4	g6?

The error that should have lost and a further demonstration how unpleasant the positions starting after 21...Rc7?! have become for Black. There are no great moves and lots of bad ones. GM Seirawan has demonstrated that White wins after 30 Nf6+ Kf8 (30...Kg7?? allows 31 Ne8+. Yet as GM Seirawan has candidly admitted, it simply had not occurred to him in the position before Black's 29th move that the Nd7 could get to e8 and therefore he had not examined the sequence starting with 30 Nf6+.) 31 Rd7 Bb4 32 Nxd5 Nxd5 33 Rxd5. White has won a valuable pawn and with Rooks on the board there is no reason that with good technique the material advantage cannot be realized into the win. It is worth adding that with opposite color Bishops and a normal one pawn advantage, the stronger side wants the major piece to be a Rook rather than the Queen.

GM Seirawan considers that Black's best chance for defending would have been to activate the Rook with 29...Rc8.

30	Bb3?!	Kg7
31	a4	

No particular harm is done by sitting on the position. However, White could have immediately obtained the characteristic endgame discussed in the note after Black's 34th move with the simple 31 Nb6 Rb8 (Only move) 32 Bxd5! Rxb7 (Forced) 33 Bxb7.

31	...	Bb4
32	Ne5	Rc8
33	Rb5	Rc1+
34	Kg2	

Now after, 34...Rc5?!, 35 Nd7! is strong. In the meanwhile White is threatening to capture the d-pawn, as well as the sequence 35 Nd3 Rb1 36 Nxb4 Rxb3 37 Nc6, with "a won Knight endgame" (Seirawan). Thus Black has nothing better than the game continuation.

34   ...   Bc3

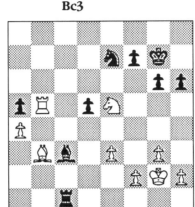

[diag. 78]

GM Seirawan had now prepared the following sequence: 35 Nd3 Rb1 36 Rb7! Nc8 (36...Bb4?? 37 Bc2) 37 Bxd5 Rxb7 38 Bxb7. Most likely this position is a theoretical draw, yet to obtain a draw Black would have to undergo a tremendous amount of harassment. Rather than playing it immediately, White decided to follow the accepted and good practice of first repeating moves before the time control at move 40, but ...

35   Rb7   Bb4
36   Rb5   Bc3
37   Rb7?

Last chance for 37 Nd3!.

37   ...   Bb4
38   Rb5

A sad necessity. Here 38 Nd3 leads to nothing after 38...Rc3! 39 Nxb4 Rxb3.

38   ...   Bc3 Draw

Of course, claimed by Black.

Queen's Gambit Declined, Semi-Tarrasch Defense

Game 22

White: Tigran Petrosian
Black: Viktor Korchnoi
Played at 1977 Quarter-Final Candidates Match, Il Ciocco, Italy,
Game 6

1	d4	Nf6
2	Nf3	d5
3	c4	e6
4	Nc3	c5

The thematic method of challenging White's superior center in the QGD is to play either ...e5 or, more often, ...c5. Here Black already "achieves" the ...c5 advance on move 4. Yet the Queen's Gambit is too strong an opening to allow Black such an easy road to equality.

5   cxd5

By far the critical continuation: Black has three replies and every one has clear deficiencies. Of course, White can aim for a symmetrical position where he has the move by playing 5 e3 Nc6 6 a3. Yet that provides much less prospects for an advantage than the text.

5   ...   Nxd5

Instead, 5...exd5 brings about the Tarrasch Defense wherein Black accepts an isolated d-pawn and hopes that his strong central pawn presence will be of sufficient compensation - see Games 24 - 26.

The opening after 5...Nxd5 is called the Semi-Tarrasch Defense, because—similarly to the Tarrasch—Black plays an early ...c5, but then turns away from the pure Tarrasch by recapturing on d5 with the Knight. The advantage of this approach is obvious: Black avoids having an isolated central pawn. Yet the disadvantage is also clear: Black has significantly less central influence than in the Tarrasch. Moreover, not only will Black be deficient in the center, but the compensation for this is not to be seen. Therefore, over the past several years, the Semi-Tarrasch has been losing popularity in international play. Grandmasters who are looking for a solid method within the Queen's Gambit Declined are increasingly choosing variations of the Orthodox Defense rather than the Semi-Tarrasch. The Orthodox Defense gives Black more central control and with winning chances no less than in the Semi-Tarrasch.

For the sake of completeness I should add that 5...cxd4 is "playable." However, the positions after 6 Qxd4 Nxd5 7 e4 or 6...exd5 7 e4! offer

Black no joy and there is no particular reason why he should aim for them.

6 e4

[diag. 79]

Why not? Black has allowed White to establish—at no cost—a powerful pawn center and there is no theoretical reason why White should not do so. Yet this most thematic plan has never had the popularity that it seems, in my opinion, to deserve. I believe there are two reasons for this, a chess reason and a "process" reason. The chess reason is that White's play must be exceedingly accurate and vigorous to exploit the strength of the isolated d-pawn that will result. Apparently many players do not feel comfortable in being placed in such a demanding situation.

The two high quality alternatives, both of which appear more often in international play, are:

(1) 6 e3, with the most common sequence being 6...Nc6 7 Bd3 cxd4 8 exd4 Be7 9 0-0 0-0. This a more routine isolated d-pawn position, with the d-pawn only on the fourth rank and with all minor pieces still on the board. This both increases White's flexibility and decreases the risk since, unlike the 6 e4 variations, Black will not have a Queenside pawn majority.

(2) 6 g3, when the thematic position results after 6...Nc6 7 Bg2 Be7 8 0-0 0-0. Then White can choose to play against the isolated d-pawn by creating it via 9 Nxd5 exd5 or White can select a superior center approach by playing 9 e4. Again, both of these approaches are rather well understood by players of closed opening systems.

The "process" reason that I mentioned earlier has to do with the matter of move orders. As far as the variations after 6 e3 are concerned some 50% of the positions arise from the Panov Variation of the Caro-Kann Defense: 1 e4 c6 2 d4 d5 3 exd5 cxd5 4 c4 Nf6 5 Nc3 e6 6 Nf3 Be7 7 cxd5 Nxd5 8 Bd3 Nc6 9 0-0 0-0, e.g., M. Adams - Y. Seirawan, Wijk aan Zee 1991. Moreover, a significant number come via transposition from the English Opening when Black has played an early ...c5 and White an early e3. For instance: 1 c4 Nf6 2 Nf3 c5 3 Nc3 e6 4 e3 Nc6 5 d4 d5 6 cxd5 Nxd5 7 Bd3 cxd4 8 exd4 Be7 9 0-0 0-0, I. Ivanov - M. Dlugy, National Open 1989.

Also the main line position given after 6 g3 results most often from a different move order than the "official one." In fact, the most common way of reaching the position after move 8 and the one after 9 Nxd5 exd5 is for White to play an early g3 and a late d4. A characteristic example of that is Sirotanovic - Ruban, Bela Crkva 1989: 1 Nf3 c5 2 c4 Nf6 3 Nc3 e6 4 g3 d5 5 cxd5 Nxd5 6 Bg2 Nc6 7 0-0 Be7 8 Nxd5 exd5 9 d4 0-0.

6 ...   Nxc3

The only correct move. Even though it strengthens White's center by transforming his b-pawn into a c-pawn, the advantages are the more significant ones: Black does not lose time with a retreat and the exchange of minor pieces decreases the cramping effect of White's superior center.

7 bxc3   cxd4

Again, with the thematic objective of exchanging minor pieces, i.e. the dark square Bishops. Everything else is clearly inferior, e.g. 7...Be7?! 8 Bc4 0-0 9 0-0 Nd7 10 Qe2 Qc7 11 Rd1 a6 12 a4 b6 13 d5 and Black has no compensation for White's vast central superiority, S. Gligoric - Sanchez, Stockholm Interzonal 1952.

8 cxd4   Bb4+

At this point Black has a valid choice. He can play first 8...Nc6, and after 9 Bc4, the tactical 9...b5. Bobby Fischer equalized easily with this in his 1972 World Championship Match, Game 9, against Boris Spassky: 10 Bd3 Bb4+ 11 Bd2 Bxd2+ 12 Qxd2 a6 13 a4 0-0!, since 14 axb5 is met by 14...Nxd4.

It is imperative for White to be in position to mobilize his d-pawn. Therefore, instead of the self-blocking 10 Bd3, correct is 10 Be2!. Then White retains a thematic and pleasant opening advantage, with one excellent example being A. Yusupov - Z. Bibli, Montpellier Candidates 1985: 10...Bb4+ 11 Bd2 Qa5 12 d5! exd5 13 exd5 Ne7 14 0-0 Bxd2 15 Nxd2 0-0 16 Nb3 Qd8 17 Bf3 Nf5 18 Rc1 Nd6 19 Qd4. White has a large spatial advantage and his d-pawn is much more dangerous than Black's extra Queenside pawn.

9	Bd2	Bxd2+
10	Qxd2	0-0

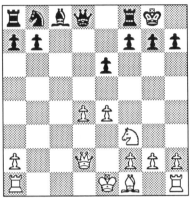

[diag. 80]

The central pawn structure has been clarified and two sets of minor pieces have been exchanged off. What you see now is what each side will have to work with. This is the starting point of the most critical and most thematic variation in the pure Semi-Tarrasch Defense. The major thematic strategic themes for each side are:

White will aim to get the d-pawn effectively to d5. There it will be in Black's side of the board, will have become a passed pawn and—White hopes—a pain for Black by virtue of both being a danger of queening and prevention of the smooth coordination of Black's forces.

In the shadow of the d5 pawn, White will mobilize his Rooks on the central d- and e-files. He will try to take advantage of his space advantage by looking to attack Black's Kingside. Because Black's Kingside is lacking in minor pieces to help with the defense, White's chances for a successful attack are good.

Black throughout has to juggle two goals:

(1) Make White's passed d-pawn as harmless as possible and keep his King sufficiently safe, and

(2) Mobilize his Queenside pawn majority to create a viable passed pawn. The chances are that this will only become possible in the endgame and thus Black will first have to survive the middlegame.

In a practical game, the situation for a knowledgeable White is much the more comfortable one: an inaccuracy by White will mean that his advantage peters out; a slip by Black will most likely lead to demolition of his position.

11   Bc4

By far the best location for the Bishop since it supports the thematic d5 advance. Of the alternatives, 11 Bd3?! is inferior since it interferes with the mobilization of the d-pawn, whereas 11 Be2 is unnecessarily modest and could in later play block off the KR from control of the e-file.

11   ...   Nc6

The normal move, with the Knight developed to its "best" square and pressure applied to the d-pawn. Yet the disadvantages also are marked: White's inevitable d5 will gain time by attacking the Knight and the Knight will be of little or no help in defending its King. In my opinion, the alternative 11...Nd7 12 0-0 Nf6 development could well be more suited to Black's needs in this position. One important example is A. Yusupov - J. Eslon, Spain 1981: 13 Rfe1 b6 14 a4 Bb7 15 Bd3 Rc8 16 a5 Qc7 17 axb6 axb6 18 Rac1 Qb8 19 Rb1 Qa8. White's spatial advantage means that he has retained his slight advantage, but Black's effective pressure on e4 makes it hard for White to build on this slight superiority.

12   0-0   b6

Fianchettoing the QB has been historically considered to be Black's soundest plan. The two respectable alternatives are:

(1) 12...Qd6 when Black hopes to apply pressure on the d-pawn with ...Rd8. Yet that   leaves Black even more vulnerable on the Kingside. In the game W. Browne - H. Olafsson, Reykjavik 1980 White obtained a very strong attack after the energetic 13 Rad1 Rd8 14 Rfe1 Bd7 15 d5! exd5 16 exd5 Ne7 17 Ng5!.

(2) 12...Ne7 remaneuvers the Knight in advance of the coming d5. However, the cost is time and a passive Knight. In Y. Seirawan - V. Korchnoi, Skelleftea World Cup 1989 White skillfully exploited these factors to achieve a pleasant advantage as follows: 13 a4 b6 14 a5 Bb7 15 Bd3 bxa5 16 Rfb1 Rb8 17 Rxa5 Nc6 18 Rab5 Ba8 19 d5!.

13   Rfe1!

As already alluded to earlier, White's play must be resolute and combine the effective mobilization of the d-pawn with attacking plans against Black's King. Therefore, inherently harmless are plans associated with Rfd1 and Rac1. For instance, 13 Rfd1 Na5 14 Bd3 Bb7 15 Qe3 Rc8 16 Rac1 Qe7 17 Rxc8 Rxc8 18 Rc1 Rxc1+ 19 Qxc1 with equality and a draw agreed, A. Zaitsev - L. Polugaevsky, USSR Championship 1968/69.

13   ...   Bb7

14 Rad1

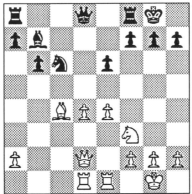

[diag. 81]

White has efficiently mobilized his forces for the coming d5 advance. Since that cannot be prevented, Black's only choice is how to prepare for it. The two main ways are:

(1) 14...Ne7—see the game.

(2) 14...Rc8: Black anticipates a discovered attack on the Bishop and prepares to control the c-file. After the obvious 15 d5, Black again has a fundamental decision to make:

   (a) 15...Na5 16 Bd3 Qd6 (16...exd5? 17 e5! leads to a killing attack for White, as first demonstrated in L. Polugaevsky - M. Tal, USSR Championship 1969.) 17 dxe6 Qxe6?! (The minor evil is 17...fxe6 when White can play against the e6 weakness with 18 Bb5! or go for an attack with 18 e5! Qe7 19 Ng5—as given by GM Dokhojan.) 18 Nd4 Qe5 19 Nf5, Y. Dokhojan - S. Webb, Europe Club Teams 1989. White has a most dangerous attack, with f4 and e5 coming up.

   (b) 15...exd5 16 Bxd5 Qc7 17 e5! (Also strong is 17 Qg5! h6 18 Qg4 Rfd8 19 h3 Ne7 20 Nd4, Swoboda - Plank, Vienna 1985.) 17...Ne7 and now instead of the insipid 18 Bxb7?! Qxb7 with equality, J. Nogueiras - M. Tal, Brussels 1988, GM Tal gives 18 Bb3! Bxf3 (If 18...Rcd8, 19 Qd6!!) 19 gxf3 Kh8 20 Qd6 or 20 Qd7, in either case with a strong initiative for White.

14 ...   Ne7

With the sensible idea of blockading the advancing d-pawn. Yet White's active development and the weakness of the c6 square allows an energetic White to keep a clear advantage.

15 d5!   exd5

16   exd5   Nf5

Up to now the game has followed W. Uhlmann - V. Korchnoi, Rovinj/ Zagreb 1970 where after 17 Bd3?! Nd6 Black had reached approximate equality. Yet perceptive thinking on GM Petrosian's part had led him to the conclusion that 17 Bd3?! is not only passive but also illogical. I mean, why should White block off two of his major pieces from the advanced, passed d-pawn?

17   Ne5!

White's Rooks, Queen, Bishop and d-pawn are harmoniously placed for central activity and therefore it is quite in order to activate the Knight, thereby threatening 18 d6 (Of course, the immediate 17 d6? allows 17...Bxf3.). As happens so often, White's logical strategy is backed with a brilliant tactical point.

17   ...   Nd6
18   Nc6!!   Bxc6?

Leads to a positionally untenable situation. Therefore, Black had to try one of the following:

(1) An unpleasant middlegame after 18...Qf6 19 Bb3.

(2) An unpleasant endgame after 18...Nxc4 19 Nxd8 Nxd2 20 Nxb7 Rab8! (20...Nc4? 21 d6!) 21 Na5! bxa5 22 Rxd2. I would rate this position as giving White 50% winning chances and 0% losing chances—always a most pleasant practical situation.

19   dxc6   Nxc4
20   Qf4!

The try for a brilliant win with 20 Qxd8?? Raxd8 21 Rxd8 Rxd8 22 c7, leads to a painful loss after 22...Rf8! 23 Rd1 b5! 24 Rd8 Nb6 (GM Marjanovic).

20   ...   Nd6

At the cost of a couple of tempos, in this way Black is able to prevent the early journey of the c-pawn to the 7th rank, e.g. 20...Qf6 21 Qxc4 Rac8 22 c7!.

21   Rxd6   Qc7
22   g3

The results of the previous play are as follows: White has a powerful far advanced passed pawn, his Rooks control the center files and the Queen is actively placed. Black's only trump—the Queenside pawn majority—is without much importance since his major pieces cannot afford to support any active pawn mobilization on that side because they have to concentrate on stopping the c-pawn and guarding the King.

White has a complete grip on the position and GM Petrosian is the right man to finish the job. Every one of his moves either increases his advantage or safeguards his own position. White has no need to hurry—prevention of potential counterplay and heading in the right direction is what matters.

22   ...   h6

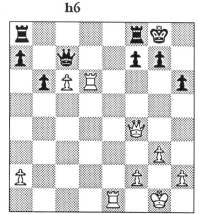

[diag. 82]

The text creates an almost imperceptible, yet quite real weakening of Black's Kingside because White's g-pawn can now be used as a battering ram to open lines. Nevertheless, Black can't do without some air for the King as otherwise he will be continually subject to various back rank mates. No relief would come from 22...Rad8 23 Rxd8 Qxd8 because with a pair of Rooks exchanged, the c-pawn becomes an even greater power.

23   Qe5!

With this and the next move, White powerfully centralizes his Queen. If now 23...Rae8, White wins easily after 24 Qxe8 Rxe8 (24...Qxd6 25 Qd7! is even easier.) 25 Rxe8+ Kh7 26 Red8, e.g. 26...Qe7 27 Rd1 Qc7 28 R8d6! b5 29 Rc1! Qxd6 30 c7.

23   ...   Rac8
24   Qd5!   Kh7

Black tries biding his time, since 24...Rfd8 loses to 25 Rd7!.

25   Re4   Kg8
26   Kg2   a6
27   h4   b5
28   g4!

With the Queen and Rooks in dominant central positions and his King off the back rank, GM Petrosian starts the decisive attack against the vulnerable h6 point.

28	...	Kh7
29	Re2	Kh8
30	g5	h5

Black must keep the Kingside as closed as possible. After 30...hxg5?! 31 hxg5 the open h-file will be decisive.

31 Rd2!

Doubling Rooks not only establishes total control of the d-file, but by having White's Rooks self-protecting, the Queen is freed to go after Black's h-pawn. This will force ...g6—another weakening of Black's King position—and then White will start exploiting the new weakness. Step by step GM Petrosian tightens the noose around Black's King.

31	...	Rfe8
32	Qf3	g6
33	R2d5!	

By closing off the diagonal from c6 to his King or Queen, White threatens to win immediately with either 34 Rd7 or 34 Qf6+. Thus Black's KR must head back to protect the f-pawn.

33	...	Rf8
34	Rf6!	

This square has been opened up for the Rook and the unstoppable threat is 35 Rd7.

34	...	Qe7
35	Rd7	Qe8
36	Rxg6!	

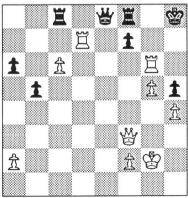

[diag. 83]

A pretty bit of tactics destroys the weakened Kingside. If now 36...fxg6, 37 Qc3+ leads to mate on g7. In time pressure GM Korchnoi allows an even simpler mate.

36   ...   Qe5
37   Qxh5 Mate

Queen's Gambit Declined, Slav Defense
Game 23

White: Helgi Olafsson
Black: Edmar Mednis
Played at Reykjavik (Iceland) International Tournament 1982

1	Nf3	Nf6
2	c4	

White's move order is a popular preventive method used by many grandmasters who like to play an early c4, i.e. an English Opening type of sequence. However, these GMs avoid the immediate 1 c4 because they do not want to face 1...e5 which can be looked upon as a Reversed Sicilian Defense with a move in hand for White. Since they have no interest in even an "improved Sicilian," Black's 1...e5 is prevented by selecting 1 Nf3 and only on the next move is the c-pawn advanced two squares.

2	...	c6

An invitation to the Slav Defense in case of 3 d4 d5. Also after other third moves by White, Black will play 3...d5 and then be in position to develop his QB to either f5 or g4, e.g. 3 g3 d5 4 b3 Bf5 or 4...Bg4. Because Black has avoided an early ...e6 he has the option of developing the QB along its original diagonal.

3	d4	d5

[diag. 84]

Via transposition of moves, the basic structure of the Slav has arisen. The "normal" move sequence would have been 1 d4 d5 2 c4 c6 3 Nf3 Nf6. In this case White would have had the choice of playing 3 Nc3.

Whites who aim for the Exchange Variation usually prefer the immediate 3 Nc3, as do those players who are more comfortable in the Meran Variation (3 Nc3 Nf6 4 e3) than in the main lines of the Slav. Of course, these "advantages" do not come for nothing, because Black has the option of the sharp variation starting with 3...e5. Therefore, in general those Whites who are not averse to the characteristic Slav variations prefer to first play Nf3.

Just a brief look at Diagram 84 shows off very well Black's pluses in comparison with the QGD, Orthodox Defense variations. Black has safeguarded his d5 strong point by using the c-pawn, thereby leaving open the c8 - h3 diagonal for the unimpeded development of the QB— which characteristically is Black's problem child in the Orthodox Defense. But again, this significant advantage is not gained for nothing. A small disadvantage is that the thematic challenge to White's superior center via the ...c5 advance will have to come at the cost of a tempo since Black has first played ...c6. A second, more important problem will appear after White's next move. Diagram 84 also immediately shows the most significant characteristic of the Slav: its inherent solidity. Not only is Black safeguarding the d5 pawn, but even if that pawn chooses to capture the c4 pawn, the d5 square remains very solid. In this way the Slav is very reminiscent of the Caro-Kann Defense against 1 e4. I have referred in my writings and lectures to the Caro-Kann and the Slav as "sister openings".

4 Nc3

This routine Knight development is by far White's most forcing approach. There also are two high class alternatives and an important mediocre one:

(1) 4 cxd5 cxd5 5 Nc3 brings about the Exchange Variation, formerly a favorite of GM Tigran Petrosian. Among the current world class players, GM Yasser Seirawan is its leading practitioner. Despite the fact that the position is a symmetrical one in a closed opening, a perceptive player has excellent chances of exploiting White's first move advantage. The current main line position occurs after 5...Nc6 6 Bf4 Bf5 7 e3 e6. Then in the game Y. Seirawan - J. van der Wiel, Wijk aan Zee 1991, White obtained the advantage after 8 Qb3 Bb4 9 Bb5 0-0 10 0-0 Bxc3 11 Qxc3 Ne4?! (Better is 11...Rc8) 12 Qa3! Qb6 13 Bxc6 Qxc6 (Worse is 13...bxc6?! 14 Ne5! when Black's c-pawn is weak.) 14 Ne5! Qb5 15 f3 and White has more of the center and will control the c-file.

(2) 4 e3 protects the c-pawn smoothly and prevents the main lines in favor of the potential Meran variation after 4...e6 5 Nc3 Nbd7. However, Black has the option of remaining in the Slav with the faultless 4...Bf5. White's prospects for an opening advantage are only slight.

(3) 4 Bg5 looks better than it is. Because—unlike the Orthodox Defense in the QGD—there is no pin, Black can obtain at least equal chances with 4...dxc4.

The position after 4 Nc3 shows up the major disadvantage of the Slav. Black has kept open the diagonal of the QB, but how is he to develop his KB? Now 4...e6 will transpose into the Botvinnik or Meran Variations, whereas 4...g6 leads to a passive version of the Gruenfeld Defense, often called the Semi-Gruenfeld or the Semi-Slav. (See the discussion in connection with Game 13.)

Black's specific problem is that the "desirable" 4...Bf5?! works out poorly because of 5 cxd5! cxd5 (5...Nxd5?! relinquishes the center to White.) 6 Qb3 and Black has to endure the abject retreat 6...Bc8 because 6...b6? is refuted by 7 e4! dxe4 8 Ne5 e6 9 Bb5+ Nfd7 10 g4 Bg6 11 h4! h5 12 Nxg6 followed by 13 Qxe6+.

| 4 | ... | dxc4 |

Thus Black is forced to give up the center, which apparently negates the whole concept of the Slav Defense's 2...c6. Yet there is also a major silver lining as a result of that move: it is not at all easy for White to recover his pawn. The two normal ways to attempt to do so are far from convincing:

(1) 5 e4 is a pure gambit of uncertain soundness. After 5...b5 6 e5 Nd5 7 a4 e6 8 axb5 (8 Ng5 h6 9 Nge4 b4) 8...Nxc3 9 bxc3 cxb5 10 Ng5 Bb7 White, at most, has compensation for the missing pawn.

(2) 5 e3 b5 6 a4 b4! leads to the following choices for White:

(a) 7 Na2 e6! 8 Bxc4 Bb7 9 0-0 Be7 10 Qe2 0-0 11 Rd1 a5 12 Bd2 Nbd7 has allowed White to recover the pawn but at the cost of an awkwardly placed QN. Black will soon get in ...c5 and comfortable equality, S. Reshevsky - V. Smyslov, USA - USSR Match 1945.

(b) 7 Nb1 Ba6 8 Qc2 b3! 9 Qd1 e6 10 Nbd2 Qd5, A. Adorjan - E. Torre, Toluca Interzonal 1982 is another gambit of uncertain value.

Therefore, at least 95% of the time in international tournaments White enters main line play with ...

5   a4

Black's ....b5 is thereby prevented and White prepares to recover his pawn. But, of course, the need for the text has damaged White two-fold: one development tempo has been lost and the Queenside (in particular the b4 square) permanently weakened. It is these factors which tend to compensate Black for having given up the center. Therefore the Slav Defense has retained its reputation as a fully satisfactory Black weapon ever since its heyday during the 1935 and 1937 World Championship matches between Alexander Alekhine and Max Euwe.

Because at the moment White has no specific threat, Black has a choice of how to proceed with his development. Historically Black's three significant variations have started with 5...Na6, 5...Bg4 and 5...Bf5. The first two have had recurring periods of popularity but currently are on the decline. The inherent problem with 5...Na6 and 5...Bg4 is that they depend more on "tricks" than a sound strategic foundation. It is 5...Bf5 that has always been considered to be Black's main line.

5   ...   Bf5

[diag. 85]

A perfect move in every way: the Bishop guards the key central e4 square, while also taking a bead on White's vulnerable Queenside. The text is the foundation for the soundness of the Slav Defense. If the variations to come turn out to be significantly inferior for Black, then the Slav Defense becomes unplayable. My best guess is that this will not happen.

For the coming play, the strategic themes for both sides are already clearly defined. These are:

White will first want to smoothly recapture on c4. Either in conjunction with that or, as is more common, thereafter, White will aim to increase his central superiority by getting in e4. The superior center then will be used as springboard for activity against Black's position. The most frequent arenas are Black's Kingside or along the d-file.

Black will complete his development in a safe and sound way. He will try to make it hard for White to get in e4 without some cost. Again, as in QGD positions, Black will work to decrease White's central superiority by challenging the d-pawn either by ...c5 or ...e5. If the position opens up, Black will look for counterplay against the vulnerable points in White's position. Most of the time these will be found along the a- to d-files.

In early play the key square for both sides is e4.

6   e3

The simplest of two main line choices. The other is 6 Ne5, with the logical point of rushing to accomplish White's early opening goals by planning 7 f3, followed by

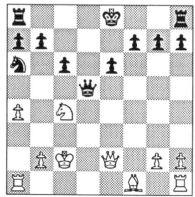

[diag. 86]

8 e4 and 9 Bxc4. Helped by some impressive successes by GM Anatoly Karpov, this variation has come back in fashion over the past five years. Black's play must be both accurate and resolute so as not to be overwhelmed by White's center. The thematic main line for both sides than is: 6...e6 7 f3 Bb4! 8 e4 Bxe4! 9 fxe4 Nxe4 10 Bd2 Qxd4 11 Nxe4 Qxe4+ 12 Qe2 Bxd2+ 13 Kxd2 Qd5+ 14 Kc2 Na6 15 Nxc4—see Diagram 86. Though Black has three good pawns for the piece and White's King appears insecure, GM Karpov demonstrated that Black's road to full equality is not easy. Current opinion is that Black does best by combining development and security as follows: 15...0-0-0 16 Qe5 f6 17 Qe3 Kb8! 18 Be2 e5!, V. Tukmakov - Solozenkin, Germany 1991, or 18 Kb3 e5!, I. Novikov - E. Bareev, USSR Championship 1990. In neither game was White able to demonstrate any advantage.

6   ...   e6
7   Bxc4   Bb4

Only so! Remember that Black must inhibit White's e4 advance. By menacing the QN—White's natural supporter of the e4 advance—Black strives to prevent that.

8   0-0   0-0

Normal and good. Nevertheless, recently a number of Slav experts have preferred a move order starting with 8...Nbd7. In the majority of cases, there will not be a difference. However, if White plays an early Nh4 and Black's QB retreats to g6, then it could be potentially dangerous for White to capture on g6. Because Black still has the option of castling Queenside, the open h-file (after ...hxg6) would give Black opportunities for an attack against White's King.

9   Nh4

An idea which has come into prominence over the past ten years: White aims for an early e4 by enabling the f-pawn to support that advance as well as by exchanging off the defending QB for the KN. Yet, the goal of playing e4 is not an end in itself but just a waystation for exploiting the central superiority for concrete objectives. Therefore as long as Black gets something useful in return for "allowing" e4, the dynamic character of the Slav will continue. (It should be added that often White first plays 9 Qb3 and then 10 Nh4.)

The standard method of aiming for e4 has been 9 Qe2 Nbd7 10 e4, with Black's most accurate response being 10...Bg6 11 Bd3 Bh5!. Black then threatens 12...e5, which White can prevent with 12 Bf4 and Black then reintroduces that "threat" by playing 12...Re8. Therefore White should play 13 e5. In the game B. Spassky - E. Mednis, Vienna (IBM) International 1986, White now "kindly" offered a draw, which I—not surprisingly—accepted. After the game GM Spassky stated that after 13...Nd5 he did not have much confidence in the standard 14 Nxd5 and had thought about playing 14 Bd2 instead. Our analysis showed that after 14...c5! 15 Nxd5 Bxd2 Black is fine.

Therefore, the main line remains 14 Nxd5 cxd5! 15 h3 a6 16 g4 and White's spatial advantage should give him a slight edge, E. Magerramov - V. Bagirov, Baku 1986.

9   ...   Bg4

Black's common response is the immediate 9...Bg6. The idea behind the text is to loosen up somewhat White's Kingside before acquiescing to that retreat. If White plays perfectly then it won't matter whether Black has chosen 9...Bg6 or the method of this game. However, in the case of "imperfect" play, Black's chances for success are greater if White's Kingside is weakened. In this game Black's approach is quite successful. In any case the only disadvantages of the text are that White gains some Kingside space and the chance to get in e4 one move earlier. However, in my estimate, Black's losing chances thereby are not measurably greater than after 9...Bg6—therefore Black's gain/loss relationship remains attractive.

The last couple of years have demonstrated that after 9 Nh4 White is not actually threatening to capture on f5 because after e.g. 9...Nbd7 10 Nxf5 exf5 the f5 pawn presses powerfully on the e4 square. Therefore Whites are now playing 10 f3 and after 10...Bg6 positions arise which are similar to those after the immediate 9...Bg6.

10	f3	Bh5
11	g4	Bg6
12	Ng2	

The idea behind this move is a sensible one: White will play e4 and wall in Black's QB - therefore why should White exchange a "good Knight" for a "bad Bishop"? Moreover, the KN can find a new attractive home on, for instance, f4 or e3.

Yet the inherently solid Slav can not be bashed so readily. In the first place, the Knight retreat costs time and, secondly, the QB is far from dead and can be redeployed effectively.

According to current theory, White's strongest continuation is 12 e4 Nbd7 13 g5 Ne8 14 Nxg6 hxg6 15 Be3 Nd6 16 Be2!, so as to try to combine the advantage of more space with the potential power of the Bishop pair. In L. Polugaevsky - E. Torre, Biel 1989, Black now lost time with 16...Ba5 and White was able to increase his advantage with 17 Kh1 Qe7 18 Rb1 Rfd8 19 b4!. GM Polugaevsky recommends as an improvement for Black the immediate 16...Qe7!?, with White only slightly better.

12	...	Nd5!

The KN must be repositioned before White blocks off the exit with 13 e4. With the KN out of the way, the QB can also be brought back to life via ...f6 and ...Bf7.

13	Qb3	a5!

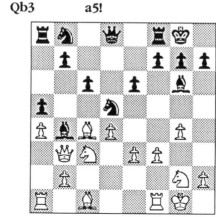

[diag. 87]

Inaccurate is 13...Qe7?! because after 14 a5! Black's Queenside would be in a bind.

14   e4

Black gets full counterplay after the active text move. In his monograph on the Slav, GM Mark Taimanov recommends 14 Bd2, adding "with advantage to White." After the developmental 14...Nd7 I would have no qualms about Black's position. At the very most, White's advantage is a tiny one. The position after 14...Nd7 is characteristic for the Slav Defense: Black is well developed, has no near term nor fundamental problems and retains prospects for timely counterplay.

14	...	Nb6
15	Be3	Nxc4
16	Qxc4	Qe7!

It is not yet clear whether Black's QN has more of a future from a6 or d7. Therefore Black delays that decision in favor of repositioning the QB. It has no future on g6 and a good one on f7.

17   h4?!

GM Olafsson overvalues his attacking prospects. Since at the moment Black's position is safe and sound, there is no reason to expect success from pawn storms. The effects of the text are two lost tempos and a weakened King position. All that is "achieved" is that Black's Bishop is forced to go where it wants to, anyway.

Extensive post-game analysis showed that correct is 17 g5! (trying to inhibit ...f6), with dynamic equality after 17...Nd7. Black then can follow up with 18...f6 and recapture with the Knight after 19 gxf6.

17	...	f6!
18	h5	Bf7
19	h6	e5
20	Qe2?!	

The opening of the game will be to Black's advantage, because it is White who has the fundamental weaknesses in the position. Necessary is 20 d5 g6 21 Na2!. Then after 21...Bd6 22 Rfd1 Na6 Black's advantage is a small one.

20	...	exd4!
21	Bxd4	

Perhaps White had overlooked that the zwischenzug 21 hxg7? is refuted by 21...Rd8.

21	...	Rd8

22   Be3

The resulting middlegame is very unpleasant for White because Black's forces will start to walk in on the weak squares. Therefore White's chances in the endgame resulting after 22 Bb6 Bc5+ 23 Bxc5 Qxc5+ 24 Qe3 Qxe3+ 25 Nxe3 g6 26 Rad1 Na6 bear investigation. Yet the holes on b3, b4 and c5 remain to torture White and no fully satisfactory continuation exists. For instance: 27 f4 Bb3 28 Rxd8+ Rxd8 29 g5 fxg5 30 fxg5 Nc5 31 Ng4 Ne6 when White's g-pawn goes lost for no compensation.

22   ...   g6
23   Bf4   Nd7

This is a more useful routing than 23...Na6 because the Knight can not only get to c5 but also the useful b6 and e5 squares. The attempt at interfering with Black's piece placement by playing 24 Bc7 Re8 25 Bg3 leaves the h-pawn in trouble after 25...Qf8.

24   Ne3   Ne5

Black's counterplay opportunities in the Slav come through loud and clear in this position: the advance of White a- , c- , d- and the Kingside pawns have left weak squares in their wake and with nothing to show for it.

25   Bg3   Qc5

The immediate threat is 26...Bc4 and White reacts to that without paying attention to his fundamental Kingside pawn weaknesses. White's best defensive chance is probably 26 Kh1, when Black can choose 26...Bxc3 or 26...Nd3—in either case with an advantage that is close to decisive.

26   Bf2?

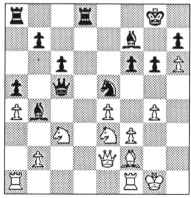

[diag. 88]

26   ...   Rd2!

Exploiting the weakness on f3—the kind of situation that Black was hoping for when essaying the 9...Bg4 10 f3 Bh5 11 g4 Bg6 sequence. Since 27 Qxd2 Nxf3+ is patently hopeless, White tries one last desperate attacking chance.

27   Ned5   Qd6!

Black wants to win material for nothing. Now 28 Qe3 cxd5 leaves White a piece down (29 f4 Nc4) and his position in shambles.

Because Black is so obviously winning, it seemed to me that White gets undeserved swindling chances after 27...Rxe2 28 Nxf6+ Kh8 29 Nxe2.

28   Bh4   Bxc3
29   Nxf6+   Kh8 White resigns

White is already a piece down with more damage to follow.

Queen's Gambit Declined, Tarrasch Defense

Game 24

White: Miguel Quinteros
Black: Larry Christiansen
Played at Cleveland International Tournament 1975

1	d4	Nf6
2	c4	e6
3	g3	d5
4	Nf3	

As of now we have the Catalan Opening and after 4...dxc4 or 4...Be7 it would continue to be so. However, Black decides on a strategically completely different approach ...

4	...	c5

Rather than preparing to smoothly defend d5 as in the Closed Variation of the Catalan or to make White lose some time in recapturing the pawn after ...dxc4, Black lashes out at White's center. At the moment Black's pawns have more central influence than White's. Of course, it would be too good to be true for Black to achieve this at no risk.

5	cxd5	

The only way to challenge Black's ambitions. If now 5...Nxd5, the opening most likely transposes into one of the variations of the Semi-Tarrasch. White can enter the Semi-Tarrasch by playing 6 Nc3 or can aim for more flexibility by delaying the immediate QN development in favor of first playing 6 Bg2 and 7 0-0.

5	...	exd5

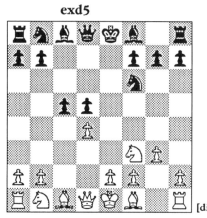

[diag. 89]

177

Thereby Black establishes the central pawn formation characteristic of the Tarrasch Defense to the QGD. The normal move order for reaching this position from the QGD would have been 1 d4 d5 2 c4 e6 3 Nf3 c5 4 cxd5 exd5 5 g3 Nf6. Speaking of move orders, the official move order for the Tarrasch Defense—as it appears in reference books and monographs on openings—is 1 d4 d5 2 c4 e6 3 Nc3 c5 4 cxd5 exd5 5 Nf3 Nc6. Then 6 g3 brings about the Rubinstein variation, which has been considered White's most effective method against the Tarrasch for well over seventy years. Please note that if White in our game now continues with 6 Nc3 and Black responds with the normal 6...Nc6, then by transposition the normal position of the Rubinstein variation against the Tarrasch Defense is reached. In this game White delays Nc3 until he has completed Kingside castling. This is a common occurrence in GM games when the Tarrasch Defense arises by transposition and if White has not played an early Nc3. There is no disadvantage in delaying Nc3 in this case and the advantage is increased flexibility for White if Black chooses something else rather than main line play.

What of the essence of the Tarrasch Defense, i.e. its characteristic pawn formation? As can be seen, Black will have more central pawn presence: White's d-pawn can be exchanged off for Black's c-pawn and then Black's d-pawn on the 4th rank will control more key space than White's e-pawn which will be either on the 2nd or 3rd rank. BUT, Black's d-pawn will be an isolated pawn and White's fianchettoed KB is ideally placed to bring pressure on it. The over-all strategic themes of the Tarrasch Defense are:

White will try to apply strong piece pressure on d5 to keep Black tied up because of the need for protecting his weakness.

Black will try to use the central influence of the d-pawn to fashion active minor piece play against White's position.

The "inventor" of the Tarrasch Defense is Dr. Siegbert Tarrasch (1862 - 1934), the famous German grandmaster, chess writer and theoretician. Always quite strong in his likes and dislikes, Dr. Tarrasch felt that his defense is the only correct method against the Queen's Gambit. He is quoted as saying: "The future will decide who has erred in estimating this defense—I or the chess world." In fact both sides can be considered to have been right. The Tarrasch Defense is fully playable, yet so are many other defenses against the Queen's Gambit and none of them lead to easy equality for Black. Among recent World Champions, Boris Spassky used the Tarrasch as his principal defense for part of the 1960s and Garry Kasparov gave it a successful fling in the early 1980s before his unhappy experiences with it in his 1984/85 Karpov match caused a change of mind.

6	Bg2	Nc6
7	0-0	Be7

Though it may appear that Black risks the loss of a tempo by playing an early ...Be7 (because White's dxc5 will "force" the Bishop to move again as it captures on c5), Black has nothing better. For instance, 7...Be6 8 Nc3 h6 9 b3 Rc8 10 Bb2 cxd4 11 Nxd4 Nxd4 12 Qxd4 Bc5 13 Qa4+ Rc6 14 e4! d4 15 Nd5, with a large advantage for White, G. Garcia - M. Chandler, Jurmala 1983.

Therefore Black should get on with completing his Kingside development.

8   Nc3   0-0

Now the main line position in the Tarrasch Defense has been reached. For well over 30 years this has been the starting point for international play, is so currently and I expect that it will continue to be so for the foreseeable future. The reason is straightforward: both sides have efficiently completed Kingside development and are ready for the dynamic play to come. Because Black's build-up has been perfectly executed, White cannot afford to tarry. White must immediately apply pressure on d5. There are only two ways to do this: the 9 dxc5 of this game and the 9 Bg5 of Games 25 and 26.

9   dxc5

[diag. 90]

An absolutely crystal clear plan: White exposes Black's d-pawn as an isolated pawn and will set about attacking it. Moreover, this is done in an effective way since the 9...Bxc5 recapture will have cost Black a tempo compared to e.g. 6 dxc5 or 7 dxc5. Black now has the choice of two radically different responses, though perhaps of approximately equal value:

(1) 9...d4—this pure gambit is the game continuation.

(2) 9...Bxc5 is the obvious response. After the expected 10 Bg5 Black again has two choices:

  (a) 10...Be6 11 Bxf6 Qxf6 12 Nxd5 Qxb2 13 Nc7 Rad8 14 Qc1 Qxc1 15 Raxc1 Bb6 16 Nxe6 fxe6 17 Rc4 h6 18 h4, L. B. Hansen - R. Antonio, Novi Sad Olympiad 1990. Though, according to theory, such endgames are only slightly superior for White, in real life the e6 weakness causes major practical problems for Black.

  (b) 10...d4 11 Bxf6 Qxf6 12 Nd5 Qd8 13 Nd2 Bh3 14 Bxh3 Qxd5 15 Qb3!?, V. Ivanchuk - S. Marjanovic, Erevan 1989. The endgame is slightly superior for White after 15...Qxb3 16 Nxb3 Bb6 17 Rfd1. Therefore GM Marjanovic chose the middlegame complications after 15...Qh5 16 Qxb7 Ne5 17 Qe4 Rae8 18 Kg2, yet these also were slightly in White's favor. Nevertheless, to me alternative (b) is much more attractive in a practical sense than alternative (a).

9 ...   d4

This pawn sacrifice is the way Dr. Tarrasch used to handle "his" defense. For the pawn Black gets space in the center, pressure on White's position and forces White to misplace his QN. Nevertheless, this variation is currently out of fashion in GM play. It is true that Black does not get quite full compensation for his pawn and therefore White retains a slight over-all edge. Yet it is equally true that in the 9...Bxc5 lines White also winds up with a slight edge. Therefore, on an objective "numerical" basis both continuations should be equally valued and therefore equally popular. However, the lack of popularity of 9...d4 can be explained by the approach that the present day GM uses in selecting his repertoire. Because Black's compensation is not quite sufficient, there is fear that in case of an inferior move, there will be no compensation remaining and that the player will be simply a pawn down. However, in a normally slightly inferior position, a "normally inferior" move will only lead to an increased inferiority, but still without permanent damage. Therefore in a practical game it is "safer" to play 9...Bxc5 than 9...d4 because the risk of "severe punishment" after an inferior move will be less.

This situation, however, only applies strictly to the perhaps top 200 - 500 players in the world. Everyone else will find that the gambit gives excellent chances for success without any undue increase in the risk of losing. Players who don't mind being a pawn down if they have some initiative to show for it will be comfortable on the Black side.

The strategic themes after 9...d4 are rather clear:
White needs to hold on to the extra pawn, complete the development

of his pieces to as active locations as possible, prevent Black's pieces from unduly encroaching White's position, and aim to lessen Black's pressure by exchanging pieces.

Black wants to use the forward d-pawn to cramp White's position and as a shield for active piece placement behind it. Black's natural arena will be the Kingside. Moreover, Black must be prepared to play the whole game down the sacrificed pawn.

10 Na4

The Knight sits awkwardly on the edge here, but the pawn must be protected. After 10 Nb5?! Bxc5 White will be lucky to hold equality.

10 ... Bf5

A perfect square: the Bishop watches the Kingside, the Queenside and the key d3 and e4 central squares.

11 a3?!

For a long time theory approved of this simple way of safeguarding the pawn: White will play 12 b4 and be materially secure. Yet it is inherently naive to underestimate the strength of Black's prospects. Good opening play demands good development. Because Black has gained more central space, White must develop his remaining pieces quickly and actively. Therefore correct is only 11 Bf4! Be4 (11...Ne4?! 12 b4! Nxb4 13 Nxd4) 12 Rc1! Qd5 13 Qb3!, giving Black the following choices:

(1) A middlegame after 13...Qh5?! requiring extremely accurate play by White. However, after 14 h3! Bd5 15 Qxb7 Ne4 16 g4! White can safeguard his material gain as follows: 16...Qg6 17 Nxd4! Rfe8 18 Nf5 h5 19 f3 hxg4 20 fxg4 Rad8 21 Rcd1, Petersons - Koblencs, USSR 1964. The three pawn advantage will be enough to win if White shows a modicum of care.

(2) The endgame after 13...Qxb3 14 axb3 Rad8. Black's compensation is not full, but White's material advantage is somewhat devalued by having a double pawn. Even with best play by White—as follows—15 Ne1! Bxg2 16 Kxg2! Nd7 17 Nd3 Rc8 18 Rfd1 b5! 19 cxb6 axb6, White's advantage is small (GM Kasparov).

11 ... Be4

Black thereby establishes his QB as the more active light square Bishop and prepares the coming Queen activation.

12 b4 Qd5

13   Nb2   b6!

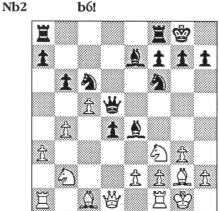

[diag. 91]

Fine play: Black lessens White's central influence (d6 square) and opens the a-file for pressure against White's Queenside. GM Christiansen was only 18 when this game was played but already possessed the exceptional feel for attacking prospects in an unbalanced position. Like Kasparov, GM Christiansen has never quibbled about a pawn. His mind is on greater things, i.e. the King.

14   cxb6   axb6
15   Bd2?!

Much too passive. The active 15 Bf4 is in order. It also has the specific point that Black's next move is prevented.

15   ...   Ne5!
16   Ne1   Bxg2
17   Nxg2   Rfd8!

Already Black has more than enough compensation for the pawn: he has strong control of the center and excellent attacking chances against White's Kingside which has become seriously weakened as a result of the exchange of the KB. In addition, White's only trump—the Queenside pawn majority formed by having the extra pawn—has been immobilized. Moreover, White's position is so passive that he can hardly undertake anything. In such situations poor moves come very easily.

18   Nf4   Qd7
19   Nfd3?

GM Christiansen considers the text to be the decisive error, because the KN will now be prevented from being an efficient helper to protect the Kingside, while the QN on b2 remains a spectator. He considers the immediate 19 f3 to be White's best, with Black retaining an edge after

19...b5! and a potential ...Nc4.

19	...	Ng6!

Of course, White would welcome a routine exchange of pieces. Black, on the other hand, needs to retain as much attacking material as possible.

20	f3	Nd5
21	Qb3?!	

White does not appreciate the danger from the coming attack. The Queen is needed on the Kingside rather than the Queenside. Therefore White should at this moment leave it home and play 21 Rf2 or 21 Nf2 followed by 22 Nbd3.

21	...	h5!

The start of the thematic attack against White's weakened Kingside. White does not come close to discovering a satisfactory defense and I doubt if one exists.

22	Kh1	Qe6
23	Rae1	h4
24	g4	h3!
25	g5	

White prevents the threatened 25...Bh4, but the Black Knight can make marvelous use of that square also. Moreover, the g-pawn is now an incurable weakness.

25	...	Nh4!
26	Rf2	Ng2!
27	Ra1	Qf5

[diag. 92]

While White is sentenced to trying to limit the coming damage, Black increases the pressure. Since 28 f4 Qe4 is hardly palatable, White decides to give up the g-pawn. Yet relief is quite temporary.

| 28 | Ne1 | Nde3 |
| 29 | Qd3 | Qxg5 |

The pawn sacrificed twenty moves ago has been recouped and the bind over White's position remains. There is no defense in 30 Nxg2 hxg2+ 31 Kg1 because 31...Bd6! threatens 32...Bxh2+! and 32 Bxe3 is also refuted by 32...Bxh2+! (33 Kxh2 dxe3). White therefore tries to get his QN into the game, but it is too little and too late.

| 30 | Qe4 | Qh4! |
| 31 | Nbd3 | |

Instead 31 Qxh4 Bxh4 leads to loss of the Exchange for White. What happens after the text is no better.

31	...	Qxe4!
32	fxe4	Nxe1
33	Nxe1	

Or 33 Rxe1 Bh4; or 33 Bxe1 Nc2.

| 33 | ... | Nc4 |
| 34 | Bf4 | |

Or 34 Nf3 Nxd2 35 Nxd2 Bxb4.

| 34 | ... | Bxb4 |

The pressure along the a-file as a result of the perceptive 13...b6! has won a pawn and with more damage to come.

| 35 | Nc2 | Bc3! |
| 36 | Rg1 | d3! |

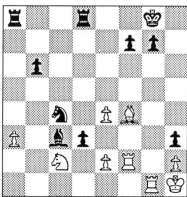

[diag. 93]

Enabling the KR to join the fray means that the end is near. In any case, forced now is 37 exd3. Instead White's try at tactics boomerangs immediately.

37	**Rf3?!**	**d2**
38	**Rd3**	**Rxd3**
39	**exd3**	**Nb2 White resigns**

After 40 Ne3 Bd4 41 Nd1 Bxg1 42 Nxb2 Bd4 43 Nd1 Rxa3 44 Bxd2 Ra1 White not only loses the Knight but gets mated too. Black won because he understood perfectly the strategic themes of the position after 9...d4, whereas White was oblivious of what he should be aiming for.

* * * * *

GAME 25

White: Edmar Mednis
Black: Nikola Padevsky
Played at Kragujevac (Yugoslavia) International Tournament 1977

1	**c4**	**c5**
2	**Nf3**	**Nf6**
3	**Nc3**	

The game has started as the Symmetrical Variation of the English Opening and Black can continue in that mode with 3...Nc6. He can also break the symmetry with 3...d5, with 3...g6 or with ...

3	**...**	**e6**

Another fully playable response without, however, putting yet the cards on the table.

4	**g3**	

White also keeps his options open. If White plays the immediate 4 d4, Black has the choice of staying in the English Opening with 4...cxd4 5 Nxd4 Nc6 or 5...Bb4, or going for the Tarrasch/Semi-Tarrasch complex with 4...d5.

4	**...**	**d5**

Announcing that Black is satisfied to transpose into the Queen's Gambit Declined, but as yet not disclosing his preference for which variation it is to be. The major independent alternative here is 4...b6, bringing about the Hedgehog Variation within the English Opening.

5	**cxd5**	

It is necessary for White to clear the center. After 5 Bg2?!, 5...d4 is unpleasant; after 5 d4?! cxd4 6 Nxd4 (6 Qxd4 Nc6), 6...e5 7 Nf3 d4 is annoying.

5   ...   exd5

It is to be the Tarrasch Defense, with both sides now quickly heading for the main line.

6	d4	Nc6
7	Bg2	Be7
8	0-0	0-0
9	Bg5	

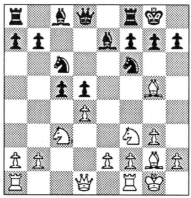

[diag. 94]

This continuation has been steadily gaining popularity and currently is by far White's preferred choice. The logic behind the move is impeccable: White develops the QB to an active square and the pressure on d5 increases the power of the coming dxc5 capture. The strategic themes at this moment are obvious:

White threatens 10 dxc5, aiming to win the d-pawn. White's follow-up plans will depend on how Black reacts to this threat.

Black must do something about this threat. The various approaches include attempted counterplay, direct protection, indirect protection and direct prevention.

The strategic themes will depend on which approach and specific continuation within it Black chooses. However, Black should never forget the inherent basis of the Tarrasch Defense: to obtain active piece play as compensation for the isolated d-pawn (or sacrificed c-pawn).

Of the various Black responses, the more significant ones are:

  (1) Attempted counterplay
    (a) 9...h6?! 10 Bxf6 Bxf6 11 dxc5 d4 (Or 11...Be6 12 Qd2 Na5
        13 Rad1 Nc4 14 Qc1 Rc8 15 b4, with White up a safe

pawn—Kasparov) 12 Ne4 Be7 13 Qd3, Vilela - Braga, Havana 1984. White is a pawn up.

(b) 9...Bg4?! 10 dxc5 d4 11 Bxf6! (In Bokor - Ostojic, Debrecen 1967, Black did not get sufficient compensation for the pawn after 11 Na4 Qd7 12 a3 h6 13 Bf4. Nevertheless, 11 Bxf6! is in White's interest: a piece is exchanged off, good squares are gained, the QN is not stuck on a4.) 11...Bxf6 and now both 12 Nb5 and 12 Ne4 are clearly in White's favor.

(c) 9...Bf5?!—see the game continuation.

(2) Directed protection with 9...Be6
This is considered a reputable line, yet as discussed in the note to White's 9th move in Game 24, after the normal sequence 10 dxc5 Bxc5 11 Bxf6 Qxf6 12 Nxd5 Qxb2 13 Nc7 Rad8 14 Qc1, both the theoretical and practical chances are all White's.

(3) Indirect protection with 9...b6
Black does not lose a pawn because after 10 dxc5 bxc5 11 Bxf6 Bxf6 12 Nxd5 he recovers it with 12...Bxb2. In the game E. Sveshikov - Filipenko, USSR 1978 White obtained an advantage after 13 Rb1 Rb8 14 Nd2 Ba6 15 Ne4 Qa5 16 Qc2, because of the vulnerability of Black's c-pawn.

(4) Direct prevention
(a) 9...c4 looks reasonable yet suffers from the fact that with the release of pressure on d4, White immediately gains central influence, while Black's central pawn structure remains vulnerable. White's best method is now considered to be 10 Ne5! Be6 11 Nxc6! bxc6 12 b3 Qa5 13 Na4 Rfd8 14 e3. If now 14...Rac8, Black has serious pawn weaknesses after 15 Bxf6 gxf6 (15...Bxf6 16 Nc5!) 16 bxc4 dxc4 17 Qc2, A. Yusupov - S. Lputjan, USSR 1979; if instead 14...c5, White gets a very strong Kingside attack with 15 Bxf6 gxf6 16 dxc5 Bxc5 17 Qh5, L. Polugaevsky - H. Pfleger, Buenos Aires Olympiad 1978.

(b) 9...cxd4 - see Game 26.

9 ...   Bf5?!

After the game the Bulgarian GM told me that he had played the text "a few times long ago." The problem with it is clear: it lacks a sound strategic basis. White is menacing Black's d5 and rather than pay attention to that, Black develops the QB to a routine square. The only meaningful point of the move is that after 10 dxc5?! d4 11 Na4, Black's QB is well placed whereas White's QB is on g5 rather than on the correct f4 square. Please note that by transposition we have entered the variation 9 dxc5 d4 10 Na4 Bf5 which is demonstrated in Game 24. Then the correct move is only 11 Bf4!, rather than 11 a3?! as played or any other move.

10   Rc1!

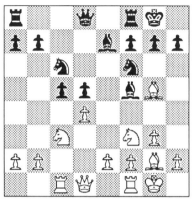

[diag. 95]

By increasing the pressure on c5 and being ready to protect White's c-pawn after the threatened dxc5, White trims the sails of Black's 9...Bf5. As a matter of fact, Black now must change his sails and play 10...c4, when White has a comfortable edge after 11 Ne5! Rc8 12 Bxf6 Bxf6 13 f4.

10   ...   h6?

This has invariably been Black's theoretical move, but Black's concept of the resulting position is just plain wrong. It is wrong because Black has not bothered to explore the differences between that position and that which occurs in the gambit line after 9 dxc5 d4 10 Na4 Bf5.

11   Bxf6   Bxf6
12   dxc5   d4
13   Nb5

To continue using the naval metaphors, it can be said that there is a sea change between this position and that after 9 dxc5 d4 10 Na4 Bf5. There White's QN was awkwardly and passively placed on the edge of the board; here the QN has a fantastic location on b5, both menacing d4 and being ready to jump to the wonderful d6 square. Moreover, Black has invested a whole tempo in playing 10...h6? to force White to have this joy. At the very best, Black has no compensation for the pawn. In truth he must be careful that things do not get worse.

13   ...   Be4

The first obvious point to be made is that the active 13...d3 is parried simply by 14 Nd6. The text is an attempted improvement over the 13...Qd7 of H. Donner - N. Padevsky, Beverwijk 1968. There Black got a satisfactory game after 14 Nd6 Be6 15 a3 a5 16 Ne1 a4 17 Nd3 Bb3 18 Qd2 Be7 19 Nc4 Rad8 20 Na5 Nxa5 21 Qxa5 Bg5 22 f4 Bf6. However, it is not difficult to suggest improvements for White. For instance 15 Qa4! Rab8 16 Ne1 Bg4 17 Rc2 led to a significant advantage in E. Lundin - H. Westerinen, Oslo 1971; as did 16 b3 Bd5 17 Rfe1 in M. Najdorf - D. Yanofsky, Groningen 1946. Best of all is probably the immediate 14 Qa4!—as in this game.

The strategic themes have been clarified and are:

White wants to make Black's advanced d-pawn harmless. The best way to ensure this is to activate White's pieces and keep them active. White's "dream" is to capture the d-pawn; however an exchange of the e-pawn for the d-pawn under favorable conditions will be sufficient for keeping a significant advantage.

Black needs to make use of the central space gained as a result of having the d-pawn in White's part of the board so as to apply strong pressure on White's position. The primary route for this is along the half-open e-file. (Note: We know that Black cannot achieve his aim if White plays correctly.)

14   Qa4!

I considered the obvious 14 Nd6 Bd5 15 Nxb7 Qb8 16 Nd6 Qxb2 17 Rc2 and concluded that it is favorable for White also. Yet I saw no reason to release the bind on Black's position. The text has multiple advantages: the Queen is actively placed, a Rfd1 is made possible, as is Nd6 followed by b4.

14   ...   Qe7
15   Rfe1!

[diag. 96]

A simple move of uncommon strength. Not only is the valuable e-pawn protected, but, moreover, White threatens the thematic 16 Nd6 Bd5 17 e4!, forcing the desirable 17...dxe3 18 Rxe3 exchange.

GM Padevsky is by nature a fast player, but the time he took on his previous move and the coming one—while chain smoking—assured me that he realized that he was in deep trouble.

15   ...   a6

After his long think, Black decides to go for a "cheapo," i.e. 16 Nbxd4?? Nxd4 17 Nxd4 Bxg2 18 Kxg2 (18 Nf5 Qe4) 18...Qe4+ wins a piece for Black. Yet from a thematic viewpoint, the text just chases the Knight where it wants to go. Though Black has no good moves, the best of the unsatisfactory bunch are probably 15...Rfd8 or 15...Bd5.

16   Nd6!   Bd5
17   Nxd4!!

White could, of course, ensure a large advantage with 17 e4!, having a fine position and a pawn plus. However, because of the active, harmonious placement of his pieces, White has a stronger, tactical possibility. No matter how Black responds, White is sure to come out with at least a two pawn advantage. The text marks the successful completion of White's strategic objective:: the elimination of Black's advanced d-pawn—and at no cost, to boot!

17   ...   Bxg2

After the significant alternative capture, 17...Nxd4, White wins as follows: 18 Bxd5 Nxe2+ 19 Kf1 Nxc1 20 Rxe7 Bxe7 21 Nxf7! Rxf7 (21...Bxc5 22 Qc4) 22 Qc4.

18   N4f5   Qe6
19   Kxg2   g6

In lost positions the only hope is counterplay. Routinely losing is 19...Bxb2 20 Rb1 Bc3 21 Rec1 Bf6 22 Rxb7, e.g. 22...Nd8 23 Rb6 Qxe2 24 c6.

20   Nxh6+   Kg7
21   Ng4   Bxb2
22   Rb1!

White's material advantage is more than enough to win and therefore it is important to keep his forces active. The passive 22 Rc2?! Bd4! would give Black some practical chances for resistance.

22   ...   Bd4
23   Rxb7   Bxc5

After 23...Qd5+ 24 e4 Qxc5, decisive is 25 Rc7.

24	Qxc6	Bxd6
25	Qf3	**Black resigns**

[diag. 97]

He is down two good pawns, has no compensation for that and is burdened by major Kingside weaknesses.

* * * * *

GAME 26

White: Laszlo Vadasz
Black: John Nunn
Played at Budapest International Tournament 1978

1	Nf3	d5
2	c4	

White's move order does prevent the "Reversed Sicilian" possible after 1 c4 e5, but the attempt to reach a desired English/Catalan variation is not without some risk. In other words, for White to play this move order he must be prepared to cope with the ambitious 2...d4. With perfect play, White can retain a slight advantage; otherwise he will very easily start suffering a spatial inferiority.

2	...	e6
3	g3	c5
4	Bg2	Nc6
5	0-0	Nf6

Here also 5...d4 is feasible. However, at that time the Tarrasch Defense was a regular part of GM Nunn's opening repertoire and thus he was quite content to continue classical development. White now chooses to turn the Reti/Catalan opening into the Queen's Gambit Declined.

6	cxd5	exd5
7	d4	Be7
8	Nc3	0-0
9	Bg5	cxd4
10	Nxd4	

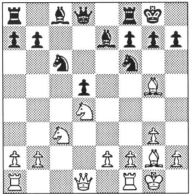

[diag. 98]

This is currently the main, main line of the Tarrasch Defense and I expect it to continue to be so for many years to come. Black prevents the threatened dxc5 by being the first to capture. White's recapture, 10 Nxd4, interferes with the Queen's pressure on d5 and makes the Knight vulnerable to an attack. These factors give Black the necessary time to smoothly safeguard his isolated pawn. On the other hand, White's KN is thereby activated and the diagonal of the KB opened. All in all, prospects are great for interesting, dynamic play.

10	...	h6

The text is an integral part of Black's modern approach. Chasing away the QB obviously significantly enhances the security of the d-pawn and it comes at no additional cost. (As remarked above, the "cost" of this method is the activation of White's KN and KB as a result of 9...cxd4.) It makes no particular sense for White to play 11 Bxf6 because after 11...Bxf6 12 Nb3 d4 13 Ne4 Be7 the space gained by the advanced d-pawn compensates for its isolated status. The important reference here is Y. Seirawan - G. Kasparov, Niksic 1983: 14 Rc1 Qb6 15 Nec5 Rd8 16 Rc4 Bxc5 17 Nxc5 Qxb2 18 Qc2 Qxc2 19 Rxc2 Rb8 when White should have recovered his pawn with 20 Nxb7 for equal chances (Kasparov). The immediate attempt at counterplay with 10...Qb6 is not quite satisfactory because of 11 Nxc6! bxc6 12 Na4! Qa5 13 Qc2 Be6 14 Rfc1 Rac8 15 Nc5! Bxc5 16 Qxc5 Qxc5 17 Rxc5 Ne4 18 Bxe4 dxe4 19 Kf1, L. Polugaevsky - Hasin, USSR Championship 1961. Black's structural pawn weaknesses (isolated a- and d-pawns) give White a pleasant endgame advantage. Please compare this sequence with the game continuation.

11   Be3

11 Bf4 is not bad, but the text is better. The key principle here is that in the play against the isolated d-pawn it is important to keep tight control of the square in front of the pawn so that it can't advance. 11 Be3 helps with this; 11 Bf4 does·not.

After the text we have indeed a classical isolated d-pawn position. For such positions the following strategic themes apply:

White needs to find a way to enhance the pressure on d5. For this the Queen will have to be developed and at least one Rook placed on the d-file.

Black needs to achieve active minor piece play in conjunction with pressure along the half-open e-file. Black's attacking prospects will be on the Kingside.

11   ...   Re8

A long period of experimentation has led to the clear conclusion that the text is Black's best move: the Rook is perfectly placed on the e-file and it is faultless to do so immediately. Because White has not yet indicated what force deployment he will choose, a decision in regard to an immediate minor piece development is premature. Thus, for instance, 11...Bg4 allows White to obtain an advantage as follows: 12 Qa4! Na5 13 Rad1 Nc4 14 Bc1 Qc8 15 Qb5! Nb6 16 Bf4 Bh3 (16...Rd8?! 17 Rc1! is very strong for White, G. Kasparov - S. Palatnik, USSR 1981) 17 Qd3 Bxg2 18 Kxg2 (Kasparov). As can be seen, Black's pieces are tied to the defense of the d-pawn, rather than ready for active play.

Despite extensive and intensive investigation, theoretical and practical, chess theory is far from resolving the question of what now is White's best move. Each of the following moves have their adherents: 12 a3, 12 Nb3, 12 Rc1, 12 Qc2, 12 Qb3 and 12 Qa4. Regarding the latter I want to add that Black's best response is considered to be 12...Bd7. Just such an example shows why the flexible 11...Re8 is now universally preferred over any other move. Because it is far from clear which is White's best approach of playing against the isolated d-pawn per se, I have chosen as the illustrative game the alternate method of handling isolated d-pawn positions.

12   Nxc6   bxc6

[diag. 99]

At first glance White's 12 Nxc6 may look insane: Black's d-pawn is isolated no more and Black's center is strengthened. Yet this method is recognized as one good way of playing against isolated d-pawn positions. Whether it is effective in a particular position depends of course on that specific situation. We already saw that it worked well against 10...Qb6. There White did have the significant plus that after 11 Nxc6 bxc6, 12 Na4 gained an important tempo.

The strategic themes now become:

For White, the new object to attack is the c-pawn. For ultimate success at least one Rook will have to be deployed along the c-file. To keep the c-pawn vulnerable, it is crucial to control the square in front of it. Therefore White wants to put his Knight or QB on c5. (Again, refer to the sequence after 10...Qb6.)

For Black, the over-all objective remains unchanged: to look for attacking chances on the Kingside, abetted by pressure along the e-file. Of the minor pieces, only White's KB is directly helpful in protecting its King. Therefore, one way of making White's Kingside more vulnerable to an attack is to exchange off the KB.

13 Qa4!?

An interesting maneuver: White wants to place the Queen on c2, without allowing ...c5, as could happen after 13 Qc2 c5. After the text, the c-pawn is under attack and 13...c5? loses to 14 Nxd5!. Unfortunately, the text also has a minus side: Black's QB is given a developmental tempo, even though it is to the modest d7 square.

Therefore, the following two logical alternatives are of significant importance in judging the merits of 12 Nxc6:

    (1) 13 Bd4. In Y. Razuvaev - J. Nunn, London 1983 the interesting course was: 13...Nh7!? 14 Na4 Ng5 15 Rc1 Ne6! 16 Rxc6 (16 Be3!?) 16...Bd7 17 Rc1 Nxd4 18 Qxd4 Bf6 19 Qd1

Rb8 20 b3 Bxa4 21 bxa4 d4 when Black's secure d4 pawn is full compensation for White's extra doubled a-pawn.

(2) 13 Na4 Qa5 (ECO D, Revised calls the position after 13...Bd7 14 Qc2 Qc8 15 Rfd1 Bh3 equal. This seems questionable since Black is a whole tempo behind our game continuation and White can exploit this with the immediate 16 Rac1.) 14 Rc1 Bg4 15 b3 Qa6, with equality, N. Kelecevic - G. Makropoulos, Pernik 1981. As an improvement for White, the immediate 14 b3 makes sense, to be able to respond to 14...Bg4 with 15 h3.

13	...	Bd7
14	Qc2	Qc8
15	Rfd1	Bh3

Black's previous move clearly prepared the activation of the QB, but where should Black want to have White's Queen when he plays ...Bh3? During the game GM Nunn considered the zwischenzug 15...Bf5 so that after 16 Qa4 the a4 square is not accessible to the Knight and then 16...Bh3. Obviously 17 Bxh3?! Qxh3 18 Qxc6? is bad because of 18...Ng4.

Instead of 16...Bh3, GM Kasparov in ECO D considers Black's best line to be 16...Qb7 17 Bd4 Red8 and calls this position "equal." It seems to me, however, that after 18 Rac1 or 18 Rd2 White still has some pull.

16 Bh1?

An instructive strategic error. Such a method of retaining the fianchettoed Bishop is often used, if the Bishop has valuable scope along its h1 - a8 diagonal. But that is not the situation here because 12 Nxc6 has strengthened Black's d-pawn, leaving the KB with little to do. Even from a defensive standpoint the KB's role is modest, with Black's QB as an attacker much superior to White's KB as a defender. If White did want to retain the KB, then the proper method was 16 Bf3 and after 16...Bg4, 17 Bh1. At least, White then is a full tempo ahead of the game continuation.

White's correct plan was the strategically consistent one: to apply pressure on the c-pawn and dominate the important c5 square. Therefore 16 Na4! is in order, after which GM Nunn was planning 16...Qe6 and rated this position as slightly superior for White.

16 ... Ng4!

Given his chance, GM Nunn exploits Black's potential with vigorous energy and wonderfully creative tactics. As will be seen, a major tactical feature is White's back rank weakness as a result of the power of the QB on h3.

17	Bd2	Qe6
18	Be1	Rad8!

So that the coming attack can have maximum effect, Black first mobilizes all of his forces. The immediate 18...Qf6 (threatening 19...Ne3) can be parried by 19 Qd3 followed by 20 Qf3, with approximate equality.

19   e4!

White correctly starts some activity as otherwise he risks being smothered alive. For instance, 19 Bg2?! Bxg2 20 Kxg2 d4 when Black will have very strong pressure along the e-file.

19   ...   Qf6!

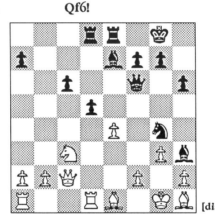

[diag. 100]

With a tactical threat which White overlooks. Necessary now is 20 Bg2!, with White only slightly worse.

20   exd5?

Did White really think that Black had left hanging a valuable center pawn?

20   ...   Ne3!!

The rude awakening. The Knight is poisoned (21 fxe3?? Qf1 Mate)— a clear consequence of White's 16th move—and Black wins the Exchange for a pawn.

21	Qa4	Nxd1
22	Rxd1	cxd5
23	Nxd5	Qe6

Materially White is not badly off, having a pawn for the Exchange and retaining a healthy pawn formation. If White could consolidate his King position, his chances for a draw are excellent. Therefore Black must aggressively exploit his initiative. GM Nunn's execution of this is exemplary.

24   Ba5?!

24 Nc7? loses immediately to 24...Qe2; after 24 Nf4 strong is 24...Qg4. Perhaps the best defensive chance is 24 Nxe7+ Qxe7 25 Bc3.

24   ...   Bc5!
25   Qc2

Of course, 25 Bxd8? allows mate starting with 25...Qe1+!, while 25 Qc4? is met by 25...Bxf2+! 26 Kxf2 Rxd5! with any capture on d5 allowing 27...Qe3 Mate.

25   ...   Bb6!
26   Nxb6

Again, if the QB doesn't guard the e1 square (i.e. after 26 Bxb6?), Black mates starting with 26...Qe1+. After 26 Bc3, the prosaic 26...Qe2! spells curtains for White.

26   ...   Qf5!!

One more tactical shot involving back rank mate motifs.

27   Rxd8

A last try. If now the careless 27...Qxc2?? it is White who wins after 28 Rxe8+ Kh7 29 Be4+.

27   ...   Rxd8   White resigns

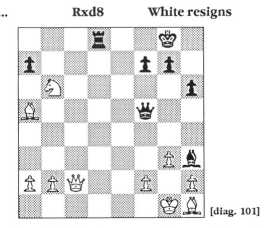

[diag. 101]

This final position definitely deserves a diagram. The only way to prevent immediate disaster is 28 Qc1 Qxa5 29 Nc4, but after 29...Rc8 30 b3 Qxa2 White's position is hopeless.

Queen's Indian Defense
Game 27

White: Tigran Petrosian
Black: Viktor Korchnoi
Played at 1977 Quarter-Final Candidates Match, Il Ciocco, Italy,
Game 12

1	d4	Nf6
2	c4	e6
3	Nf3	

GM Petrosian was one point behind and this was scheduled to be the last game. Thus to level the match he needed a win here. Nevertheless he remains true to his opening repertoire and avoids the sharper 3 Nc3 because of his dislike for facing the Nimzo-Indian Defense.

3	...	b6

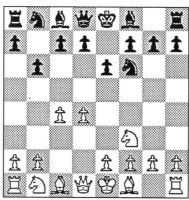

[diag. 102]

GM Korchnoi selects the Queen's Indian Defense (QID). Other good alternatives are the Bogo-Indian (3...Bb4+), Queen's Gambit Declined (3...d5) and the invitation to the Benoni Defense with 3...c5.

The central objective of the QID is the same as for the Nimzo-Indian: control of e4. The approach is also the same: piece pressure, rather than the ...d5 pawn advance of the QGD. Black's aim is to have sufficient central influence but without the symmetrical tendencies of the Orthodox variations of the QGD. He thereby aims to increase his winning prospects and hopes that by avoiding any structural deficiencies the risk of a loss is also minimized.

The general strategic themes for both sides are:

White will aim to assume control of e4. In particular if White gets in the pawn advance e4—without allowing Black concessions—White can expect a substantial central superiority, because the basic theme behind the QID will have been negated. As a secondary point, White will be on the look-out to see whether Black's ...c5 advance can be profitably countered by d5, giving White a large spatial advantage, while deadening Black's QB.

Black has two needs:

(1) Retain control of e4 as long as is reasonable to do so.
(2) Challenge White's superior center as soon as it is safe to do. From Diagram 102 we can see that White has two pawns on the fourth rank while Black has none. To have sufficient central influence Black will have to get at least one pawn to the fourth rank. In most cases, ...c5 is the thematic advance, while some variations call for both ...c5 and ...d5, and a few for just ...d5.

4   e3

The start of what I have called the "Quiet Line" and long a part of GM Petrosian's repertoire. It is an unassuming yet healthy system. White will complete the development of his Kingside with Bd3 and 0-0 and then develop the Queenside. Since White plans to fianchetto the QB, the text move does not inherently lock it in. Once White's development is complete, he expects that his slight central superiority will lead to some initiative in the middlegame. Because White's Bishops (KB on d3, QB on b2) will be pointed in the direction of Black's Kingside, that is where White's opportunities in the majority of cases will be.

Other sound moves are 4 a3, 4 Nc3 ("risking" the Nimzo-Indian after 4...Bb4), 4 Bg5, 4 Bf4 and 4 g3, which is the most popular one. This is presented in Games 28 and 29.

4   ...   Bb7
5   Bd3

Black has a choice of sound approaches to select from: he can imitate White by first playing 5...Be7 or can immediately make his decision for central influence and play 5...c5 or 5...d5.

There is a fourth possibility, a more dynamic and challenging one, and it is hardly surprising that the Great Fighter selects this one. (It also has appeared in GM Petrosian's games with Black.)

5   ...   Bb4+!?

This check has a number of things in its favor. By developing with a threat, Black gains time for quick castling and also indirectly reinforces his control of e4. Moreover, it forces White to abandon any hopes for straightforward play. GM Petrosian's exceptional strength has been a deep understanding of strategic positions and now he has to juggle a number of dynamic considerations instead of being able to select the best way of heading in the known direction.

Though White has three valid ways of covering the check, only one has independent importance for the QID. The other two are:

(1) 6 Nc3 transposes into the Nimzo-Indian Defense and is exactly the variation appearing in Game 16.

(2) 6 Bd2 is sound but harmless. After 6...Bxd2+ 7 Qxd2 (Or 7 Nbxd2 d6 8 0-0 Nbd7 9 Qc2 0-0 10 Rad1 Qe7, with approximate equality in F. Samisch - A. Alekhine, Dresden 1926. There is nothing in 11 e4 because of 11...e5 when Black has a satisfactory position from the Bogo-Indian.) 7...d6 8 Nc3 Nbd7 9 Qc2 0-0 10 0-0 Qe7 11 Ng5 (Again, 11 e4 e5 12 d5 leads to nothing after 12...a5 followed by 13...Nc5) 11...h6 12 Nge4 c5! (Voronkov), Black has sufficient central influence, faultless development and equal chances.

6   Nbd2   c5!?

The only consistent follow-up to 5...Bb4+. After the routine 6...0-0 7 0-0 Black is playing a normal position where the Bb4 risks being misplaced. There is even less strategic basis to 6...Ne4?!, because after 7 0-0 f5 8 Qc2 Bxd2 9 Nxd2 Qh4 10 f3 Nxd2 11 Bxd2 0-0 12 b4!, T. Petrosian - M. Taimanov, USSR Championship 1951, White has at no cost gained substantial space on the Queenside and center. When added to two potentially active Bishops, this gives White a clear strategic advantage. Please compare this position to the related one from the Nimzo-Indian Defense: 1 d4 Nf6 2 c4 e6 3 Nc3 Bb4 4 e3 b6 5 Bd3 Bb7 6 Nf3 Ne4 7 Qc2 f5 8 0-0 Bxc3 9 bxc3 0-0 10 Nd2 Qh4 11 f3 Nxd2 12 Bxd2. Here White is handicapped by having doubled c-pawns and also as a consequence of that, an isolated a-pawn. Black therefore is fully equal—see Game 16 for additional discussion.

7   dxc5

This simple capture entails making a major decision because White is decreasing his central superiority. If Black recaptures with the Bishop, White's d-pawn has been exchanged for the c-pawn; if Black recaptures with the b-pawn, then the d-pawn has been exchanged for Black's b-pawn. For such an exchange to be effective, White must get compensation elsewhere.

I believe that White does best with the immediate 7 a3! Bxd2+ 8 Bxd2. Black has no way of taking advantage of White's loss of time, e.g. 8...Ne4?! is answered by 9 Bxe4! Bxe4 10 Bc3, forcing the undesirable

10...f6 (10...0-0?! allows 11 dxc5 bxc5 12 Qd6!). Then White gains a strong initiative after 11 Nd2! Bg6 12 dxc5 bxc5 13 h4! h5 14 Qf3 Nc6 15 Ne4 Qe7 16 Rd1 0-0 17 Nd6, A. Petrosian - A. Chernin, Palma de Mallorca 1989. Therefore Black has to satisfy himself with normal, though modest development, e.g. 8...d6 9 Bc3 Nbd7 10 0-0 0-0. After 11 Nd2 cxd4 12 Bxd4 (12 exd4?! d5 allows Black ready equality.) 12...Nc5 (Now after 12...d5?! 13 cxd5 White's Bishops will be a terror against Black's Kingside.) 13 Bc2 e5 14 Bc3 a5 15 f3 Qc7 16 Rc1 Rfd8 17 Qe1, L. Portisch - U. Andersson, Turin 1982, White has a bit more space and the two Bishop potential and thereby a slight advantage.

7 ... **Bxc5**

[diag. 103]

Forced, since after 7...bxc5?! 8 0-0, followed by 9 Nb3 Black's KB will be out on a limb. However, in positions where the KB has been developed to e7, the recapture with the b-pawn is a valid alternative.

Our diagram shows a strategically unbalanced dynamic situation. At the moment the three developed Black minor pieces are placed considerably more actively than White's three developed minor pieces. On the other hand, only White has a centrally important pawn on the fourth rank and once White completes the development of the QB after a3, b4 (or b3), Bb2, he will have some spatial advantage and good central development of his minor pieces. Moreover, his Bishops will be well trained on Black's Kingside.

The above considerations lead to the following important strategic themes:

White wants to quickly develop his QB so as to negate the potential of the currently more active Black minor pieces. Because Black's minor pieces are generally pointed in the direction of White's Kingside, White should ensure that Black cannot develop attacking prospects there.

Black must try to take advantage of his active minor pieces to apply pressure against White's Kingside. If Black cannot exploit his slight potential for initiative, he will feel somewhat uncomfortable once White completes his minor piece development.

8   0-0?!

The "automatic" text shows that White has not appreciated the sophisticated thinking behind 6...c5!? and apparently expects the routine 8...0-0 in response. Then by transposition of moves the position possible after the routine 6...0-0 would have arisen: 7 0-0 c5 8 dxc5 Bxc5.

The immediate castling not only slows down White's high priority development of the QB but actually makes White's King more vulnerable. White's most perceptive move order is, I believe, 8 a3 a5 (8...Nc6 9 b4) 9 b3 Nc6 10 Bb2 and only after 10...0-0, 11 0-0. The kind of position White should be aiming for is shown by the course of the following "old" game: 8 Qc2 0-0 9 0-0 Nc6 10 a3 Rc8 11 b4 Be7 12 Bb2 h6 13 Qb3! Qc7 14 h3 d6 15 Rac1, V. Smyslov - W. Unzicker, Baden-Baden 1957. White's Kingside is secure, he has more space and two Bishops on open diagonals and therefore a normal opening advantage.

8   ...   Nc6!

In conjunction with the next move, GM Korchnoi demonstrates a new, purposeful execution of Black's strategic theme: make maximum use of the active piece development to start menacing White's King. By avoiding the routine Kingside castling, Black not only saves one tempo but also enables Black's h-pawn and KR to become participants in the attack. In addition, since White's pieces are more suited to menace Black's Kingside than Black's center, Black's uncastled King is perfectly secure.

It is noteworthy to add that even though GM Korchnoi only needed a draw, all along he selected the plan required by the position. As will be seen, most of the time this plan required the sharpest and therefore apparently most dangerous play.

9   a3   Qc7!
10   b3

After 25 minutes reflection White pulls back from the active 10 b4, because after 10...Bd6 11 Bb2 a5!, Black gains permanent control over the important c5 square. Moreover, if White aims for exchanges with 11 Ne4? Nxe4 12 Bxe4, 12...f5! 13 Bd3 Ne5! leaves him busted. Yet even after the safer text, GM Korchnoi fashions a powerful attack.

10   ...   Ne5!
11   Nxe5?!

White underestimates Black's initiative. The careful 11 Be2 was in order.

11	...	Qxe5
12	Ra2	Bd6!

Forcing White to weaken his Kingside and, in combination with the next move, allowing Black to effectively reposition his pieces so that they don't get in each other's way. Up to here GM Korchnoi had used 50 minutes (time limit was 40 moves in 2.5 hours) to decide on his near term game plan. With the major decision made—to attack White's Kingside —he played the next part fairly quickly. The clear benefit of playing in accordance with the strategic theme of the position is that the flow of the moves comes much more readily.

13	g3	Qc5
14	e4?!	

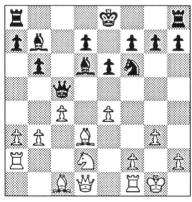

[diag. 104]

GM Petrosian is normally the consummate defender, with the exquisite ability to pick up the whiff of the slightest breeze thousands of miles away. But in this game his antenna has been turned off. Though the goal of closing the diagonal of Black's QB is of course sensible, the text is not the way to do so because of the major disadvantage involved: the e-pawn now becomes vulnerable to Black's QB, access to f2 is freed and the key d4 square permanently weakened. On a normal day GM Petrosian would have instinctively chosen the correct 14 Be2! followed by 15 Bf3.

14	...	h5!
15	b4	Qc7
16	Re1	h4
17	Nf1	hxg3
18	hxg3	a5!

Note how well Black is playing the whole board. After he has loosened up White's Kingside, he proceeds to do the same to White's Queenside. Because White's development is backward and passive, Black has no need to worry about leaving his King in the center. Even though it is White who needs a win, he is stuck in a defensive crouch with no recognizable winning prospects. Such a fate can easily befall those who select a centrally disadvantageous course, i.e. 7 dxc5, without appreciating the strategic themes involved.

19   Rb2

The only way to protect b4, though at the cost of giving up the a-file. The alternative, 19 b5, is hardly palatable since c5 goes totally into Black's possession and White's c-pawn becomes a vulnerable backward pawn.

19	...	axb4
20	axb4	Be5

At the half-way point of the first session, Black can look forward with confidence to the future: his position is excellent and he is also well ahead on time, having used 1 hr. 7 minutes to White's 1 hr. 31 minutes.

21	Rc2	Ra1
22	Qe2	Qb8

The Queen is on the way to a8 from where it will help control the a-file and apply pressure on the e-pawn. White's position is already inferior enough that trouble can come quickly, e.g. 23 Nd2? is refuted by 22...Bxg3! and 23 Bb2? is bad because of 23...Bxb2 24 Rxb2 Rxe1 25 Qxe1 Qe5! 26 Qe2 Ng4! followed by 27...Qh5 (GM Marjanovic).

23   Kg2?!

Walking voluntarily into a nasty pin can hardly be recommended. The sensible defensive plan is 23 Bd2, when 23...Rxe1 24 Bxe1 Qa8 leads to nothing after 25 Ra2. Black should therefore keep up the pressure with 23...Ra3.

23	...	Qa8
24	Nd2	Ra4!
25	b5	Kf8

[diag. 105]

Black's fine 24th move has succeeded in immobilizing White's Queenside pawns, while also establishing control of c5. Black also has control of both Rook files and pressure against the e-pawn. Even though Black does not need a win, he does have to move. Therefore the practical question becomes: what next? The text, played after 9 minutes of thought, is something like a "pass."

26 Nf3   Bd6
27 Ng5

Not an attacking move as such, but a way of protecting the e-pawn without blocking off the QB, as happens with the Knight on d2. Of course, the pincer 27 e5?? self-destructs White after both 27...Bxe5 and 27...Bxf3+ 28 Qxf3 Rh2+.

27 ...   Bc5
28 Bb2   Ke7
29 Rcc1   Ba3!

The exchange of the dark square Bishops will give Black increased control of those squares. It is already apparent that as far as the light square Bishops are concerned, it is Black who has the superior one.

30 Ra1   Bxb2
31 Qxb2   Rxa1
32 Rxa1

After 32 Qxa1 Black can ensure a match victory by selecting the riskless, slightly superior endgame after 32...Qxa1 33 Rxa1 Ra8. After the text Black retains a pleasantly superior middlegame: control of dark squares, superior Bishop and good attacking chances against White's King. GM Korchnoi also has a very comfortable time situation, having 30 minutes left to GM Petrosian's 10 minutes.

32 ...   Qb8

33   Qd4?!

White used up eight of his remaining ten minutes for this useless move and from now on was in severe time trouble. White has no constructive plan available; still 33 Qa3+ d6 34 f4 is a better bet.

33   ...   e5!
34   Qc3

Of course, White drops the Queen after 34 Qxb6?? Bxe4+, while 34 Qe3 Rh2+! 35 Kg1 Qh8 36 Qf3 Rh5! 37 Ra7 Qb8! also is untenable.

34   ...   Rh5
35   Qb4+   d6
36   Qd2

By forcing ...d6, White has given himself the opportunity that a possible Ra7 will mean an attack on a pinned Bishop.

36   ...   g6

A most annoying move to face in time pressure: Black overprotects his Rook and forces White to come up with a move that does not make matters worse.

37   Be2?

Black's "strategy" brings immediate results. For drawing chances, 37 Rh1 is the best hope; for "winning" prospects 37 Ra2 or 37 Rd1 make some sense.

37   ...   Nxe4

Thank you.

38   Nxe4   Bxe4+
39   f3   Bb7
40   g4   Rh7 Draw

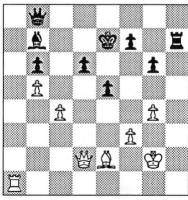

[diag. 106]

White is a pawn down in a miserable, lost position. Yet, as Black needs only a draw to advance to the Semi-Finals, a draw offer is not only the gentlemanly but also the practical thing to do.

* * * * *

Game 28

White: Lev Polugaevsky
Black: Viktor Korchnoi
Played at 1977 Semi-Final Candidates Match, Evian, France, Game 2

1	d4	Nf6
2	c4	e6
3	Nf3	b6
4	g3	

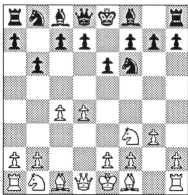

[diag. 107]

White's most principled and popular variation: first he will aim to neutralize Black's fianchettoed Bishop by the counter-fianchetto of his own light square Bishop and then will look for a way to start the fight for the key e4 square. At some time the exchange of Bishops could be in White's interest since this would tend to decrease Black's control over e4. Also the fianchettoed KB will be in position to indirectly prepare the possible d5 and e4 advances.

4	...	Bb7

Obvious, normal, logical, perfect ... and yet over the past several years the eccentric appearing QB development to a6 has become equally popular. This is presented in Game 29.

5 Bg2   Be7

Because the QID is inherently a conservative opening, the conservative text—preparing castling—is Black's usual choice. However, similarly to Game 27, 5...Bb4+ is playable and is being played. Now, unlike Game 27, White's best move is 6 Bd2 and after 6...Bxd2+ 7 Qxd2! 0-0 8 Nc3 d6 9 Qc2! c5 10 0-0 cxd4 11 Nxd4 Bxg2 12 Kxg2 Qc8 13 b3 Nc6 14 Rfd1, L. Portisch - U. Andersson, Indonesia 1983, White's spatial advantage and more active development gave him a slight edge.

Black is not sufficiently developed to yet afford either one of the full central pawn advances:

(1) 5...d5?! 6 0-0 Be7 7 Nc3 0-0 8 Ne5! leads to a favorable variation of the Catalan for White, because now it is White's fianchettoed Bishop which has more scope than its Black counterpart.

(2) 5...c5?! runs into tactical trouble after 6 d5! exd5 7 Nh4 when White will recapture on d5 with advantage. For example: 7...b5!? 8 cxd5 d6 9 0-0 g6 10 a4 b4 11 Nd2 Bg7 12 Nc4 Ba6 13 Qc2 0-0 14 a5 Bxc4 15 Qxc4 Nbd7 16 Nf3 Re8 17 Nd2 Qe7 18 e4, I. Novikov - V. Gavrikov, Lvov 1987 when Black has no compensation for the light square weaknesses on the Queenside nor for White's central superiority. White's advantage is larger than in the main lines of the QID.

6   0-0

Because the variation at hand is strictly a strategic, slow moving one, early castling by both sides is considered to be both most flexible and faultless. White can try to sharpen play with the immediate 6 Nc3 so that after 6...0-0 7 Qc2, the threat is 8 e4. The complications that result after 7...c5! 8 d5! exd5 9 Ng5 probably lead to dynamically equal chances after 9...h6! 10 Nxd5 Bxd5, whether White recaptures with the c-pawn or Bishop.

Of course, White can sidestep the above complications by responding to 6...0-0 with 7 0-0; Black can prevent them with the immediate 6...Ne4 when 7 Qc2 Nxc3 8 Qxc3 will transpose to our game and 7 Bd2 to the variation discussed after move 8.

6   ...   0-0
7   Nc3

This normal developing move also helps to prepare the potential d5 and e4 advances. White does have an extremely sharp alternative, 7 d5!?, called the Pomar Variation, after Spanish GM Arturo Pomar. The tactical point is to open up White's KB diagonal after 7...exd5 with 8 Nh4. Polugaevsky resurrected it successfully in his next match against

Korchnoi, at Buenos Aires 1980. If Black's play is inexact, White can indeed generate a very dangerous initiative. However, Black's position at the moment is faultless and the passage of time has allowed sufficient defenses to be discovered. The following method has the currently highest reputation: 8...c6 9 cxd5 cxd5! 10 Nc3 Na6 11 Nf5 Nc7 12 Bf4 Re8! 13 Bd6 Bf8 14 Qb3 Bc6 15 Bxf8 Rxf8 16 Rad1 Re8 17 Rfe1 Re5, with equality and a draw agreed in O. Romanishin - Y. Razuvaev, Jurmala 1987.

7   ...   Ne4

[diag. 108]

The text is the accepted method of preventing White from enlarging his central influence. In response, 8 d5?! is ineffective because White winds up with weak doubled pawns after 8...Nxc3 9 bxc3. Again, the direct 7...d5 transposes into an uncomfortable-for-Black Catalan after 8 Ne5!—as I alluded to earlier. The other central advance, 7...c5?!, is significantly worse, because then 8 d5! negates all of Black's objectives in playing the QID, while ensuring a large spatial and central superiority for White.

8   Qc2

The traditional, main line continuation: the Queen controls e4 and prevents the creation of doubled c-pawns. Yet there also is a slight strategic deficiency: after the expected 8...Nxc3 9 Qxc3 sequence, e4 remains safely in Black's hands and because c3 is an awkward square for the Queen, it will cost a tempo to reposition it.

It is for these reasons that two other continuations have been gaining reputation over the past 15 years:

   (1) 8 Nxe4 Bxe4 9 Ne1 Bxg2 10 Nxg2 has eliminated Black's control of e4, but at the cost of allowing two sets of minor pieces to be exchanged. This means that the importance of

White's remaining central superiority has been decreased. Still, White's prospects for a continuing advantage can not be underestimated. (My book "From The Opening Into The Endgame" explores this variation at length.) Black must be resolute in challenging White's center. A model example of this is U. Andersson - L. Polugaevsky, Haninge 1990: 10...d5! 11 Qa4 c5! 12 Be3 cxd4 13 Bxd4 dxc4 14 Qxc4 Qc8 15 Rac1 Na6 16 Nf4, when instead of 16...Qxc4 17 Rxc4 (White went on to win this slightly superior endgame), GM Polugaevsky recommends the more active 16...Rd8! 17 Be3 Qb7!, with approximate equality.

(2) 8 Bd2 only looks paradoxical. In fact both of Black's immediate captures work out poorly: (a) 8...Nxc3 9 Bxc3 has greatly helped White's minor piece development while leaving Black with the unresolved question of how to bring his QN into the game, and (b) 8...Nxd2?! 9 Qxd2 has caused Black to lose control over e4 while, again, furthering White's development. The gain of the Bishop pair is no compensation because in the resulting centrally inferior situation the Bishops will have little scope.

The correct approach for Black is to take advantage of the inherently passive location of the Bd2 to start active central play. A well regarded method is 8...Bf6! 9 Rc1 c5! 10 d5 exd5 11 cxd5 Nxd2 12 Nxd2 d6 13 Nde4 Be5! 14 Qd2 Ba6! 15 Rfe1 g6, J. Brenninkmeijer - J. van der Wiel, Holland 1991. Here the position is sufficiently open so that Black's Bishops are good compensation for White's greater space and central potential.

| 8 | ... | Nxc3 |
| 9 | Qxc3 | |

For the benefit of those not familiar with this variation, it is worth pointing out that the tactical 9 Ng5?? fails to 9...Nxe2+ 10 Kh1 Bxg2+. Nor is the strengthening of the center with 9 bxc3?! promising, since here the doubled pawns are more of a weakness than strength. After 9...Nc6! 10 Nd2 Na5! 11 Bxb7 Nxb7 12 e4 c6 followed by 13...d5 Black has sound equality (GM Matanovic).

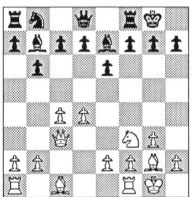

[diag. 109]

The strategic themes and needs for each side have become clear and are as follows:

White's first order of business is to develop his QB. Then White should aim to increase his central space by aiming for the e4 and/or d5 advances. In most instances the help of Rooks will be required, with the most frequent placement as follows: QR on d1, KR on e1. However, bearing in mind that the existing central superiority is on the left side of the board, if the anticipated line opening will be on the Queenside, then the Rook placement will be: QR on c1, KR on d1.

White's most likely sphere of activity will be along the d-file, with pressure to be extended on the Queenside.

Black's first need is to decide which pawn he will use to make his central stand: c-, d-, or f-pawn. If Black plays ...c5 or ...d5, his sphere of activity will be the center/Queenside; after ...f5 his prospects will be on the Kingside. Once this decision is made, then Black wants to develop his QN as quickly as possible.

9 ... f5

The text is Black's most unbalancing approach. He overprotects e4 and enables the active posting of the KB on f6. The demerits are also clear: the development of the QN (and thereby also the QR) is delayed and a potential weakness on e6 created.

The two strategically safer alternatives are:

   (1) 9...Be4 prepares to follow up with ...d5, when the QB would be outside the pawn chain, rather than inside, as after the immediate 9...d5?!. To hope for an advantage White needs to aggressively apply pressure along the c-file: 10 Bf4! c6 11 Rfd1 d5 12 cxd5 Qxd5 13 Ne1 Bxg2 14 Nxg2 Rc8 15 Ne3 Qd8 16 Nc4 Nd7 17 e4 b5, so far J. Smejkal - J. Ambroz, Czech Championship 1978, when instead of the passive 18 Nd2?!,

White could have retained a slight edge with 18 Ne5!.
(2) 9...c5 is Black's highest rated method in going for a draw. In what seem like "countless" games between GMs Andersson and Karpov, that has been the result. Of course, not everybody can handle slightly inferior positions as well as Anatoly Karpov. A typical case of such care is the game U. Andersson - A. Karpov, London 1982: 10 Rd1 d6 11 b3 Bf6 12 Bb2 Qc7 13 Qd2 Rd8 14 dxc5 dxc5 15 Qf4 Na6 16 Qxc7 Nxc7 17 Bxf6 gxf6 18 Nd2 Bxg2 19 Kxg2 Kf8 20 Ne4 Ke7 21 Nc3 Na6 22 Rxd8 Rxd8 23 Rd1! Rg8! (Black's weakened Kingside can become a problem in a pure Knight endgame. Keeping Rooks on cuts down on potential activity by White's King.) 24 Kf3 h5 25 e3 Nb4 26 h4 Draw.

10   b3

Simple and good. However, Black does have more immediate problems to solve after the ambitious 10 d5!?, with the idea 10...exd5 11 Ne1. In J. Timman - J. Ehlvest, Linares 1991 White gained a clear advantage after 11...d4 12 Qxd4 Bxg2 13 Nxg2 Rf7 14 Be3 Nc6 15 Qd5 Bf6 16 Rab1! Ne7 17 Qd3 d6 18 Rfd1 Qc8 19 b4. Black has permanent weaknesses on d5, e6, f5 and no compensation anywhere. Instead of 13...Rf7, GM Timman suggests 13...Nc6 and 13...Kh8 as possible improvements, but I don't see how these mitigate the structural problems in Black's position.

I think that Black has to recognize that in the QID modest goals should be the early aim. Therefore the developmental/defensive 10...Bf6 11 Qc2 Na6 12 Rd1 Qe7 13 Nd4 Nc5 makes sense. In N. Krogius - R. Holmov, USSR Championship 1965, Black was very close to equality after 14 Be3 Bxd4!? 15 Bxd4 d6 16 b4 Nd7. Black will close the center with 17...e5 and then White's slight spatial superiority will be of little practical significance.

10   ...   Bf6
11   Bb2   Nc6

This immediate QN development is made possible by tactics, because the dangerous looking 12 Ne5 is defanged by 12...Nxd4! 13 Qxd4 Bxg2 14 Kxg2 d6, which led to an approximately equal endgame after 15 Qe3 dxe5 16 Bxe5 Bxe5 17 Qxe5 Qd6 18 Qxd6 cxd6, J.H. Donner - M. Euwe, Holland 1954. However, from a longer range strategic perspective, the text has the disadvantage of blocking the diagonal of the QB.

It is for this reason that with the passage of time, GM Korchnoi has gravitated to the more modest 11...d6 12 Rad1 Qc8 13 Qd2 Nd7. In ECO E, Revised, GM Ehlvest evaluates the position after 14 Ne1 Bxg2 15 Nxg2

Rf7, J. Timman - V. Korchnoi, London 1984 as equal. It seems to me, however, that White's central superiority should count for something. A possible improvement in Black's piece placement is 12...Qe7 (instead of 12...Qc8), as played in V. Tukmakov - P. Nikolic, Reggio Emilia 1987/88. Since Black's chances are on the Kingside, the Queen's location on e7 seems more suited for that.

12 Rad1

With White's QR well placed on the d-file, White will now unpin the d-pawn with 13 Qc2 or 13 Qd2 and then be ready for 14 d5. Black needs to arrange a satisfactory way of coping with that. It is apparent that his QN will will have to be prepared to move again.

12 ... Ne7

Black gets out of the way of the coming "d5 express" and prepares to reposition the Knight further on g6 for the Kingside play to come.

However, less than a year later, in the game A. Miles - V. Korchnoi, Wijk aan Zee 1978, he selected a more flexible Knight redeployment: 12...Qe7! 13 Qd2 (13 Qc2 is also met by 13...Nd8). 13...Nd8!, with the point that from d8 the Knight can get to both the center (e6) and the Kingside (f7). This turned out to be important after 14 d5?! Bxb2 15 Qxb2 d6! 16 dxe6 Nxe6, with already a slight edge for Black. Instead of 14 d5?!, correct is 14 Ne1 Bxg2 15 Nxg2, with perhaps a tiny advantage to White.

13 Ne1

Because the Black QB has remained the clearly superior white square Bishop, it is strategically advantageous to exchange it off.

13 ... Bxg2
14 Nxg2 g5!

[diag. 110]

Both necessary and good. Black gets ready to start counterplay on the Kingside, while preventing White's Knight from reaching the attractive f4 square. If Black does nothing, White will soon play e4 and then enjoy a riskless substantial superiority in central space.

The strategic themes in the coming middlegame are as follows:

White will aim for an early e4, with the objective of rolling Black up along the d- and e-files. In addition, any opening of the position will give White strong attacking chances against Black's weakened Kingside.

Black must be ready to counter White's central play with action along the f-file. This will most likely involve playing ...f4, prepared by a previous ...Ng6. If White delays his central play, Black could aim for ...e5 himself after ...Ng6, Qe7, d6.

15   Qc2

This direct, active method of aiming for e4 is best. The alternate approach is to prepare this with f3, as in V. Pirc - M. Euwe, Amsterdam Olympiad 1954: 15 Qd2 Ng6 16 f3 Qe7 17 e4 fxe4 18 fxe4 Bg7. Black can then use the open f-file to exchange Rooks. The substantial reduction of material will minimize the importance of White's central superiority and bring Black very close to equality.

15	**...**	**Ng6**
16	**e4**	**f4!**

The fighting response, thematic and correct. After the fearful 16...fxe4?!, Black's only "compensation" for central inferiority is a weakened Kingside. After the text, Black's increased space on the Kingside is reasonable compensation for White's superior center. In addition, White's Knight at present is without offensive prospects. Moreover, it will soon become apparent that White's imposing center is not quite the power that it seems to be because it will be difficult to get both the d- and e-pawns to the fifth rank.

17	**e5**	**Bg7**
18	**Qe4**	

This move is all right by itself, but in hindsight is the start of muddling play. Because it will be very difficult for White to get in d5 and since, without that advance, White's QB on b2 has nothing to do, it makes sense to bring it to a location where it has more scope. Therefore I like GM Keene's suggested 18 Ba3!, with White having a slight advantage due to having more space. After 18...Rf7, White can then proceed as discussed in the next note.

18	**...**	**Qe7!**
19	**Rd3?!**	

White has an optically attractive position, but lacks a readily available way to progress. For instance, 19 d5?! can only be counterproductive after 19...exd5 20 Qxd5+ Qf7 when the weakness of White's e-pawn will mean that the best that he can do is an exchange of this pawn for Black's d-pawn, with no resultant chances for an advantage.

Over the immediate future, either one of these plans seems thematic to me:

(1) Safeguard the Kingside with 19 f3 followed by 20 g4, or

(2) Get the Knight to a useful location via 19 Ne1 and 20 Nd3.

In due course, White can then prepare the d5 advance. Instead, GM Polugaevsky embarks on a series of obscure Rook maneuvers which turn out to be a waste of time.

19	...	Rad8
20	Rfe1?!	

Since this does not stop Black's response, the immediate 20 Rfd1 would have saved a tempo.

20	...	d5!
21	exd6	Qxd6
22	Red1?!	

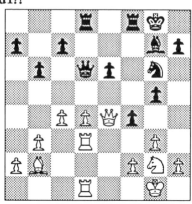

[diag. 111]

While it is true that the immediate 23 Qxe6+? leads to a trapped Rook after 23...Qxe6 24 Rxe6 Ne5! 25 Rd1 Kf7, releasing the pressure on the e-pawn is just plain ridiculous. White's formerly "strong" d-pawn will turn out to be vulnerable, while Black's backward e-pawn becomes secure. Correct is the modest 22 Rdd1, normalizing the Rook placements.

22	...	Qe7!

Preparing the coming Queen regrouping. Black improves his position, step by step, while White just gropes around.

23	Ne1	Qf6

24	R1d2	Qf5!
25	Qxf5?	

White took no time at all on this capture. If he had thought just a bit he would have seen the error of his ways. White's position, of course, has become unpleasant, but a reasonable defense is 25 Re2!, protecting the Queen and keeping an eye on the e-pawn.

25   ...   exf5!!

Though quite obvious in hindsight, this recapture had completely eluded GM Polugaevsky's foresight. Black gets rid of his vulnerable e-pawn and ensures that he will have a healthy mobile Kingside majority. White has no hope for active play and the "nice" d-pawn is more of a weakness than strength.

26   Ng2

The eleven minutes White spent on the text show how unexpected Black's move was. White simply lacks an attractive continuation. After e.g. 26 Nf3 the tournament bulletin gives the following good-for-Black line: 26...g4 27 Ne5 Nxe5 28 dxe5 Rxd3 29 Rxd3 f3! 30 Rd7 Re8! 31 Rxc7 Rd8! 32 h4 Rd1+ 33 Kh2 Rd2.

26	...	g4!
27	Nxf4	Nxf4
28	gxf4	Bh6
29	Re2	Bxf4

With some more fine moves GM Korchnoi has fashioned an advantageous, active endgame. The thematic Kingside play envisioned first with 9...f5 and reinforced by 14...g5! has brought Black an active pawn majority there, thereby placing White's King in great danger from a potential pawn storm. White's position is close to critical, and moreover, he has also started to run short of time, having only ten minutes left to move 40, whereas Black had 30 minutes remaining. Please note again that since Black has been playing throughout in accordance with the strategic themes of the 9...f5 variation, his moves have come "easier."

30   Re6?

This strategic blunder, unaccountably played almost instantly, does make White's position critical because Black can now establish control of the open e-file. White had to select his move with great care. For instance, 30 Rd1?! is inferior because after 30...Rf6! Black threatens the powerful 31...Rh6. Instead, necessary is 30 Re1! so that after 30...Rf6 White has 31 Bc1 and after 30...Rde8! White can contest the e-file with 31 Rdd1. Black remains significantly better after 31...Bd6, yet White has chances to put up a tough defense.

	30	...	**Rfe8!**
	31	**Rf6**	

31 Rxe8+ Rxe8 32 Kf1 leaves the h-pawn hanging; 31 d5?? Rxe6 32 dxe6 leaves the Rook en prise.

	31	...	**Re1+**
	32	**Kg2**	**Rf8!**
	33	**Rxf8+**	**Kxf8**

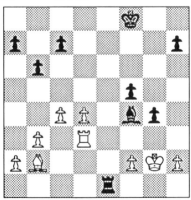

[diag. 112]

Black's Rook has penetrated White's position and the Kingside pawns will form a fence around White's King. GM Korchnoi simply squishes his opponent.

	34	**d5**	**Bd6**	
	35	**Bc3**	**Rc1**	
	36	**Bd2**	**Rc2**	
	37	**a4**	**f4**	
	38	**h3**	**f3+**	
	39	**Kf1**	**h5**	
	40	**hxg4**	**hxg4**	**White resigns**

The game was adjourned after Black's 40th move, but White resigned without resuming play.

He had sealed 41 Ke1, whereupon 41...Bc5! keeps White in a hopeless hammerlock (42 Be3 Re2+ 43 Kf1 Bxe3 44 Rxe3 Rxe3 45 fxe3 Ke7! is a lost K + P endgame; 42 Kd1 Ra2 43 Kc1 Bxf2 44 Kb1 Rxd2 45 Rxd2 g3 queens the g-pawn). If instead 41 Rd4, GM Robert Byrne gives the following convincing variation: 41...Rb2 42 Be1 Rxb3 43 Rxg4 Rb1 44 Re4 Bb4 45 Re6 Kf7 46 Re3 Kg6 47 Re6+ Kf5 48 Re3 Rxe1+ 49 Rxe1 Bxe1 50 Kxe1 Ke4 51 Kd2 Kd4 with an easily won K & P endgame.

*   *   *   *   *

Game 29

White: Tigran Petrosian
Black: Viktor Korchnoi
Played at 1977 Quarter-Final Candidates Match, Il Ciocco, Italy, Game 8

1	d4	Nf6
2	c4	e6
3	Nf3	b6
4	g3	Ba6

[diag. 113]

If I would know nothing about the theory of this variation—similarly to the proverbial "man from Mars"—and if I would see a weak player use the text, I would shake my head and murmur something like "he knows nothing about the QID nor about chess." After all, doesn't "everybody" know that the QB belongs on b7? It is true that 4...Bb7 is perfect in every way; nevertheless, the "amateurish" appearing 4...Ba6 has, over the past decade, become a valid main line alternative. Consider, e.g., the following anecdotal evidence: the, as I write, current Chess Informant (#51) features nine games with 4...Bb7 and nine games with 4...Ba6. The father of the variation, GM Aron Nimzovitch, would be proud to learn that more than fifty years after his death, his brainchild has finally reached full respectability.

The concept behind the text is perceptive, but the execution of it sufficiently difficult that it has taken such a long time for GMs to believe the concept. GM Nimzovitch's deep insight was that since the natural protection, 5 e3?!, is inferior because as a result of 4 g3 White can hardly afford to develop his KB on e2 or d3, White needs a less natural way and that every one of them will lead to some awkward placement of a White piece. However, it is not at all easy to exploit such a misplacement and

Black can easily wind up with a misplaced piece (i.e. the Ba6) himself. As a general conclusion I would state that 4...Ba6 is only suitable for the stronger players, whereas 4...Bb7 can be handled satisfactorily by the "weak" and "strong" alike.

The over-all strategic themes of Nimzovitch's variation are: White's approach must be two-fold:

    (1) Protect c4 with as little negative side effects as possible, and

    (2) Take advantage of the fact that Black's QB is missing from the central h1 - a8 diagonal, by aiming for control of the e4 and d5 squares.

Since one of White's pieces will get misplaced as a result of the protection of c4, Black must exploit this temporary misplacement. Because White can choose a number of methods, Black better know all the relevant variations cold.

The following is a brief look at the major White options:

    (1) 5 Qa4 was for well over 40 years White's main response, because the Queen not only defends the pawn but also exerts pressure against Black's Queenside. Yet the negative side has over the last 15 years also come to the fore: the Queen has not only given up support of White's d5 advance, but is itself vulnerable to an attack. At present, among top GMs only U.S. Grandmaster Maxim Dlugy has it as a regular part of his opening repertoire. Black has two viable approaches:

        (a) 5...c5 6 Bg2 Bb7! 7 dxc5 (Now 7 d5? just loses a pawn.) 7...bxc5 (7...Bxc5 is equally good.) 8 Nc3 Be7 9 0-0 0-0 10 Rd1 d6 11 Bf4 Qb6, with approximate equality, A. Karpov - L. Polugaevsky, Biel 1990.

        (b) 5...c6 6 Nc3 b5!? 7 cxb5 cxb5 8 Nxb5 Qb6 9 Nc3 Bb4 10 Bd2 (Giving back the pawn after 10 Bg2 Nc6 11 0-0 Bxc3 12 bxc3 Bxe2 13 Re1 may offer White a minute edge.) 10...0-0 11 Bg2 Nc6 12 Rb1 Rab8 13 a3 Bxc3 14 Bxc3 Rfc8 15 Qc2 Ne7! 16 0-0 Ned5 17 Rfc1 Qb3! 18 Qxb3 Rxb3 19 Nd2 Nxc3 20 Rxc3, Draw, G. Kuzmin - E. Mednis, Riga Interzonal 1979. Black will recover the sacrificed pawn and enjoy full equality.

    (2) 5 Qc2 also gives up support of d5 and Black equalizes after 5...c5! 6 Bg2 Nc6 7 dxc5 bxc5 or 7...Bxc5.

    (3) 5 Qb3 misplaces the Queen for a different reason: 5...Nc6! 6 Nbd2 d5! 7 Qa4 Bb7 8 cxd5 exd5 9 Bg2 Qd7 10 0-0 Bd6, with equality, Huzman - A. Mikhaljchishin, Lvov 1988. White's QN stands poorly, as does the Queen, whereas

Black has active piece placement to compensate the slight weakness of the c6 square.

(4) 5 Nbd2 again breaks the communication between White's Queen and the possible d5 advance, allowing Black to obtain approximate equality after 5...Bb7! 6 Bg2 c5.

(5) 5 b3—see the game continuation.

5   b3

This simple method has over the past ten years become White's overwhelming choice of guarding c4, not because it has no disadvantages, but because it has less than other methods. At this moment White has no misplaced pieces and therefore 5...c5?! fails to 6 d5.

5   ...   Bb4+

This check is part of the sophistication behind 4...Ba6. However, White's methods have also been refined and at the current stand of theory he can expect to retain a normal opening advantage. This has caused Blacks to start exploring aggressively the complications resulting after 5...d5 6 Bg2 dxc4!? 7 Ne5 Bb4+ 8 Kf1 Nfd7. We are only in the early stages of this investigation, but I would expect that after 9 Nxc4 (9 Bxa8 Nxe5 is unclear) White will retain an opening advantage due to his superior center.

6   Bd2

Forced because 6 Nbd2? Bc3 7 Rb1 Bb7! leaves White horribly tangled up, with Black threatening both 8...Bxd4 and 8...Be4. The attempt to escape with 8 Bb2 came to naught in K. Shirazi - J. Benjamin, U. S. Championship 1984: 8...Ne4! 9 Rg1 Qf6! 10 Bc1 Nc6 11 e3 Nb4! (12 a3 Na2 followed by 13...Nxc1).

6   ...   Be7!

[diag. 114]

This retreat forms the perceptive point of the check: to force White's QB onto the undesirable d2 square. There it takes away d2 from the QN, is on the wrong diagonal and interferes with the configuration of White's forces in general. For the coming action in the center White's QB is best placed on the central diagonal and, specifically, the faultless b2 square.

Of course, Black can play 6...Bxd2+, but after 7 Qxd2! c6 8 Bg2 d5 9 0-0 0-0 (9...dxc4 10 Ne5) 10 Qb4 Ne4 11 Rc1, A. Karpov - N. Short, Amsterdam 1988, White has a pleasant advantage because of the following factors: superior center, potentially more active Bishop, pressure against Black's Queenside, dark square weaknesses in Black's position. Moreover, White has no misplaced piece—therefore Black has not realized the objective behind 4...Ba6.

The strategic themes from Diagram 114 are as follows:

White needs to ensure that his QN and QB are harmoniously developed. Moreover, White has to anticipate that Black will transpose into a Closed Catalan Opening and be ready for that. Since White's thematic central advance in the Closed Catalan (CC) is e4, White has to aim for it after proper preparation.

Black must try to exploit White's clumsy QB placement on d2. The most effective way is to transpose into a Closed Catalan with ...c6 and ...d5.

7   Nc3

This normal move looks better than it is, the problem being that the Nc3/Bd2 combination is poorly coordinated for a Closed Catalan Opening. Of course, hindsight has been of major help in drawing this conclusion. A very large amount of GM activity has demonstrated that White does best in simply satisfying himself with as close as possible the normal configuration against the Closed Catalan. Therefore best is 7 Bg2 c6 8 Bc3! d5 9 Nbd2 Nbd7 10 0-0 0-0 11 Re1 c5 12 e4!. Compared to the CC, White's QB is on c3 rather than on b2, whereas Black's QB is on a6 instead of b7. Even though the Bc3 is slightly misplaced, the fact that Black's QB does not control e4 is of greater significance. Therefore White can look forward to a normal opening advantage, no matter how Black's d-pawn captures: (1) 12...dxe4 13 Nxe4 Bb7 (Or 13...Nxe4 14 Rxe4 Bb7 15 Re3) 14 Ned2, G. Kasparov - V. Ivanchuk, Tilburg 1989; (2) 12...dxc4 13 Nxc4 Bb7 14 Qd3!, A. Karpov - A. Khalifman, Reykjavik World Cup 1991.

7   ...   d5?!

The perceived threat (8 e4) is no threat at all but the weakening of Black's Queenside pawn structure after the text is permanent. Even though the flexible 7...0-0 also is playable, I feel that most thematic is

7...c6!, preparing 8...d5, e.g. 8 Bg2 d5 when White lacks a comfortable way of guarding c4 (9 Ne5 Nfd7!). Moreover, after 8 e4, Black can also respond with 8...d5!, and after 9 e5, 9...Ne4. According to current theory, the main line positions resulting after 10 Bd3 Nxc3 11 Bxc3 c5 12 dxc5 bxc5 offer equal chances.

| 8 | cxd5 | exd5 |

The centrally correct recapture, yet the result is a weakened pawn chain on the Queenside. Therefore, 8...Nxd5 9 Bg2 (9 e4!? is an ambitious plan worth considering) 9...Nd7 may well be a more comfortable road for Black. What is thematically wrong about Black's choice of variations is that White's QN + QB wind up very well placed for this central configuration.

9	Bg2	0-0
10	0-0	Nbd7
11	Ne5!	

[diag. 115]

Because of the threatened 12 Nc6, Black's response is forced. White then has a favorable case of the central pawn structure discussed in connection with Game 21, because White's KB already exerts strong pressure against Black's d-pawn.

11	...	Bb7
12	Bf4	Re8
13	Rc1	Nf8

Black prepares to meet the threatened 14 Nb5 with 14...Ne6, yet now White is able to execute favorably the same minor piece exchange as in Game 21.

| 14 | Bg5! | Ne6 |
| 15 | Bxf6 | Bxf6 |

16 e3

The same type of position has arisen as with the "Korchnoi Method" against the Tartakower Variation of the QGD. (See Game 21.)

Black has a slightly weakened Queenside pawn formation and a stultified central pawn structure. White will try to weaken Black's Queenside some more by advancing his pawns on that flank and also will look for an opportune moment to break in the center with e4. Because of the closed nature of the pawn chain, Black's Bishop pair is without scope and in general Black is without meaningful counterplay. Basically all that Black can do is react to try to contain White's plans. Over-all White has a slight, yet pleasant plus in a maneuvering type of situation. Black has unquestioned prospects of holding his own, but with little hope for more. GM Petrosian no doubt felt quite satisfied here: his brilliant victory in Match Game 6 (See Game 22) evened the score and here he stands comfortably better.

16 ... c6

Here and in the future, GM Korchnoi, somewhat uncharacteristically, selects a passive, careful, "batten down the hatches" approach. The alternative is the attempt at counterplay with 16...c5!?, as played in L. Portisch - G. Sosonko, Tilburg 1984. White did retain a slight edge after 17 Re1 Nc7 18 f4 Be7 19 Ne2 Bf8 20 Qd2, but, according to GM Portisch, if Black had now continued actively with 20...a5! (instead of 20...Ne6?!) his chances for reasonable counterplay would have been good.

17 Nd3   Qd6
18 Re1   Rad8

The attempt at counterplay with 18...c5?! does not quite work because of 19 dxc5 bxc5 20 Na4 Rac8 21 e4!, with GM Marjanovic providing the following analysis:

(1) 21...Bd4?! 22 exd5 Bxd5 23 Ndxc5! Bxg2 24 Nxe6 Rxc1 25 Qxc1 Bc6 26 Nxd4 Rxe1+ 27 Qxe1 Qxd4 28 Nc3, with White a sound pawn up.

(2) 21...dxe4 22 Ndxc5 Qxd1 23 Rexd1 Nxc5 24 Nxc5 Bg5 (24...Ba8 25 Nxe4) 25 Rc4 Ba8 26 h4, followed by 27 Nxe4. White again is a pawn up, though Black has some drawing chances in the Rook + opposite color Bishop endgame after 27...Bxe4.

19 b4!   Re7
20 a4   Rdd7
21 Qb3   Rd8
22 Red1   Red7

White has gained additional space on the Queenside, while Black has decided that keeping the status quo is his best approach. GM Petrosian now tries to establish the most fruitful piece deployment for the potential pawn advances a5/b5/e4. The time situation is: White has used a bit over 1.5 hours (time limit is 40 moves in 2.5 hrs), while Black is at the two hour mark.

23	Ne2	g6
24	Nef4	Rc7
25	Rd2	Bg5
26	Nxe6	fxe6

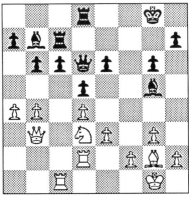

[diag. 116]

An unavoidable further slight weakening of Black's pawn formation. Worse is 26...Qxe6?, because of 27 b5! followed by 28 bxc6 when Black's isolated d-pawn will be indefensible. After the text, 27 b5 can be satisfactorily parried by 27...c5. Therefore, White first doubles Rooks on the c-file and will try to combine a direct attack on the c-pawn with a b5 advance. White continues to enjoy a pleasant, riskless, moderate size advantage.

27	Rdc2	Rdc8
28	Bh3	Kg7
29	Nf4	Re8

After 29...Bxf4?! 30 exf4 Black has chronic weaknesses on the dark squares and his e-pawn becomes extremely vulnerable.

30	Rc3	Bc8

GM Korchnoi spent seven minutes on this move and now had only 3 minutes left for the last ten moves. Though GM Petrosian still had twenty minutes remaining, he spent half of that time on his next two moves—moves which amounted to just a simple riskless Knight redeployment. Black's position, though cramped, is not at risk of unexpected attacks and thus there is little expectation of a blunder by him; the prospects of a blunder by White must be rated as nil.

31 Nd3   Bd7
32 Ne5   Rec8

With sophisticated maneuvers GM Petrosian has increased the pressure. Still, to achieve something permanent, White will need to break with either b5 or e4. The obvious preparation for e4 is the careful 33 R1c2. Yet after five minutes of reflection, White essays ...

33 e4??

The former World Champion has decided that it's time for action. The tactical justification for the text is that 33...dxe4? is not playable because of 34 Nxd7 followed by 35 Bxe6, winning the Exchange. However ...

33 ...   Bxc1

White had overlooked that he has opened the KB's diagonal. It's safe to say that his jaw must have dropped ten feet. The result is not only physical but also psychological damage.

34 Rxc1   dxe4?

No doubt Black was jumping for joy as he was playing 33...Bxc1, but on his very next move he gives back all of his bounty. Correct is the careful 34...Be8, threatening both 35...c5 and 35...dxe4.

35 Nxd7   Qxd7

After 35...Rxd7 36 Bxe6 Qxd4, White gets his material back with 37 Qe3!, and reestablishes equality, e.g. 37...Qxe3 38 fxe3 Rdc7 39 Bxc8 Rxc8 40 Rxe4.

36 Bxe6   Qxd4

[diag. 117]

Now after the obvious 37 Bxc8 (or first 38 Rd1) 37...Rxc8 38 Rd1 followed by 39 Rd7+ and 40 Rxa7 White can establish material and positional equality. Instead ...

37   Rc4??

Much worse than 33 e4??. That can be excused as momentary blindness, but the text is criminal negligence.

37   ...   Qa1+

Thank you, very much.

38   Kg2   Rf8

Good enough to win, but considerably stronger is 38...Re8! since 39 Rxe4 Rde7 followed by 40...Qf6 leaves White in an unbreakable pin.

39   Rxe4   Re7
40   Bd5!

Just getting out in the nick of time, though the position remains lost.

40   ...   Rxe4
41   Bxe4   Qf6
42   Qc2   Rc8
43   a5   bxa5

The sealed move. White's position is hopeless: an Exchange down in an inferior position, while having no reasonable "swindling" chances.

44   bxa5   c5
45   Qc4   Re8
46   Bd5   Qd4
47   Qb3   Re2
48   Qb7+   Kh6
49   Qf7   Rxf2+

Black had this sacrifice in mind when playing his 46th and 47th moves—otherwise he would not have allowed the incursion of White's Queen. With the text, Black forces a K & P endgame where he is a pawn up. Though this endgame is only won by one tempo, it is a "clear" tempo and can be calculated readily enough. I would not be surprised if this was already prepared during adjournment analysis.

50   Qxf2   Qxd5+

[diag. 118]

There is no way White can prevent the exchange of Queens: 51 Kg1 Qd4; 51 Kf1 Qf5; 51 Kh3 Qf5+.

51	Qf3	Qxf3+
52	Kxf3	Kg5
53	Ke4	Kg4
54	Kd5	Kh3
55	g4	Kxh2!
56	Kxc5	Kg3
57	g5	Kf4 **White resigns**

The conclusion would be 58 Kc6 Kxg5 59 Kb7 h5 60 Kxa7 h4 61 Kb8 h3 62 a6 h2 63 a7 h1=Q.

Torre Attack
Game 30

White: Julian Hodgson
Black: Edmar Mednis
Played at Stavanger, Norway International Tournament 1989/90

1	d4	Nf6
2	Bg5	e6

GM Hodgson has developed a dynamic repertoire based on an early Bg5 in d4 openings. Thus after 1 d4 Nf6 he may play the immediate 2 Bg5 (as here) or 2 Nf3 e6 3 Bg5. This game was the 10 AM game in a two round day and thus did not allow for much specific preparation. Quickly reviewing Chess Informant #47, I was intrigued by Game #88, J. Hodgson - I. Rogers, Wijk aan Zee II 1989. Black's set-up appeared to be equally viable after 2 Bg5 e6 and 2 Nf3 e6 3 Bg5. GM Rogers' method seemed to combine strategic soundness with an unbalanced position—an attractive mix for a Round 5 game where my opponent was a half point ahead. Yet soon I was to rue my uncritical credulity...

3	e4	h6
4	Bxf6	Qxf6
5	Nf3	

This is an important position in the Torre Attack and usually arises from the move order 1 d4 Nf6 2 Nf3 e6 3 Bg5 h6 4 Bxf6 Qxf6 5 e4. White has the dual advantages of edge in development and superior center, while Black looks forward to eventually exploiting the latent strength of the Bishop pair. An interesting fight is in store.

Let us now backtrack for a few moments to consider the basic starting point of the Torre Attack: 1 d4 Nf6 2 Nf3 e6 3 Bg5 [see diag. 119]. This opening is named after the Mexican GM Carlos Torre who popularized it in the 1920s. It can be looked upon as an attempt to improve on the Colle Opening (1 d4 Nf6 2 Nf3 e6 3 e3). In both, White aims for quick development behind a stabilized center, followed by an attack against Black's Kingside. In the

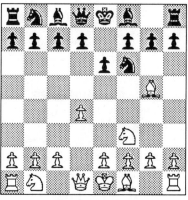

[diag. 119]

Colle, White is usually handicapped by an inactive QB; in the Torre the QB is immediately developed to an active location. Black has three basic approaches to choose from:

(1) Solid, unpretentious development with 3...d5 or 3...Be7.

(2) Counterplay on the Queenside, starting with 3...c5.

(3) Immediately forcing the QB to declare its intentions with 3...h6. This is by far Black's most ambitious plan, in the hope that the early QB development can be labeled "premature." White has two alternatives:

  (a) 4 Bh4, with Black going after the QB as follows: 4...g5 5 Bg3 Ne4. The position resulting after 6 Nbd2 Nxg3 7 hxg3 Bg7 has become recognized as quite comfortable for Black. White's build-up is too modest to hope to exploit Black's slight Kingside weakness; moreover, Black has gained space there as a result of his advanced g-pawn. Black will castle Queenside and look for opportunities to exploit his Bishop pair potential. This variation is fast disappearing from the opening repertoire of Whites.

  (b) 4 Bxf6 Qxf6 5 e4 is the modern way of handling this important Torre variation. We are now back to the actual game.

[diag. 120]

The strategic themes are:

White must try to exploit his edge in development, superior center and the awkward placement of Black's Queen to fashion an attack. Some line opening will be required for this.

Black must catch up as best as possible with his development and then try to partly neutralize White's central superiority. Black's over-all objective is to reach a satisfactory middlegame where his Bishop pair can start to demonstrate its power.

Over the next moves White succeeds brilliantly in realizing his objective; Black fails.

5   ...   d6

Here and on the next move, ...g6 followed by ...Bg7 is a good alternative. I was satisfied to blithely follow GM Rogers' analysis.

6 Nc3   Nd7
7 Qd2   c6
8 0-0-0   e5?

The text is given a ! mark and the position after it is rated equal by GM Rogers in Chess Informant 47, Game 88, but the move is as wrong as can be because Black opens the game before his development is sufficiently complete. The correct method of getting in this desirable advance is to first ensure that Black can castle, as demonstrated in the Rd. 9 (last round) game J. Hodgson - B. Carlier: 8...Be7! 9 Kb1 e5 10 h4 Nb6 (But not 10...Nf8? because White again has 11 dxe5! dxe5 12 Nb5!.) 11 a4! Bg4 12 a5 Bxf3 13 gxf3 exd4! 14 Qxd4 Qxd4 15 Rxd4 Nd7. I think that Black here is very close to full equality.

9 dxe5!

The strategic refutation: White's superior development sets up a tactical shot in case Black recaptures "thematically." In the Hodgson - Rogers game White played 9 h4—criticized by Rogers, who suggested 9 Kb1 with equality.

9   ...   dxe5??

For a fleeting moment I considered the possibility of White playing 10 Nb5, but dismissed it out of hand as "no danger." Hindsight tells us that the unappetizing 9...Nxe5 is forced, with White gaining a clear increased central and developmental edge with 10 Nd4!.

10   Nb5!!

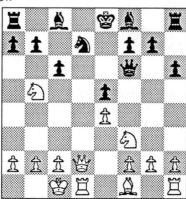

[diag. 121]

The tactical refutation: 10...cxb5 loses after 11 Bxb5 Qe6 (Or 11...Qf4) 12 Nxe5 Qxe5 13 Bxd7+ Ke7 14 Bxc8.

10   ...   Kd8

Not only can't the sacrifice be accepted, but there also is no satisfactory way of declining. Subsequently I found the following predecessor: J. Klinger - D. King, Lucerne 1989: 10...Rb8 11 Nxa7 Nc5 12 Nxc8 Rxc8 13 b4 Qe6 14 bxc5 Bxc5 15 Qc3 Bd6 16 Bc4 Qe7 17 Rxd6 Qxd6 18 Rd1 Qe7 19 Qxe5 Qxe5 20 Nxe5 0-0 21 Rd7 Black resigns.

11   Qc3?

With this natural move White goes from a forced win to nothing. After the game GM King showed us that the winning sequence requires the interpolation of the check on a5: 11 Qa5+ b6 12 Qc3, because the weakness of c6 is decisive. The game type continuation 12...cxb5 13 Bxb5 Bd6 loses to the simple 15 Qc6. Hodgson had rejected the check because of concern about 12...a6 and only later discovered the similar refutation: 13 Nd6! Bxd6 14 Qxc6.

11   ...   cxb5!

Forced and good.

12   Bxb5   Bd6
13   Rxd6!?

White played this quickly, but overlooked Black's 14th move. However, Black also can defend after 13 Rd2 by 13...Re8 14 Rhd1 Re6.

13   ...   Qxd6
14   Rd1   Qc7
15   Qb3?

White's long think prior to playing this told me that he wasn't happy any more. Instead of the text, correct is 15 Qxe5 after which I didn't see anything better than 15...Qxe5 (15...f6 16 Qe6 leaves Black's King very exposed in the center.) 16 Nxe5 Ke7 17 Bxd7 Bxd7 18 Nxd7 Rhd8. White then has two pawns for the Exchange (a slight material advantage), but Black's position is healthy and since White's extra pawns are one on each side, there is no prospect of him achieving two connected passed pawns. I rated the endgame as equal and wouldn't have minded accepting it after the shock of 10 Nb5!!.

15   ...   Rf8!

My original plan was to force White's Bishop to declare its intentions after 15...a6 as I judged the simplification 16 Bxd7 Bxd7 17 Qxf7 as in my interest. But then I noticed that White has 16 Qxf7! axb5 17 Qxg7 Re8

18 Qf6+ Re7 19 Qf8+ with perpetual check. By now I wasn't satisfied with a draw anymore.

16   Nh4

This direct attempt should have led nowhere. More perceptive is 16 Bxd7! Bxd7 17 Nxe5, as suggested by GM Yuri Averbakh. After 17...Qxe5 18 Qxb7 Qc7 19 Qxa8+ Ke7 20 Qd5 Be6 the attacking chances provided by Black's extra piece count for more than White's three pawns, but material is equal and White's chances for a draw reasonable.

16   ...   a6

Envisioning the coming Exchange sacrifice, as it seemed to me that development of the Queenside is Black's overriding priority. I was reluctant to play 16...g6 because I felt that White can exploit my Kingside weaknesses starting with 17 Qe3, yet now 17...Qb6 18 Qxh6 Kc7! seems more than fully satisfactory.

17	Qa3	Re8
18	Nf5	axb5!?
19	Qxa8	g6
20	Nd6	Re6
21	Qa3	

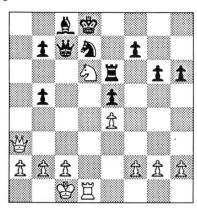

[diag. 122]

White must keep up the pressure since 21 Nxf7+? Ke7 22 Nxh6 Ra6 traps White's Queen.

21   ...   Qc6!

Gives the King the c7 fleeing square while protecting b5 and d7. Moreover, in case the Nd6 moves, White's e-pawn will be under attack.

22	Rd5	Qa6
23	Nxf7+	Kc7

24 Qb3

During the game I was unsure whether Black has any advantage remaining in the endgame after 24 Nxh6 (24 Qxa6? bxa6 25 Nxh6 Bb7 is obviously hopeless.) 24...Qxa3 25 bxa3. White then has three pawns for the piece and both sides have ugly Queenside pawns. Subsequently, I worked out a clear advantage for Black after 25...b6!: (1) 26 Rxb5 Nc5! 27 f3 Ba6 28 Rb4 Bf1; (2) 26 f3 Ba6 27 Ng4 (or 27 Nf7 Re7 28 Nd6 Kc6) 27...Rd6!. In all cases Black's piece is more valuable than White's pawns.

24 ... b4!

The liberation of Black's Queen finally makes his advantage clear. Yet there was a practical handicap caused by my previous thinking: I had less than 4 minutes for my last 16 moves, while GM Hodgson had close to an hour.

25	Qxb4	Qf1+
26	Rd1	Qxf2
27	Nd6	Qc5
28	Nb5+	Kb8
29	Qb3	Rb6!

It is worthwhile to force the weakening 30 a4.

30	a4	Rc6
31	Kb1	Qc4
32	Qxc4	Rxc4
33	Nc3	Rc6
34	Nd5	

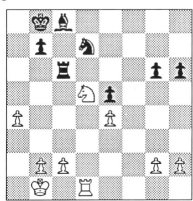

[diag. 123]

With this move White offered a draw. Because he only has two pawns for my piece, it was easy to refuse the offer. However, on my next move, the immediate 34...Nc5! is better.

34	...	Rd6
35	Rf1	Nc5
36	Rf8	Re6
37	a5	Nxe4
38	Nb6	Rc6
39	Nd7+	Kc7
40	Nxe5	Rc5

And here 40...Re6! is a lot stronger. My main aim, understandably, had been just to reach move 40 while retaining my material advantage. However, over the past several moves I had stopped keeping score, while GM Hodgson's scoresheet was faulty and thus only after Black's 42nd move did we stop blitzing.

41	Nxg6	Rxa5
42	Rf4	Ng5
43	h4	Ne6
44	Rf7+	Bd7
45	g4	Kd6
46	Ne7?!	

This unnecessarily hasty move eases Black's task considerably. Correct is 46 Rh7.

46	...	Nd8!
47	Rg7	Bxg4
48	Ng8	Be6!

Leads to a theoretically interesting and important endgame. My judgement was that after 48...h5 49 Nf6 (49...Bf3? 50 Rd7+ Ke6 51 Rxd8 Kxf6 52 Rf8+) White would still achieve the exchange of the h-pawns but with considerably better piece placements than in the game. The idea behind the text is to take advantage of White's momentarily misplaced pieces to apply decisive pressure against the c2 pawn.

49	Nxh6	Rh5
50	Rg6	Kc7
51	Ng4	Rxh4

[diag. 124]

Because White had played so quickly, my last was the sealed move to end the first session. The game was to be resumed at 9:30 PM (after the Rd. 6 play from 4 - 8 PM). It is clear that the double threat of 52...Rh1 mate and 52...Rxg4 forces White's response. But what then?

52   Nf2   Bf5!!

In the brief snatches of time after this round and after Round 6, I had first looked at the "obvious" 52...Rh2, yet after 53 Rf6 there was no clear way of making progress. Once White is able to consolidate with b3 and Nd3 it is not clear whether Black has a 100% certain theoretical win, because White's pawn formation is very sound. Of course, Black could continue playing for a win hour after hour after hour, yet ultimate success is not guaranteed.

Only shortly before resumption of play did the text move enter my mind. It is the ultimate execution of the move 48 plan: first the Bishop is placed on the key diagonal and only then will the Rook look for its best location.

53   Rg3?

This routine move is hopeless. The only try I had seen was the paradoxical looking 53 Rf6! Rf4 54 Ne4!. Therefore, in place of 53...Rf4, I had considered playing 53...Bh7, with the final decision to be made during play.

53   ...   Nc6!
54   Nd3?!

Loses immediately, but there is no satisfactory defense to the threats of 54...Nb4, 54...Nd4, 54...Rh2. For instance, 54 b3 Rh2 55 Nd3 (55 Rf3 Bxc2+) 55...Nd4 etc.

54   ...   Bxd3!

55 cxd3

Forced because 55 Rxd3 loses to 55...Rh1+ 56 Ka2 Nb4+. The split pawns that result after the text are defenseless against Black's active pieces.

55	...	Nb4!
56	Kc1	Rh2!
57	d4	Rc2+
58	Kb1	Rd2
59	b3	Rxd4
60	Kb2	Rd3
61	Rg4	Nc6
62	Kc2	Rh3
63	Kb2	Na5
64	Ka3	

At first I couldn't understand White's move, i.e. what does White have after 64...Rxb3+ 65 Ka4 b6? As I looked again, I saw the diabolical plot: 66 Rg7+ Kb8 67 Rg8+ Kb7 68 Rg7+ Ka6 69 Ra7+!! Kxa7 stalemate. Therefore ...

64	...	Nxb3
65	Kb4	b6! White resigns